IronFit Secrets

for Half Iron-Distance Triathlon Success

Also by Don Fink and Melanie Fink:

Be Iron Fit, Second Edition

Mastering the Marathon

IronFit Strength Training and Nutrition for Endurance Athletes

IronFit
Secrets

for Half Iron-Distance Triathlon Success

Time-Efficient Training
for Triathlon's Most
Popular Distance
**DON FINK and
MELANIE FINK**

LYONS PRESS
Guilford, Connecticut

An imprint of Globe Pequot Press

Lyons Press is an imprint of Globe Pequot Press

Ironman, Ironman Triathlon, and Ironman 70.3 are registered trademarks of the World Triathlon Corporation

IronFit is a registered trademark of Don Fink

All exercise photos featuring Yvonne Hernandez are provided courtesy of Lynn Kellogg/ www.trilifephotos.com.

Cover photograph: Jessi Stensland (www.gojessi.com) by Action Sports International

Illustrations by Tom Debiasse

Text design/layout: Mary Ballachino
Project editor: Ellen Urban

Library of Congress Cataloging-in-Publication Data is available on file.

ISBN 978-0-7627-9293-1

Printed in the United States of America

10 9 8 7 6 5 4 3 2 1

To our loving parents, Esther and Martin
and Claire and Richard

Contents

Introduction viii

Chapter 1: Triathlon's Most Popular Distance 1
Chapter 2: The Eight Essential Half-Iron Workouts 10
Chapter 3: The Crucial Training Principles, Training Cycles,
           and Practice Races 24
Chapter 4: Heart Rate Training for the Half Iron-Distance 35
Chapter 5: Sixteen-Week Half Iron-Distance Training Programs 44
Chapter 6: The Half Iron-Distance Functional Strength and Core
           Program, Warm-Up Routine, and Flexibility and
           StretchingProgram 84
Chapter 7: Mastering Transitions: "The Fourth Sport" 117
Chapter 8: Half Iron-Distance Race Strategies, Fueling,
           and Hydration 128
Chapter 9: Effective Goal Setting and Race Selection 151
Chapter 10: Half Iron-Distance Equipment from A to Z 158
Chapter 11: Healthy Eating for Ultimate Fitness 171
Chapter 12: Perfecting Technique 185
Chapter 13: Mental Training: Powerful Secrets to Self-Confidence . . . 202
Chapter 14: Building and Maintaining Excellent Health 210
Chapter 15: Recovery and Maintenance Training 218

Acknowledgments 226
Appendix A: Additional Maximum Heart Rate Estimation Formulas . . . 227
Appendix B: Glossary 229
Appendix C: References 233
Index 236
About the Authors 244

Introduction

The Half Iron-Distance has grown to become triathlon's most popular race. Over half a million athletes will race this distance worldwide in the coming year, and the number of races continues to grow at an amazing rate.

The Half Iron-Distance Triathlon includes a 1.2-mile open-water swim, followed by a 56-mile bike ride and a 13.1-mile run. (The metric equivalents of these distances are a 1.9 km swim, a 90 km bike, and a 21.1 km run.) These distances are exactly half those of the full Iron-Distance. Many around the world also refer to the Half Iron-Distance as "Middle Distance" and "Long Course," but most triathletes simply refer to it as the "Half."

At the time *Be Iron Fit* was written eight years ago, only a handful of races existed at the Half Iron-Distance level. These were considered more of a stepping stone on the way to the Iron-Distance dream, little more than a tune-up or dress rehearsal for the full Iron-Distance. Today that has all changed in the triathlon world.

The Half Iron-Distance being the most popular triathlon, the number of races has skyrocketed and continues to grow with no end in sight. There are now several major race series spanning the globe featuring this triathlon distance, and there are also hundreds and hundreds of additional independent races worldwide. The estimated over half a million athletes who will race the Half in the coming year will possibly be more than twice the number who will race the full Iron-Distance.

Why has the Half Iron-Distance grown to become triathlon's most popular distance? It's because it is the perfect distance for the vast majority of busy athletes who also have demanding career and family responsibilities. While the full Iron-Distance is doable, it takes very careful planning and a lot of sacrifice to accomplish the goal while also keeping the rest of life in balance. In contrast, the Half—still a very substantial and challenging distance—provides a much more accessible opportunity to compete at a high level while also maintaining a positive and sustainable lifestyle balance.

Despite the Half Iron-Distance's soaring popularity, a general misunderstanding exists regarding how best to prepare for it. Because the word *Iron* is often part of the race's title, many athletes assume that you prepare for it just like the full Iron-Distance Triathlon. We have even had athletes over the years ask us if they should just take one of the training programs in *Be Iron Fit* and do half of it.

This assumption is not correct, as you prepare quite differently for these two races. Cutting the training in half would in no way approach the goal of maximizing your performance. These races are competed at different intensity levels, with different approaches, and, as a result, the training is different as well.

IronFit Secrets for Half Iron-Distance Triathlon Success provides a clear path to maximizing an athlete's success at this popular racing distance. If you want to optimize your Half Iron-Distance performance, you have come to the right place. It's all right here. This book contains the training programs and the information you need to achieve your Half Iron-Distance dream.

You can benefit most from this book if you already have a basic level of triathlon knowledge. Perhaps you have participated in shorter-distance triathlons, road racing, cycling, or open-water swim competitions. Or perhaps you have already completed a Half Iron-Distance Triathlon, and you want to train smarter and race faster. We will take you through everything you need to do to accomplish your Half Iron-Distance goal.

As with all of our books, *IronFit Secrets for Half Iron-Distance Triathlon Success* is not written with a lot of technical talk and scientific lingo; instead, we present information in a clear and useful way, spelling out exactly what you need to do, and when you need to do it. No complicated formulas, no guesswork—just a clear, step-by-step path to achieving your goal. We provide you with effective training, efficient time management, and "been there, done that" knowledge.

We start with a presentation of the eight essential training sessions and how they fit into the proper training cycles for the Half. From there, we discuss the crucial training principles for this race, including how to make heart rate training work for you. It's important to take full advantage of the essential workouts, how they should be arranged in proper training cycles, and how they are influenced by the crucial training principles, for athletes to optimize their training results. And, essentially, to avoid what we refer to as "junk training."

With an understanding of these topics, we then present three detailed sixteen-week Half Iron-Distance training programs. These programs are designed to be user-friendly, and can be put to immediate use. Guidance is also provided to help you select the program that best fits your goals, experience level, and available training time.

While the sixteen-week programs cover all of the specific training sessions in swimming, cycling, and running, this book also provides a highly effective warm-up routine, a functional strength and core training program, and a stretching and flexibility routine, all specifically designed for success in the Half. We also present specific training and guidance on the Half Iron-Distance's "fourth sport," the two transitions known as T1 and T2, often overlooked even though they are key aspects of the race.

From there we cover proper technique in the three sports, and provide tools for improving and fine-tuning your form. Next, we discuss the necessary equipment for Half Iron-Distance success, including suggestions on the most economical ways to "buy speed."

Also covered is a thorough discussion of race selection, racing strategies, and how to set exciting and motivating goals. We present proven techniques and approaches for building powerful self-confidence and maintaining good health and optimal racing body weight.

Finally, we offer specific guidance on exactly what you should do in the "off-season" to best prepare for the next season, and to ensure continued improvement year after year.

One more important point: It's going to be fun! Preparing for and achieving the Half Iron-Distance dream is not about discomfort and sacrifice. It's about enjoying the challenge and appreciating the journey. *This will surely be one of your most enjoyable and rewarding adventures ever, from start to finish.*

Like we said at the outset, if you want to maximize your performance and achieve your Half Iron-Distance dream, you have come to the right place. So turn the page and let's get started!

CHAPTER 1

Triathlon's Most Popular Distance

And all may do what has by man been done.

—Edward Young

The recent exploding popularity of the Half Iron-Distance Triathlon has been the most exciting trend in the endurance sports world. What was once just a handful of races years ago has now expanded into hundreds of events worldwide.

The Half Iron-Distance Triathlon includes a 1.2-mile swim, followed by a 56-mile bike, and then a 13.1-mile run. (The metric equivalents of these distances are a 1.9 km swim, a 90 km bike, and a 21.1 km run.) These are exactly half of the distances for the full Iron-Distance Triathlon. Many around the world also refer to the Half Iron-Distance as "Middle Distance" and "Long Course," but most triathletes simply refer to it as the "Half."

Twenty years ago, you would have been hard-pressed to find a race at this distance; they were few and far between. Fortunately, some of the classic races from that era are still with us today, going strong. Races like Eagleman in Maryland, Buffalo Springs Lake in Texas, and Wildflower in California— always some of our favorites—are now even better.

But today these classics are joined by a countless number of new races at the Half Iron-Distance. The largest, the Ironman 70.3 series, boasts over seventy races worldwide, and has been adding races every year. Several other major North American–based race organizations, including the Rev 3 Series and the HITS Series, have races at this distance in the double figures. The popular European-based Challenge-Family series, with races all over the world, is also rapidly growing in its offering of Half Iron-Distance Triathlons. Many of these major race series have their own championship race as well. Furthermore, there is also a European Championship at this distance, as well as National Championships in the United States and many other countries.

Lynn Kellogg (www.trilifephotos.com)

There are hundreds of independent races as well. The race schedule website TriFind.com lists over a hundred Half Iron-Distance races in North America, and USA Triathlon, the governing body for triathlon in the United States, sanctions over two hundred races at what they classify as the "Long Course" distance.

All of this excitement over the Half is quite remarkable given this race distance's history. Overshadowed by the popularity of the shorter Olympic Distance Triathlon (also known as the Standard Distance Triathlon) and the longer full Iron-Distance Triathlon, the Half Iron-Distance found itself the Rodney Dangerfield of triathlon distances . . . getting no respect. At best, it was considered nothing more than a training race—a stepping-stone on the way to achieving the full Iron-Distance dream.

This is clearly no longer the case. Everything has changed for the Half Iron-Distance. While still used by many as great preparation for the full Iron-Distance, the Half is now a major force in the triathlon world in its own right and has become the most popular distance.

How did this happen? Why did this great change take place? The short answer is, time and money.

The full Iron-Distance Triathlon requires athletes to commit a significant amount of time toward preparation. Sure, it's doable, and our book *Be Iron Fit* demonstrates how smart training and efficient time management can help practically any athlete to achieve his or her Iron-Distance dream. But it takes strict planning and a lot of sacrifice to accomplish the goal, often temporarily pulling the rest of life out of balance. It's something a lot of athletes want to do once, twice, or even a few times, but it's not something they want to do every year. Athletes want the challenge of a truly epic endurance sports event, but more often than not, they want it to be of a size and scope that can fit into their lives on a more regular basis.

This is the reason so many athletes find the Half Iron-Distance to be the perfect distance for them. This is especially true for the vast majority of athletes who have demanding careers and family responsibilities. While still a very substantial and challenging event, the Half provides a much more accessible opportunity to compete at a high level while also maintaining a healthy lifestyle balance.

The Half Iron-Distance race experience is also extremely enjoyable. While top pros will complete the distance in less than four hours, the average finishing time is closer to six hours. This means that if the race starts at 7 a.m., most athletes will cross the finish line by around 1 p.m., and still be able to have a wonderful afternoon enjoying the post-race festivities, celebrating with family and friends at the awards ceremony, and meeting other like-minded athletes—a truly wonderful way to spend a spring or summer day. In fact, if you like to meet inspiring, healthy, and fitness-minded people, there are few better places to be.

The Half is also more logistically accessible for most athletes. As mentioned earlier, there are hundreds and hundreds of races spanning the globe. There are many more races available at the Half Iron-Distance than the full Iron-Distance, so it's far more likely that athletes will have a local race available to them, helping them to avoid the time, expense, and inconvenience of planning a major trip to a full Iron-Distance race.

Finally, there are simple economics. The entry fee for some major full Iron-Distance races exceeds $600, and that does not include the costs of travel and accommodations usually associated with these races. On the other hand, most athletes can find a great local race at the Half Iron-Distance, with race fees of less than half that amount, and, in many cases, closer to one-third of it.

If local, there will be much less travel time and expense as well. In fact, in many situations, athletes can sleep in their own beds the night before a race

AN IRONFIT MOMENT

The "Big 10" Time Management Tips

While the time required to prepare for a Half Iron-Distance Triathlon is significantly less than that required for a full Iron-Distance, it is still a significant time commitment. Every bit of efficient time management can really help you to maintain a satisfying lifestyle balance.

Following are ten of the most successful time management tips for the Half Iron-Distance triathlete in training:

1. Train in Time, Not Miles

All miles are not the same; sometimes they take longer than expected. This makes estimating your training time more difficult. The most efficient way to train is by time, not distance. A 60-minute run is a 60-minute run. Put it in your day planner and plan around it just like you would any other appointment. All of the training plans in this book are designated in time, not distance, to make planning your training time as easy as possible.

2. Take Advantage of Indoor Training Options

Indoor training options like treadmills and indoor bike trainers provide greater flexibility and efficiency. With indoor training options you don't need to schedule your training around weather conditions and darkness. You also don't need to spend more time bundling up with lots of extra clothing if you live in a colder climate. You'll spend less time washing, drying, and folding clothes, too. While we are likely to do most of our training outside, take advantage of time-efficient indoor training whenever you can.

3. Morning Workouts

If possible, train first thing in the morning. Not only are our energy levels typically higher in the morning, but if we do train first thing in the day, we don't risk something unexpected arising during the day to derail our planned training sessions. Traffic backs up, trains don't run on time, your boss keeps you late . . . Stuff happens. There are an infinite number of unexpected events that can spoil your training session if you don't get it done early in the day. Plus, when you train first thing, you will feel wonderful about it all day.

4. Lunchtime Workouts

In addition to trying to get a good portion of your training completed first thing in the morning, if possible, you should also take advantage of lunchtime workouts. Depending on your work or lifestyle situation, this may not be possible for all; but if it is, it's a wonderful opportunity for effective time management. A great example of this can be seen in the "Just Finish" training program in Chapter 5, which averages about six hours of training per week. If you can just squeeze in four 45-minute lunchtime training sessions per week, you'll be able to knock off half of your training time right there.

5. Masters Swimming Sessions

If you are fortunate enough to have a good local Masters Swimming program available to you, take advantage of it. Masters swim sessions are typically about an hour long and are scheduled at specific meeting times each week. All you need to do is put the two weekly times that work for you into your day planner and then just "show up" like you would for any other appointment on your calendar. The rest will take care of itself. Your Masters Swimming coach will have the workout planned for you, and the other swimmers in your lane will provide you with all the motivation you need.

6. The "Mom Shift"

As you will see as you read the inspiring athlete profiles in this book, there are many very successful Half Iron-Distance triathletes who are full-time stay-at-home mothers. Many moms find that they actually can make more time available for training during the week than they can on the weekend. When their kids are home, they are involved in more family activities. Many of these successful moms do what we call the "Mom Shift." They take whichever of the sixteen-week training programs they are using in Chapter 5 and they shift all of the days ahead by three days (give or take one day). What this does is put their longest training days on Tuesday and Wednesday, instead of Saturday and Sunday. If you are a stay-at-home mom, or if you work weekends, you may benefit from this time management technique.

7. Take Power Naps

Our bodies repair themselves, get stronger, and recover while we are sleeping. Unfortunately, the first casualty of a busy triathlete's lifestyle is proper sleep. Look to see if you have any opportunities during your day for a brief nap to help restore and reenergize. The most popular places to do this include while commuting on trains or buses. Many successful athletes squeeze in a quick 20- to 30-minute nap on the way to or from work. This is great for your health, and will help you to more fully absorb the good benefits of our training. Set the alarm on your phone, though; you don't want to risk sleeping through your stop.

8. Lay Out Your Clothes and Equipment in Advance

If you plan to work out first thing in the morning, get everything ready the evening before. This includes your exact clothing, footwear, equipment, and fueling and hydration. This way, you won't waste time looking for items in the early-morning hours; you can just get up and go.

Likewise, if you want to be able to squeeze a workout in as soon as you get home from work, take this same approach. Have everything ready to go before you even arrive. This way you can change your clothes and go as soon as you get home, greatly increasing your chances of getting in a quality session.

Or, if you plan to stop at a fitness center or other training location on the way home from work, make sure you have a bag packed in the car in advance, with everything you'll need.

9. Be Willing to Sacrifice the Perfect to Get the Good

If you've planned for today's workout to be 60 minutes in duration, but you're a little behind schedule and can only manage a 50-minute workout, seriously consider just doing a shorter version of the same workout. Many athletes make the mistake of trying to squeeze the workout in later in the day, but "later in the day" never happens, and the workout is skipped altogether. It's usually better to do most of the workout now rather than risk missing it completely. So, unless you are absolutely sure that you will have room in your schedule to squeeze it in later in the day, or properly use your "slide day" (see Chapter 2), do as much of it as you can now and then just move on to the next day in your training schedule.

10. Commute and Complete Errands via Running and Cycling

Many athletes are very successful at combining their training with other activities, saving significant amounts of time. This, of course, depends greatly on your lifestyle situation, but many of us miss these opportunities for great time management. Can you commute to work via bike a couple of times a week? Can you run to the soccer field to see your kid's game? Can you do any of your regular errands via bike? Just finding one or two opportunities a week to combine regular activities with training will make a significant difference in your overall time management.

We hope the above time management tips will help you to find more training time in your schedule. Please consider these tips as you decide on which of the three sixteen-week training programs in Chapter 5 will fit you the best.

and drive to the starting line in the morning. This is very helpful when trying to maintain a healthy and balanced lifestyle.

Because of these factors, the exploding popularity of the Half is likely to continue. As an example of this, membership in USA Triathlon (the governing organization of triathlon in the United States) has grown by over 300 percent in the last ten years.

The future of triathlon is bright, and the future of the Half Iron-Distance is even brighter.

Following is the first of ten motivating profiles of an inspiring Half Iron-Distance Triathlete.

HALF IRON-DISTANCE SUCCESS STORY: MAUREEN CULLEN

Maureen Cullen, who is married with three children, raced her first triathlon nine years ago, soon after the birth of her first child. At that point she had swum only once or twice over the previous ten years, and she didn't even own a bike.

That all seems like a very long time ago, as today Maureen's extensive résumé of endurance sports accomplishments includes age-group victories at major Iron-Distance events; qualifying for and racing in the Ironman World Championship in Kona, Hawaii; qualifying for and racing in the 70.3 World Championship in Henderson, Nevada; and qualifying for and racing in the Boston Marathon multiple times.

What makes all of this even more amazing is that in addition to being a full-time wife and mother to three children, Maureen also works as a race director for local all-women running events, coaches her kids' sports teams, and does volunteer work at local charities. Maureen Cullen is an exceptional example for all of us in the endurance sports world, and a wonderful representative for triathlon.

Among Maureen's many talents are her excellent time management skills. She employs many of the "Big 10" time management techniques presented earlier, especially the use of early-morning workouts. Maureen tries to get a large portion of her training completed first thing in the morning, so as to have the least impact on the rest of her family.

Maureen also tries to involve her family in as much of her training and racing activities as possible. In the case of her husband, that's easy, as he enthusiastically trains for and competes in triathlons as well, but she'll also invite her kids along for the warm-up or cooldown portions of her runs, or perhaps for a swim at the pool or in the nearby ocean.

Another one of the "Big 10" time management techniques Maureen regularly uses is frequent indoor training. She will set her kids up with arts and crafts, or some other fun activity, right next to her on the indoor bike trainer so they can all be together. Not only does this promote more quality family time, but Maureen's regular demonstration of a willingness to consistently work hard to achieve her goals can only serve as a very powerful example for her children.

The IronFit training approach has helped Maureen not only to train efficiently, but also to reach amazing levels of performance and accomplishment. Concerning her experience with the Iron-Fit methods and her remarkable success, Maureen stated, "It has been an incredible journey, and through it all my family and friends (especially my children) have seen me set goals and work toward achieving them, hopefully leading by example. By figuring out ways to make it work, and by not making excuses, IronFit training methods allow for that balance."

Maureen has raced the Half Iron-Distance the most often in the past and plans to focus primarily on this event in the upcoming season. Watch for Maureen Cullen and her family at the races, enjoying the journey and living the dream.

CHAPTER 2

The Eight Essential Half-Iron Workouts

Knowing is not enough; we must apply.
Willing is not enough; we must do.

—Johann Wolfgang von Goethe

This chapter presents the eight essential training sessions needed to optimally prepare for the Half Iron-Distance Triathlon. This is not the training program itself, but the basic building blocks which, when properly organized together, can be designed into the optimal training program for you.

Of course, it is not just about swimming, cycling, and running every day and then showing up on race day to compete in a Half Iron-Distance Triathlon. There are eight specific types of workouts that need to be properly designed and ordered in an athlete's program. There is also a specific way each of these sessions should be executed to maximize training results.

While one might assume an athlete would use the exact same workouts to prepare for both the Half and the full Iron-Distance triathlons, this is not the case. These two races are different, and we prepare for them in different ways.

The eight key Half Iron-Distance workouts are the following:

1. Transition Sessions
2. The "415-20-45 Brick"
3. Alternating "Long and Longer" Runs
4. Higher-Intensity Bike and Run Sessions
5. Cycling Power Hill Repeats
6. The IronFit Swim Approach: Masters, Drills, Intervals, and Open Water

7. High-rpm Cycling Spins

8. Strategic Rest Days / Slide Days

We will clearly explain each of these eight sessions in full detail, in a straightforward and easily understandable way. Where applicable we will explain what each session's duration should be, how frequently it should be completed, and at what level of training intensity.

Most important, these workouts will be fun. Training does not have to be "all pain and no gain." Our eight key workouts are designed to be both highly productive and highly enjoyable.

Each training session within a great training program has a specific purpose, and each works hand in hand with the other training sessions to most efficiently maximize fitness. Grouping the right workouts together in the proper order produces truly synergistic training; anything less than this approach amounts to what we call "junk training."

The following is a presentation of each of the eight key workouts.

Transition Sessions

Transition sessions, also known as "bricks," are a key component of triathlon training. These are workouts that include two sports separated by only a quick change from the clothing and equipment of one sport to the clothing and equipment of the other sport.

The most common example is the bike-to-run transition session. This workout begins with a bike ride for a specific amount of time. Once the time on the bike has been completed, the athlete stops briefly (preferably for 5 minutes or less), changes from cycling gear to running gear, and then runs for a specific amount of time.

This is an essential training session for triathlon because it prepares the body to do exactly what it is challenged to do in the race. We don't cycle fresh—we cycle after the effects of a swim; and we don't run fresh—we run after the effects of a swim and a bike. This session teaches the body to become comfortable with this and to handle the transitions more effectively.

Each of the training programs in Chapter 5 includes transition sessions as a key component, and both the Competitive and Intermediate Programs include two transition sessions per week for most weeks of the program. The "Just Finish" Program includes only one transition session per week in the first half of the program, but then also introduces a second weekly transition session during the peak training weeks.

The most challenging of the two transitions in a triathlon is the bike-to-run transition (aka, T2), much more so than the swim-to-bike transition (aka, T1). The way the bike affects our muscles makes running difficult, especially for the untrained athlete. This is why the Chapter 5 programs all focus specifically on bike-to-run transition sessions.

While no specific swim-to-bike transition sessions are included in any of the three programs, it is suggested that at least on some of the days that include both a swim and a bike session, you start your bike session shortly after your swim session has been completed (preferably within 5 minutes). This will help your body to better prepare to make this transition on race day.

A great day to do this type of swim-to-bike transition session in the Intermediate and "Just Finish" Programs is Thursday, as these two programs both have a swim session and a bike session planned for that day. For the Competitive Program, however, Wednesday is the best day to do this type of swim-to-bike transition session, as there is both a swim and a bike-to-run transition session planned for the same day, which provides an excellent opportunity for a "double brick" training situation; in other words, a swim session followed by a bike session, then followed by a run session.

The "415-20-45 Brick"

Of all the possible ways to use transition sessions to prepare for a Half Iron-Distance Triathlon, there is one that is so beneficial it belongs in a category all its own. In fact, if we had to pick one magic bullet session in Half Iron-Distance training, the "415-20-45 Brick" would be it.

The "415-20-45 Brick" is a special five-hour transition session, and as you will see in the Chapter 5 training programs, this session will appear as follows:

Trans: 4:15 hr. Z2 Bike (at 3:50, insert 20 min. Z4) (QC)
45 min. Z2 Run

We will fully present and explain the abbreviations and the heart rate zones used above in Chapter 5, but for now, in plain language, this session is structured as a five-hour transition session, which begins with a 4:15 (4 hours and 15 minutes) bike portion in heart rate zone 2 (moderate intensity). Then, at the 3:50 point of the bike portion, the athlete increases the intensity to heart rate zone 4 (high intensity) for a period of 20 minutes. Following this 20-minute-long, higher-intensity insert, the athlete returns to heart rate zone 2 (moderate intensity) for the remaining 5 minutes of the 4:15 bike portion. Immediately following the bike portion, the athlete quickly changes from cycling gear into running gear (preferably within 5 minutes) and then goes for a 45-minute run in heart rate zone 2 (moderate intensity).

Jen Luebke: Pro Triathlete and Half Iron-Distance Competitor
Tom Robertson Photography

These "415-20-45 Bricks" are very challenging, and go a long way toward preparing the athlete both mentally and physically for the Half Iron-Distance Triathlon.

The 4:15 ride itself is a very worthy test. While some are faster and some are slower, the majority of trained athletes can cover between 60 to 90 miles (at 14 to 21 mph) in heart rate zone 2 (abbreviated as "Z2"; moderate intensity) by the time of the peak training weeks of the Competitive and Intermediate Programs in Chapter 5. To be able to cover more than the Half Iron-Distance bike portion and to quickly transition into running gear and then to complete a substantial run distance is a huge confidence builder and confirmation of fitness.

What makes the effort even greater is the fact that we include a very challenging 20-minute, higher-intensity spurt just prior to the run. This makes the run that much harder, and it forces your body to recover quickly from the effects of the bike portion to run smoothly. Again, this is an enormous indicator of preparedness for the Half Iron-Distance, both physically and mentally.

It is important to mention that while the "415-20-45 Brick" is our most challenging session in our Half Iron-Distance training program, it is also the most rewarding. When you complete this session you are going to feel great. Not only will you have the earned feeling of real accomplishment, but you will also have the earned feeling of confidence that you can achieve your Half Iron-Distance goal.

Because of the length of this session, it is included on some Saturdays in the Competitive and Intermediate Programs in Chapter 5, which works best for most athletes. As with all of our training, we build up to the "415-20-45 Brick" gradually and safely over several weeks. We start with shorter Saturday transition sessions, and then gradually build it up to the five-hour level.

While the "Just Finish" Program does not include a "415-20-45 Brick" due to time constraints, it does include a shorter version of this session, which mirrors the purpose of the "Just Finish" Program itself: It provides what the athlete needs to "just finish" the Half Iron-Distance Triathlon, and to do so in good health and in good spirits.

There is also a variation of the "415-20-45 Brick" to help simulate actual race conditions and pace that we will briefly touch on here. In the Competitive Program in Chapter 5, we will also include one five-hour transition session with a 40-minute Z3 insert toward the end of the bike portion, instead of a 20-minute Z4 insert. (Note: We will include a slightly different version of this session in the Intermediate Program in Chapter 5 as well.) This session in the Competitive Program will appear as follows:

Trans: 4:15 hr. Z2 Bike (at 3:30, insert 40 min. Z3) (QC)
45 min. Z2 Run

We will further discuss heart rate zone 3 (middle intensity) in Chapters 4 and 5, and why we generally minimize our training time in it, but the important point for now is that we include this slightly different version of this session to help provide a better taste of what "race pace" will feel like in our Half.

Alternating "Long and Longer" Runs

Long runs, which we define as runs lasting 90 minutes or more, are essential to Half Iron-Distance preparation. Developing aerobic running endurance is crucial, because not only do athletes need to be able to complete a 13.1-mile half marathon, but they also need to be able to do it after they have already completed a 1.2-mile swim and a 56-mile bike.

Most athletes tend to realize this, and thus include long runs as part of their training. The problem comes, however, when they either do not correctly build these runs into their overall plan, don't adequately space them out with enough time in between, or don't grow the durations of these runs at the proper rate of increase. Many athletes make the common mistake of running too far, too fast, and too soon, which will almost always lead to injury. Not a good plan.

We want to gradually build the duration of our weekly long runs at the proper rate of increase, and then we want to strategically place them among our other workouts of the week to maximize training benefit. The optimal time of the week for most athletes to schedule long runs is the day after the longer transition sessions, which in some situations will be a "415-20-45 Brick." Because these longer transition sessions are scheduled on Saturday in the training programs in Chapter 5, the best day to schedule our long runs is Sunday.

The reason this works so well is that when athletes awake the day after the longer transition session, they will likely still retain some of the fatigue and aftereffects in their legs and body. By executing our long run at this time, we teach our bodies to adapt to this condition, which is similar to how they will need to adapt to running on tired and sore legs during the race itself. By scheduling these two key sessions on back-to-back days, we help to optimize the training benefit.

The second trick we will use is to alternate our long runs on every other weekend in a "long and longer" pattern. The reason for this is that it often takes our bodies longer than one week to fully recover from a long run that lasts more than two hours, especially when it comes the day after a longer transition session. This is why in the Competitive and Intermediate Programs in Chapter 5, we start to alternate our long runs between 2.25 hours and 1.75 hours, once we gradually build them up to this level. This trick maximizes the training benefit of our long runs, while minimizing the risk of injury.

Higher-Intensity Bike and Run Sessions

The Half Iron-Distance Triathlon is raced at a higher level of intensity than the full Iron-Distance, so it reasonably follows that a higher proportion of our training will be in higher-intensity work as well.

The Competitive Program in Chapter 5 includes four sessions per week during the peak training phase, featuring heart rate Z4 (higher intensity) cycling and running; and the Intermediate and "Just Finish" Programs in Chapter 5 include as many as three sessions per week, featuring higher-intensity Z4 cycling and running. In fact, in the peak training phase of the Competitive Program, four out of seven (57%) total weekly cycling and running sessions include at least some higher-intensity work.

There are two basic types of higher-intensity sessions that we will use on both the cycling and running sides: Z4 Inserts and Z4 Repeats.

Following is an example of a higher-intensity Z4 Insert running session:

60 min. Z2 (at 45 min., insert 10 min. Z4)

We will fully present and explain the abbreviations and the heart rate zones used above in Chapter 5, but for now, in plain language, in this 60-minute run, we start off in Z2 (moderate intensity) and hold this heart rate zone for the first 45 minutes of the workout. Then, at the 45-minute point, we increase our effort by enough to raise our heart rate into Z4 (higher intensity). We then hold our heart rate there in Z4 for the duration of this 10-minute Z4 Insert, and then we reduce our effort by enough to allow our heart rate to return to Z2 (moderate intensity) for the remaining 5 minutes of the run.

The higher-intensity Z4 Inserts are therefore a relatively long higher-intensity effort. We include Z4 Inserts of as long as 15 minutes on the run side, and 20 minutes on the cycling side, in both the Competitive and Intermediate Programs. During the peak training phases of these two programs, we include one of each per week on both the cycling and running sides. For the peak training phase of the "Just Finish" Program, we include one cycling Z4 Insert session per week and one running Z4 Insert session every other week.

Now that we have discussed higher-intensity Z4 Inserts, the following is an example of a higher-intensity Z4 Repeats running session.

60 min. Z2 (at 10 min., insert 7 x 3 min. Z4 @ 1.5 min. jog)

In this 60-minute run session, we start off running in Z2 (moderate intensity). Then, 10 minutes into the run, we increase our effort level enough to bring our heart rate up into Z4 (higher intensity) for a total of 3 minutes. Then, exactly 3 minutes from the time we first started trying to achieve Z4, we slow down enough to bring our heart rate down into an easy Z1 to Z2 (low intensity) jog. As soon as we have jogged for exactly 1.5 minutes, we again increase our effort level by enough to raise our heart rate back up into Z4 for 3 minutes. We continue this same sequence of 3 minutes of Z4 followed by 1.5 minutes of easy Z1 to Z2 for a total of seven complete cycles. Once we have completed all seven times through, we adjust our effort level to again return to Z2, and complete the remainder of the 60-minute run (which is 18.5 minutes) in Z2.

During the peak training phases of both the Competitive and Intermediate Programs, we include one Z4 Repeats session per week on both the cycling and running sides. During the peak training phases of the "Just Finish" Program, we include one cycling Z4 Repeats session per week, and one running Z4 Repeats sessions every other week.

Cycling Power Hill Repeats

Another very important workout for the Half Iron-Distance is the cycling power hill repeats. These are especially important if your targeted Half Iron-Distance race has a hilly bike course, but even if it doesn't, these sessions are a secret to developing great cycling power.

Following is an example of a cycling power hill repeats session:

60 min. Z2 (at 10 min., insert 10 x 2 min. Z4
Hill Repeats @ Easy Spin Back Down)

We will fully present and explain the abbreviations and the heart rate zones used above in Chapter 5, but for now, in plain language, in the above session we start this 60-minute workout by cycling in heart rate zone 2 (moderate intensity) for 10 minutes. Ideally, locate a good training hill in your area (that you can cycle to the base of) within this 10-minute period.

Then, at exactly 10 minutes into this session, cycle up the hill in Z4 (higher intensity) for 2 minutes. Once you've completed the 2 minutes, safely turn around and cycle easily back to the bottom of the hill. Repeat this same sequence up and down the hill for a total of 10 times. Then, complete the time that remains in the 60-minute ride in Z2. The amount of this final portion in Z2 will vary depending on how long it took to cycle easily back down the hill after each time cycling up the hill for 2 minutes.

These sessions are very challenging, and we suspect you may be cursing us while you are doing them, but there is nothing better for building your anaerobic cycling power and speed. Furthermore, there is nothing better for building your hill-climbing confidence as well.

Tip: For best results on the uphill portion, locate the gearing that puts you in a Z4 heart rate at about a 70- to 75-revolutions-per-minute cadence. Remain seated for the first two-thirds of each hill repeat, and then stand and visualize yourself powering up to the top of the hill for the last third.

The IronFit Swim Approach: Masters, Drills, Intervals, and Open Water

The best swimming asset a triathlete can have is a good local Masters Swimming program, especially one that does a good portion of its workouts in freestyle, versus too heavy a focus on the other strokes. This situation is even better if the program has a coach who is able to watch your technique on a regular basis, offer helpful feedback, and suggest corrective drills to help you to continually improve and fine-tune your technique.

If you are not lucky enough to have a good program available to you in your area, we have designed specific freestyle swim sessions (Chapter 5) and corrective swim drills (Chapter 12) to help you to build both your swimming endurance and your swimming technique. Please also note that we have included suggested perceived effort levels for each section of the swim sessions in Chapter 5.

Here is the secret to Half Iron-Distance swimming success: It's not about swimming hard; it's about swimming smoothly and efficiently. If you just go to the pool and swim at a high level of intensity each time, you are probably not getting smoother and more efficient. The opposite is far more likely.

Remember: Swimming is just the first of three sports in the Half. We rarely want to be swimming "all out." We always want to focus on preserving our valuable energy for the long bike and run ahead. Our workouts should not be focused on a great deal of super-hard swimming. Instead, they should be focused on building solid technique and efficiency with only limited speed work at certain specific times.

The key to accomplishing this is to focus on efficiency in each and every swim workout, and to work on corrective swim drills at the beginning and end of your swim sessions, just as our swim sessions are structured in Chapter 5. Think of the drills as being the most important part of the workout, not the main sets. They are secondary.

As we will discuss in more detail later in this book, our swim preparation should also include some open-water practice, including a wet suit if you plan to be wearing one on race day. If possible, this should be in the form of an actual open-water practice race. Even if you are an experienced swimmer or triathlete, swimming in the open water is quite different from swimming in a pool. Our first time of the year in open water should not be the morning of our Half Iron-Distance race.

To best prepare for our Half Iron-Distance swim, we will first look to take advantage of a well-coached Masters Swim program. But if that is not an option, we will focus our preparation on swimming efficiency, regular drill work, and open-water practice.

High-rpm Cycling Spins

High revolutions per minute (rpm) spins on the bike are truly synergistic training sessions, as they provide great hidden training benefits. Most athletes don't even think these sessions could possibly be important because they are completed at a relatively easy Z1 heart rate. After working with hundreds and hundreds of endurance athletes, we often have to laugh at good old triathlete "reasoning"—if it doesn't hurt, it cannot be beneficial. But of course, this is not the case.

While these sessions build our cycling technique and aerobic base, they also serve to provide overall recovery from other workouts. From a training-benefit standpoint, they are kind of a "three-for."

These sessions are best completed either cycling on flat terrain or on an indoor bike trainer. We live in a relatively hilly area, so we mostly do these on the trainer.

Following is an example of a high-rpm cycling spin session:

$$60 \text{ min. Z1 (at 100+ rpm)}$$

We simply cycle at a cadence of 100 rpm or more (we suggest between 100 at 105 rpm) in an easy gear that allows us to maintain a relatively low Z1 heart rate. What you will find is that to be able to cycle at such a high rpm, you need to spin the pedals in nice, efficient circles as opposed to mashing them up and down. We will discuss the importance of "spinning circles" more in Chapter 12, but the important point to understand for now is that spinning the pedals in a circular pattern serves to make our cycling much smoother and more efficient. While we are receiving good aerobic training benefits from this session, we are also building better technique.

The other great benefit of this workout is recovery. The smooth, lower-resistant motion of this workout helps to increase blood flow to speed recovery. This is why these sessions are included on Sunday in the Chapter 5 training programs. They can be completed before the long run that day, if that is how your schedule dictates, but ideally, it's great to do these sessions after our long run of the week. They serve to jump-start our recovery and send us into our Monday rest day / slide day, with our bodies ready to fully recover and absorb all of the good benefits of our training.

From a priority standpoint, this session is probably the least important of the eight essential workouts. For this reason, it is included in the "Just Finish" Program as an "optional" workout. It is a nice-to-have, but given the goals of the "Just Finish" athlete, it's not an absolute need-to-have. If you can squeeze it in, however, it will definitely be worth your time—especially if your cycling technique is in need of improvement.

Strategic Rest Days / Slide Days

Just the mention of the term *rest day* makes many type A triathletes cringe. But rest days are absolutely essential to optimizing our training. Our bodies absolutely need the proper amount of time to recover and absorb the good benefits of our training. Many athletes cannot get their minds around this, and, consequently, many of them will be continually frustrated by injury and performance stagnation. The rest day should be viewed like any other key workout. We often jokingly refer to it with our coached athletes as "the non-workout workout."

There are one or two weekly rest days strategically built into all three of the sixteen-week training programs in Chapter 5. I say "strategically" because they are placed among the other workouts in the week at a point where they will prove most beneficial.

Now here's the secret to how you can most effectively use rest days: Instead of just referring to them as "rest days," we will designate them as "rest days / slide days." In other words, use them to slide your rest days forward or back by one day to better fit your training schedule around your overall schedule on a particular week.

For example, Monday is your rest day / slide day, but you find out that you have a commitment coming up next week on a Tuesday that will prevent you from training that day. To remedy this, simply slide Tuesday's training session forward to Monday and designate Tuesday as your rest day for that week.

All of the workouts are designed in a specific order for good reason, so we want to avoid "flipping" them during the week, if possible. Instead, if something comes up and you cannot get a planned workout in on the day it is planned for, simply slide your rest day / slide day forward or back one day to accommodate the situation. This allows you to get all of your training sessions in, while keeping them in the order they were intended, and still get the benefit of your rest days.

The three sixteen-week training programs presented in Chapter 5 use these eight essential Half Iron-Distance training sessions and build them into each program to maximize the athlete's training benefit. We have designed these programs in a way that totally eliminates guesswork. Just follow the program each day and enjoy the challenge, and the journey.

Following is the second of ten motivating profiles of an inspiring Half Iron-Distance Triathlete.

HALF IRON-DISTANCE SUCCESS STORY:
SEAN REILLY

Sean Reilly has built himself into an elite competitor during his nine years in triathlon. His personal bests include a 4:38 at the Half and a 9:29 at the full Iron-Distance, and he has become a threat to win his age group in practically any race he competes in. Sean has qualified for and competed in both the Ironman 70.3 World Championship in Henderson, Nevada, and the Ironman World Championship in Kona, Hawaii, multiple times.

Amazingly, Sean didn't start out as a top competitor; he was originally much closer to the middle of the pack than he was to the front. But through his consistent hard work year after year, Sean steadily rose through the ranks to the elite level he now enjoys. Though we credit Sean for his well-deserved success, Sean says, "The IronFit methods are fantastic because they help with time management. There are no 'junk' miles. Every workout is specific, with an intended goal in mind. I'm much faster now than I was eight years ago."

Sean Reilly is married with three children. He uses many of the time management techniques discussed in this book to ensure that his training doesn't interfere with his children's activities. Most important in accomplishing this is for him to get most of his workouts in very early in the day. Even on weekends, Sean will sometimes get up as early as 3 a.m. to be done with his training in time to enjoy the day with his family.

Sean is a high school English teacher, which in many ways is ideal for training. Not only can he train early, before work, but he can sometimes get out of work early enough for a second opportunity for training in the afternoon, before his family gets home for the evening.

While his profession is good for training, it's not quite as good for racing, because he doesn't get much vacation time, besides the summer break. As a result, Sean schedules most of his race travel for the summer months.

While Sean enjoys training for both the Half and full Iron-Distance, he finds the time requirement of the Half to be much more manageable. He sees this as the race's biggest advantage, along with the fact that the after-race recovery period is much shorter as well.

Surprisingly, Sean Reilly's very first triathlon ever was a Half Iron-Distance. It was Ironman Florida 70.3, which at the time was held at Disney World. As Sean knows well, races at fun destinations like this can provide wonderful vacation opportunities for the entire family.

Watch for Sean Reilly at the races this year, as he continues to build his racing performance in our sport's biggest events.

CHAPTER 3

The Crucial Training Principles, Training Cycles, and Practice Races

Believe with all of your heart that you will
do what you were made to do.

—*Orison Swett Marden*

Now that we know the eight essential training sessions required to best prepare for the Half Iron-Distance Triathlon, we will discuss the crucial training principles that will guide us in organizing these individual training sessions into proper training cycles. We will also discuss how to select the optimal types of training races for you, as well as how and when to build them into our overall training plan. Combining the essential training sessions and practice races with the crucial training principles, and arranging them into proper training phases, is the key to truly synergistic training.

The Overload Principle

The most fundamental concept of athletic training is the overload principle. The American Council on Exercise defines the overload principle as "One of the principles of human performance that states that beneficial adaptations occur in response to demands applied to the body at levels beyond a certain threshold (overload), but within the limits of tolerance and safety." In simple terms, our bodies either need to work harder or in a different way than they are used to working to improve. If we regularly do the exact same volume of training, we will eventually hit a plateau, and our fitness and performance will no longer improve.

We need to introduce gradual "overloads" to our training volume to stimulate improvement. We include the word *gradual* because it will only work if the proper amount of over-load is introduced. If it's too much of an overload, it can cause a break-down, and no improvement will be gained. Conversely, if it's too modest of an overload, it will not be enough to stimulate growth. The overload needs to be just the right amount to stimulate the fitness improvements we want.

We cannot count the number of times we have seen examples of both extremes. On the one side, we see so many athletes who are just creatures of habit. They basically do the same workouts week after week, and then are surprised and frustrated when they find that their efforts don't result in better racing performances. Con-sistency is very important for endur-ance sports success, but it needs to be applied in the proper way.

Adriana Nelson: World Class
Endurance Athlete
101 Degrees West

On the other side, we see just as many athletes who quickly throw them-selves into much-higher-volume workouts. They apparently have never heard the old saying, "Too much, too soon." These athletes quickly get injured, as their bodies are not ready to absorb the workouts they challenge themselves with. Enthusiasm is important for endurance sports success, yet it needs to be applied in the proper way.

These two common extremes are just not how our bodies work. Our bodies respond to gradual adaptation. This is good news for most athletes, as this often means that not only can you improve your performance with proper training, but you can also probably continue to improve your per-formance for many years to come. The programs presented in Chapter 5 are designed to do exactly that. They will help you to improve your performance year after year.

The Principles of Training Volume, Duration, Frequency, and Intensity

We have had many driven athletes come to us over the years telling us that they were confident they would achieve their goals because they were willing to work harder than anybody else. It sounds good at first, but the reality is that physical therapy centers are packed full with injured athletes who were willing to work harder than anybody else. To really break through to new levels of performance, it may not be necessary to work harder at all. The key to success for many is simply to work *smarter.*

We have also had many athletes come to us for coaching over the years who were frustrated because, despite their consistent efforts, they never seemed to get any faster. Their race times stayed pretty much the same year after year. Almost without exception, the reason for this stagnation is ineffective employment of the three variables of training volume: duration, frequency, and intensity.

What is meant by training volume? Most athletes don't actually know. Many equate volume of training with duration of training. For example, they think that to increase your volume, you need to increase the length of your workouts.

Actually, *volume* is the combination of training duration, frequency, and intensity. In other words, it is the combination of how long you train, how intense your effort level is while you train, and how frequently you train.

Training volume is best expressed by the following equation:

$$\text{Volume} = \text{Duration} \times \text{Frequency} \times \text{Intensity}$$

The first component is *duration,* which can be measured in time. For example: a 60-minute run or a 75-minute bike ride. This is what we mean by duration. All of the training programs in Chapter 5 indicate a specific duration for each and every bike and run training session.

The second component is *frequency,* which can be measured in the number of times per week that you do a particular activity. For example: A particular week in one of the programs in Chapter 5 may indicate two swims, three bike sessions, and four run sessions. So, our frequencies are simply two swim sessions per week, three bike sessions per week, and four run sessions per week.

The final component is *intensity*, which can be measured in heart rate or level of perceived effort. The higher the heart rate, the higher the intensity, while the lower the heart rate, the lower the intensity. Likewise, the higher the perceived effort, the higher the intensity, while the lower the perceived effort, the lower the intensity. The training programs in Chapter 5 indicate specific heart rate zones for every bike and run session, and specific levels of perceived effort for all swim sessions.

The Principle of Training Cycles

The majority of athletes training for a Half Iron-Distance Triathlon do not properly take advantage of the power of training cycles. Most athletes tend to bunch together a variety of training options available to them, and that's pretty much how they prepare for a race. Perhaps a couple of guys in their triathlon club meet to swim together on Tuesday and Thursday mornings, so that's when they swim. The local running club has a track workout on Tuesday evenings, so that's when they do higher-intensity running. The local bike shop does a group ride Friday after work, so that's when they do their longer bike rides. Typically, this common approach will have some initial success, but usually its effectiveness levels off and leads to performance stagnation at some point.

The reason? This approach does not take advantage of training cycles and our body's natural way of continuing to become stronger and faster. The best way to approach our training is to look at it in terms of three types of training cycles: the weekly training cycle, the "A Race" training cycle, and the annual training cycle.

All three training cycles can occur simultaneously in a highly effective overall training plan. This is why properly designing the optimal training plan is so challenging. Each workout selected for a specific day should be the best possible one to work with each of the other workouts within the week, to maximize the training benefit within all three training cycles.

Weekly Training Cycle

The Weekly Training Cycle is our weekly pattern of training sessions—the actual sequence in which we do our workouts and the day of the week on which we do them. This doesn't mean that we do the exact same workout on the same day of each week. It means we generally do the same type of workout on the same day of most weeks.

There are two reasons why this makes sense: First, our workouts need to be properly ordered and spaced to maximize their effectiveness. There are many no-no's; for example, two higher-intensity days in a row in the same sport, which does not allow for proper recovery. Doing this over the long term is more likely to result in performance stagnation and injury than it is to help you reach your potential. Workouts within the weekly training cycle need to be arranged in a way where your body can be recovering from and absorbing the benefits of one type of training session while it is being worked and challenged with another type.

Second, your training schedule needs to efficiently fit into your overall lifestyle. If we plan workouts for days or times that conflict with your work, family, or other responsibilities, then you will obviously not be able to consistently complete the training sessions. Having a relatively set weekly format allows for better planning and time management.

Please note that if the training plans in Chapter 5 do not fit your overall lifestyle schedule well, we present several suggestions on how to adjust them, including the use of "Slide Days" and the "Mom Shift."

"A Race" Training Cycle

The "A Race" training cycle is the one that is centered on one specific major race coming up. Each "A Race" cycle can range from a couple of months to several months, and while it may include several additional races, it is primarily focused on preparing for one major race.

The sixteen-week training programs in Chapter 5 are examples of "A Race" cycles. They include some possible other races (e.g., an open-water swim, a Sprint or Olympic Distance triathlon, and/or a half marathon), but the entire cycle is geared toward preparing for a Half Iron-Distance Triathlon. Most competitive age-group athletes will prepare for one to three "A Race" training cycles in a year.

Annual Training Cycle

The annual training cycle is the big picture. It's our approach to preparing for and achieving all of our goals for the entire year. It is likely to include from one to three "A Race" cycles, and is also likely to include an off-season training and maintenance phase (Chapter 15).

The important point is that all three training cycles need to work together to maximize an athlete's racing performance and to help keep the athlete healthy and improving year after year. As coaches, when we design our athletes' training schedules, we always want to be looking at this big picture. We don't want to just design a workout that seems to fit well today. What we really want to do is to design each workout with all three cycles in mind. We want it to be the best training session for our weekly training cycle, our "A Race" cycle, and our annual training cycle. When we can accomplish this, we have truly synergistic and beneficial training.

Training Phases in Our Sixteen-Week Half Iron-Distance Training Programs

"A Race" training cycles include various specific training phases, and our sixteen-week training programs in Chapter 5 are no exception. Each program is divided into two eight-week portions. The first eight weeks is our base-building phase. This phase will be almost entirely at a moderate intensity level (heart rate zones Z1 to Z2) and will focus on gradually and safely building your aerobic base and endurance. The actual week-to-week training time increases are steady and consistent. The Competitive Program's training time increases by 60 minutes each week; the Intermediate Program's training time increases by 45 minutes each week; and the "Just Finish" Program's training time increases by 30 minutes per week.

Each program will then transition into a second eight-week portion, which will include both our peak training phase and pre-race taper phase. In our peak training phase we will introduce higher-intensity training sessions into the mix. These weeks will be our most challenging, as we focus on building strength, speed, and endurance.

In the final nine days of our sixteen-week training programs, we will transition into our pre-race taper phase. During the pre-race taper we will gradually reduce our training volume as we get closer to race day. This will allow our bodies to fully recover from all of the hard training over the previous months, and to gather our energy both physically and mentally for a peak racing performance. The timing of the taper phase needs to be just right. We want it to be long enough to recover and freshen up, but not so long that we begin to decondition. The taper phases in our sixteen-week training programs are designed to accomplish exactly that.

Training Races

As mentioned earlier, "A Race" training cycles typically include additional races other than the "A Race" itself, which in our case is the Half Iron-Distance Triathlon. These races, however, should be selected with a purpose in mind, and they should be designed to contribute to our preparation, not take away from it.

For example, if you have never swum an open-water race before, it would obviously make sense to include one in your preparation for your Half Iron-Distance Triathlon. Doing so would give you valued open-water experience and greater confidence on race day. If you do have prior open-water experience but have not swum in your wet suit for a while, an open-water practice race may be beneficial.

The timing of your practice races is also crucial. For example, if you have never run a road race before, you could probably benefit from including a half marathon in your "A Race" preparation. But it would not be a good idea to schedule it for the weekend before your Half Iron-Distance Triathlon. That would spoil your planned nine-day pre-race taper, and instead of being rested, physically fresh, and mentally sharp on race day, you will more likely feel tired and flat. The point is that both the type of practice race and its timing are crucial.

We will now consider the possible race options, whether or not they are a good fit for you, and, if so, how best to build them into our sixteen-week training plan.

For most athletes, there are up to three optional training races to consider including during the sixteen-week program: an open-water swim, either a Sprint or Olympic Distance triathlon, and a half marathon. Depending on the individual, each race has the potential to provide specific elements that will benefit the athlete in the journey to the Half Iron-Distance. Of course, each needs to be properly timed and built into the athlete's training program in a way that makes the program most beneficial overall.

In the following section, we present the three possible races in the like-liest priority order for most athletes. We provide information to help you decide whether or not to include each of them, and we explain how best to build them into your sixteen-week training schedule.

Open-Water Swim

Most athletes should consider including an open-water swim competition if possible during Half Iron-Distance training. This is especially true if swim-ming is your weakest area. But even if you are a strong swimmer, there is a big difference between swimming in a pool and swimming in open water. There is also a big difference between swimming in a swim suit and swim-ming in a wet suit.

The preferable distance is about 1 mile (or about 1.5 km), and it can be substituted in for any of our planned swim training sessions. We don't suggest tapering for it, but instead use it as a training session. Because open-water swims are typically on a Saturday or a Sunday, our suggestion is to simply do it before your other bike or run training planned for that day, and to count it toward the swim sessions planned for either the week before or after. Anytime between Week 4 and Week 15 is fine for this, as long as you feel safe and comfortable in the open water.

Sprint or Olympic Distance Triathlon

Most athletes should consider either a Sprint Distance Triathlon (approxi-mately 0.5-mile swim, 15-mile bike, and 3-mile run) or an Olympic Distance Triathlon (1.5 km swim, 40 km bike, and 10 km run) to serve as a tune-up for their Half Iron-Distance race. This is less from a standpoint of condition-ing and more from one of practicing all race-day routines, including your pre-race, race, and post-race fueling and hydration; your transitions (T1 and T2); your race clothing; and your race equipment. It's the perfect "dress rehearsal," as it provides an opportunity to practice and test everything you plan to do on race day.

If you have not raced a triathlon in several months, then you should seriously consider building this type of practice race into your sixteen-week training program for your Half. And if you are new to triathlon, then doing a Sprint or Olympic Distance Triathlon as a practice race is an absolute must.

Tip: If possible, select a Sprint or Olympic Distance Triathlon with a similar course and terrain to your planned Half Iron-Distance race. It will help make your "dress rehearsal" even more beneficial.

The best weeks in the training programs to include a short-course triathlon tune-up race are Weeks 10 through 14. In Chapter 5, we will present more suggestions on how to adjust your sixteen-week training program to include a Sprint or Olympic Distance Triathlon.

Half Marathon

The third most beneficial of the three optional races is a half marathon. Most athletes with a running background would do best to skip this one, as continued training, not more racing, is more beneficial. But for those who have never run this far, or haven't completed a road race in a long time, it's a great confidence builder to complete the half marathon distance as part of your training.

The best weeks in the training program to include a half marathon are Weeks 10 through 14, and it is suggested that you just substitute this race in for one of your Sunday long runs. In Chapter 5, we will present more suggestions on how to adjust your sixteen-week training program to include a half marathon.

However many of these training races you decide to include in your sixteen-week program, our suggestion is to try to keep it as simple as possible. Trips to races involving a lot of travel time and expense may not be worth it. Try to find practice races in your area that you are able to drive to the morning of the race. We are lucky to live in an area where all three of these racing options are frequently available within an hour's drive from our home, but we realize this is not the case for many athletes. To the extent possible, try to minimize travel time and expense and weigh the pros and cons before signing up for a race far from home.

There are surely great local sources for race information in your area. Some of these include race listing websites, the local running club, bike shop, and Masters Swimming programs. There are also some good sources that cover races across the United States. Here are a few to consider:

- For open-water swim races, try US Masters Swimming (www.usms .org).
- For Sprint and Olympic Distance Triathlons, try USA Triathlon (www.usatriathlon.org).
- For half marathons, try Running the USA (www.runningtheusa .com).

Additional race web links, including international web links, are provided in Appendix C.

Following is the third of ten motivating profiles of an inspiring Half Iron-Distance Triathlete.

HALF IRON-DISTANCE SUCCESS STORY:
SHANNON SCHLAGETER

Shannon Schlageter is a full-time, stay-at-home mom with four young children. Shannon has established herself as an elite competitor over the past six years, with numerous overall and age victories in Sprint and Olympic Distance Triathlons, and she has qualified for the 70.3 World Championship. Shannon has also become a top road racer and has qualified for and raced in the Boston Marathon.

Shannon's race of choice for the foreseeable future is the Half Iron-Distance. In fact, Shannon's four "A Races" this year will be the Boston Marathon and three Half Iron-Distance events. Shannon loves how the Half is such a challenging endurance race, while also allowing for a greater overall lifestyle balance. With a combination of efficient time management and the IronFit training approach, even a mother of four can manage to excel. And while Shannon will surely try the full Iron-Distance at some point, she sees the Half as the overall best race for her.

Shannon has greatly benefited from the efficient IronFit approach to training. It allows her the flexibility to plan her training around her children, who are always her top priority. As Shannon puts it, "Their schedule usually dictates my training schedule. I try to do all my longer training days during the week while they are at school. The weekends are usually filled with their sporting events."

Shannon also likes how the Half Iron-Distance offers many more nearby racing opportunities. As Shannon stated, "I made a promise to myself that I would not let triathlon get in the way of enjoying my children's activities, and that it would not take time away from my family. Since we are so busy, I try to only pick one or two races that might require me to be away on a weekend. Otherwise, most of the races I do are in the vicinity of where we live."

Shannon's favorite Half so far is the classic Eagleman 70.3 in Maryland, but she looks forward to testing out many more Half Iron-Distance courses in the near future. Watch for Shannon at the races . . . you will usually find her at the front of the pack!

CHAPTER 4

Heart Rate Training for the Half Iron-Distance

Constant dripping hollows out a stone.

—Lucretius

Proper heart rate training is the most effective way to maximize the benefit of your limited available training time.

There is no silver bullet to preparing for the Half Iron-Distance Triathlon, but in all our many years of coaching, we can think of no single training element that has led to greater performance breakthroughs with our athletes. Heart rate training eliminates all the "junk training," and it is the most effective way to maximize the benefit of every training minute.

Surprisingly, the vast majority of triathletes have not mastered this. While many wear heart rate monitors in training, few are effectively using the information from the monitors in a productive way. They sort of view the heart rate feedback as interesting information, but they fail to put that information to good use.

As coaches, we are always excited when a new athlete comes to us for coaching who has not properly used heart rate training previously, because we know that not only will we likely be able to help the athlete break through to new levels of performance, but we will probably even be able to achieve that goal with the same (or less) training time.

Why don't most athletes fully embrace effective heart rate training? We've heard a range of different answers to this question, but the most common is that many athletes feel their bodies will naturally tell them what pace they should run or cycle at. This is not surprising, because it seems logical that you should "train how you feel" and "go at your own pace." But this is mostly a misconception about how training works. The reality is that for each race distance, there are proper heart rate zones that an athlete should train in to maximize the benefit of the training time, as well as to avoid stagnation and even injury. There is no race in which this is truer than the Half Iron-Distance Triathlon.

Another reason some athletes may not fully embrace heart rate training is because watts-based training for the bike is currently in vogue. Newcomers to endurance sports may mistakenly see heart rate training as "old school." This is not the case. While watts-based training for the bike can be a productive element in the training programs for many athletes, proper heart rate training is the core factor. We train many of our coached athletes with watts-based cycling training in addition to overall heart rate training, and we will further discuss watts-based cycling training later in this book.

Jeff Kellogg: Elite 50+ Endurance Athlete and Half Iron-Distance Competitor *Lynn Kellogg (www.trilifephotos.com)*

Because most athletes do not properly utilize heart rate training, they fall into a very common endurance sports trap. Simply put, they train at too high an intensity level on their "easy days" and too low an intensity level on their "hard days." All of their training tends to gravitate toward the very narrow range of heart rates in Zone 3. Their hard days are a little harder and their easy days are a little easier, but they all fall into about the same ten beats per minute range of heart rates. It doesn't feel this way to them, but this is how they get trapped.

What this means is that all of their workouts are pretty much the same in terms of level of effort. Every day they are locked in to the same narrow range of heart rates. This is highly ineffective training. All it's really doing after a while is training their bodies to be in those heart rates. That's about it.

While this may work for a while, and the athlete may see some initial performance improvement, eventually this approach leads to performance stagnation and increases the potential for injury. Unfortunately, these are the usual results of "junk training." The good news? If a lot of what you are doing now is "junk training," then it means you may have a lot of untapped potential, just waiting to be unleashed.

We will not focus on a lot of complicated scientific theories and technical talk in this book. After coaching hundreds of athletes for many years, we know that this is not what most athletes want. Athletes want to know exactly what they need to do each day to achieve their goals, and they want a plan they can immediately put into action. That is exactly what we provide here.

Having said this, we will offer a brief and succinct explanation of what is behind effective heart rate training.

Aerobic Versus Anaerobic

The body's two main energy systems are the following:

- **Aerobic Energy System:** An energy system that utilizes oxygen and stored fat to power physical activity. This system can support activity for prolonged periods of time, as stored fat and oxygen are available in almost endless supply. Even a very lean triathlete with a body fat percentage in the single digits has enough stored fat to run several triathlons back-to-back.
- **Anaerobic Energy System:** An energy system that utilizes glycogen (stored sugar) to power muscle activity. This system cannot support activity for long periods of time, as the body stores sugar in relatively small quantities.

While both of these energy systems work at the same time, the ratio of the two systems changes as the level of activity changes. The intensity of our training activity determines the ratio at which we are drawing from each system: the higher the intensity, the more anaerobic the activity; the lower the intensity, the more aerobic the activity.

Heart rate is an excellent indicator of where we are in the spectrum of aerobic and anaerobic ratios. At lower heart rates, the mix is more aerobic. At higher heart rates, the mix is more anaerobic. As our effort level and heart rate increases, the mix becomes more anaerobic.

For example, we race the Half Iron-Distance Triathlon at a higher level of intensity than the full Iron-Distance Triathlon. Therefore, the Half is a more anaerobic race than is the full Iron-Distance.

The important point to understand is that the benefit of an effective heart rate training program is that you are training at the proper intensity level at the right time, which serves to develop both your aerobic and anaerobic systems.

As mentioned earlier, the majority of athletes train at the wrong intensity most of the time, resulting in ineffective training; this is why we call it "junk training." The most successful triathletes understand that we need to put out a very big effort on our "hard days," and we need to restrain our effort to a moderate level on "easy days." A good heart rate training program has the athlete in the proper heart rate zone at the right time, resulting in highly effective training.

Estimating Your Heart Rate Zones

The most accurate way to determine your maximum heart rate and heart rate training zones is to be tested. Many universities and fitness centers offer these testing services at a relatively modest cost.

If it is not possible to have formal testing done, there are also various low-tech methods and field tests for estimating your maximum heart rate. The most popular of these is the "220 Minus Your Age" method. You simply subtract your age from 220 and this provides an estimate of your maximum heart rate (MHR).

For example, according to this method, a forty-year-old athlete's maximum heart rate would be estimated at 180 beats per minute: 220 − 40 = 180 MHR.

While this estimate is pretty close to being correct for the majority of forty-year-olds, we usually encourage our coached athletes to race a 5K with a heart rate monitor and determine what their maximum heart rate was for the race. This field test is usually a very good indication of your maximum heart rate.

Once you have determined your maximum heart rate, we can use it to determine the four training zones for use with the training plans presented in Chapter 5:

Zone 4: 90 to 95 percent of MHR (anaerobic training)

Zone 3: 86 to 89 percent of MHR (middle zone)

Zone 2: 75 to 85 percent of MHR (higher-end aerobic training)

Zone 1: 65 to 74 percent of MHR (lower-end aerobic training)

As an example, for a forty-year-old athlete with an estimated 180 MHR, the heart rate zones for running would be as follows:

Running Heart Rate Zones

Z4: 90 to 95 percent of 180 MHR = 162 to 171 beats per minute (BPM)

Z3: 86 to 89 percent of 180 MHR = 155 to 161 BPM

Z2: 75 to 85 percent of 180 MHR = 135 to 154 BPM

Z1: 65 to 74 percent of 180 MHR = 117 to 134 BPM

Because cycling stresses our bodies in different ways than running (e.g., sitting vs. standing, and more balanced vs. less balanced), our heart rates for cycling are usually about 5 percent lower than our running heart rate zones. In other words, when cycling we obtain the equivalent training effect at a heart rate about 5 percent lower than when running.

In the following table, we apply 95 percent (a 5 percent discount) to the same forty-year-old athlete's running heart rate zones to estimate heart rate zones for training on the bike:

RUNNING ZONES	CYCLING ZONES (95 PERCENT OF RUNNING ZONES)
Z4 = 162 to 171 BPM	Z4 = 154 to 163 BPM
Z3 = 155 to 161 BPM	Z3 = 147 to 153 BPM
Z2 = 135 to 154 BPM	Z2 = 128 to 146 BPM
Z1 = 117 to 134 BPM	Z1 = 111 to 127 BPM

While this 95 percent guideline provides a pretty close estimate for the majority of athletes, we usually encourage our coached athletes to do a 100 percent effort 15-minute cycling time trial (do this on a flat, safe course with no traffic) with a heart rate monitor and confirm their maximum heart rate for the bike. This field test is usually a very good indication of your maximum cycling heart rate. If your field test results differ, adjust your heart rate zones accordingly.

In Appendix A we present two additional formula approaches for determining maximum heart rate for your consideration.

If formal testing is not possible, using the "220 Minus Your Age" estimate (or one of the alternative methods in Appendix A), and then double-checking your results with both the 5K run and 15-minute cycling time trial, will provide most athletes with good heart rate zones to work with in the Chapter 5 training programs.

The Dreaded "Gray Zone"

As mentioned above, the Z3 heart rate zone (about 86 to 89 percent of maximum heart rate) is the natural zone of choice for many athletes. If we ask athletes to run or cycle "as they feel," this is where they very often end up; they tend to naturally gravitate toward Z3.

It's almost funny when we start to work with some new athletes and we begin to plan workouts for them in all four training zones (Z1, Z2, Z3, and Z4). They actually have a difficult time *not* training in Z3. When we ask them to run in Z2, they try to, but then drift up into low Z3. The feedback they give us is that Z2 feels like they are just jogging. When we ask them to run in Z4, they try to, but then drift back down into high Z3. They say no matter how hard they try, they cannot run hard enough to keep their heart rate up in Z4. Amazingly, all of their training is locked into this very narrow range of heart rates.

After years of gravitating toward this same range of heart rates, they now have a very difficult time being anywhere but in this zone. This is obviously not ideal. How could essentially running the same workout week after week and year after year properly develop your energy systems and improve your performance? The answer is, it won't.

Some athletes and coaches refer to this heart rate range as the *gray zone*. It tends to be too hard for our moderate days, when we are focusing on building our aerobic system, and not hard enough for our higher-intensity days, when we want to focus on building our anaerobic system. Ironically, it's a vicious cycle: By pushing too hard on our moderate days, we are too tired to push hard enough on our higher-intensity days. Athletes trap themselves into the dreaded gray zone, which eventually leads to performance stagnation and even injury. The good news is that when these same athletes learn to properly separate their training into Z1, Z2, Z3, and Z4, they almost always break through to new levels of performance.

If this sounds like you, don't despair. There is hope. Just discipline yourself to follow the program and consistently stay in the proper zone, even if it feels too slow or too fast at first. Keep your Z2 work within Z2, and save your energy so that you can push harder and get your higher-intensity work into Z4.

AN IRONFIT MOMENT

Lactate Threshold

Many athletes are familiar with the term *lactate threshold,* but few really understand what it is and what it means in the context of effective training. Lactate threshold is the heart rate level at which lactate begins to accumulate at a faster rate in the muscles than the body can clear.

Lactate is produced in our bodies when performing a physical activity. The accumulation of lactate has a negative impact on the muscles' ability to perform. Lactate threshold is not a constant. It changes relatively quickly for several reasons, including changes in your fitness level. Daily variations of up to several heartbeats per minute are common.

Another way to look at lactate threshold is that it is approximately the heart rate a well-trained athlete can maintain for about one hour at 100 percent effort. This is helpful, as it implies that for any distance you race that takes you less than one hour, you should be mostly at a heart rate *higher* than your lactate threshold; and for any distance that takes you longer than one hour to complete, you should be mostly at a heart rate *under* your lactate threshold.

Following is the fourth of ten motivating profiles of an inspiring Half Iron-Distance Triathlete.

HALF IRON-DISTANCE SUCCESS STORY:
ANDREW WINTER

Andrew Winter's first triathlon experience was when he joined his corporate relay team for a Sprint Triathlon in Singapore, back in 2004. He didn't enjoy the stifling Singapore heat and humidity, and he vowed "never again" for the sport of triathlon.

Fortunately, with the Singapore race a distant memory, Andrew competed in a Sprint race in Genova, Italy, in 2010, and this time he was hooked. Since then Andrew has thrived in the sport, and his many accomplishments already include a 5:03 Half Iron-Distance Triathlon, a 9:49 full Iron-Distance Triathlon, and a 3:06 marathon.

Andrew's rapid endurance sports progress is especially note-worthy given the very full life that he lives. He is the director of operations for an international container shipping company, and frequent traveling is a big requirement of his job. Often his trips are scheduled on short notice, which makes planning for his training especially challenging.

Andrew has a very understanding and supportive family, including his wife, who has her own business, and two young daughters. But they make it all work exceptionally well, and Andrew's success at the races clearly confirms this. Between a very supportive family, great time management skills, and Andrew's effective use of the IronFit training approach, he actually makes it all look pretty easy.

To date, Andrew has raced the Half Iron-Distance three times, all at the very popular race in Majorca, Spain. Each time he successfully utilized the IronFit "90-95-100" Perceived Effort Approach (Chapter 8), and not only performed very well, but also greatly enjoyed the entire Half Iron-Distance experience.

Andrew also favors the Half Iron-Distance's lessened training time requirement, more reasonable race entry fee, and its over-all positive experience. Andrew has raced more full Iron-Distance races in the past, but due to his great success and enjoyment of the Half Iron-Distance, it may likely prove to be his race of choice in the future.

Watch for Andrew and his wonderful family at the races this year, as he continues to lower his Half Iron-Distance times and live the dream.

CHAPTER 5

Sixteen-Week Half Iron-Distance Training Programs

Do not wait to strike till the iron is hot; but
make it hot by striking.

—*William B. Sprague*

In this chapter we present three detailed sixteen-week Half Iron-Distance
training programs. Each program is based on the athlete's available time to
train and level of competitiveness.

The Competitive Program includes approximately 200 total training
hours, with an average of about 12.5 hours per week, and a maximum week
of about 15.3 hours. The Intermediate Program has about 150 total training
hours, with an average of about 9.4 hours per week, and a maximum week
of about 11.8 hours. The "Just Finish" Program tops out at about 100 total
training hours, with an average of about 6.3 hours per week, and a maximum
week of about 8 hours.

Following is a summary comparison of the three sixteen-week programs:

TRAINING PROGRAM	AVERAGE HOURS/WEEK	PEAK HOURS/WEEK	TOTAL HOURS (APPROX.)
Competitive	12.5	15.3	200
Intermediate	9.4	11.8	150
"Just Finish"	6.3	8.0	100

Consider the time management techniques presented in Chapter 1 and
in the athlete profiles, and conservatively estimate your weekly training time
availability. Once you have completed this analysis, simply select the program that best fits you, your goals, your experience level, and your available
training time.

Each program tells you exactly what to do each and every day throughout the sixteen-week period. There are no complicated formulas or overly general workout descriptions. Having worked with hundreds of athletes for many years, we know that this is not what athletes want. Athletes want clear direction on exactly what they need to do and when they need to do it. This is exactly what each of these programs provides. They are designed to be efficient, productive, and enjoyable.

Each program starts with an eight-week base-building phase and then transitions into a second eight-week phase featuring higher-intensity training. Finally, each training program concludes with a nine-day pre-race taper phase to have you rested, sharp, and race-ready at just the right time for your Half Iron-Distance challenge.

Abbreviations in Sixteen-Week Training Programs

Following is an explanation of the abbreviations used in each of the sixteen-week training programs:

Z1   Heart rate zone 1 (heart rate zones are discussed in Chapter 4).

30 min.   Thirty minutes.

1:15   One hour and 15 minutes.

100+ rpm   Pedal bike at a cadence of 100 or more pedal revolutions per minute.

Trans   Transition sessions are a combined bike/run session, where we transition from one sport to the other in 5 minutes or less (discussed in Chapter 2).

QC   Quickly change from cycling gear to running gear.

Z1 to Z2   Train at a heart rate anywhere within zones 1 and 2 (heart rate zones are discussed in Chapter 4).

30 min. Z2 (at 20 min., insert 5 min. Z4)

Begin the 30-minute session in your Z2 heart rate. At 20 minutes into the session, increase your heart rate to Z4 (by increasing your effort level) for 5 minutes. At the completion of the 5 minutes, return to Z2 for the remaining 5 minutes of the session.

PU   Pickups are temporary increases in effort by about 10 to 15 percent.

Spin   Easy recovery cycling in an easier gear.

Jog   Easy recovery running at a slower pace.

Sample bike training session: 45 min. Z2 (at 10 min., insert 5 x 4 min. Z4 @ 2 min. spin) Begin your 45-minute bike session at a pace that will maintain a Z2 heart rate. At 10 minutes into the session, increase your heart rate to Z4 (by increasing your effort level) for 4 minutes, and then decrease gearing for an easy 2-minute spin. Repeat this sequence five times. After completing five sequences, return to a Z2 heart rate for the remainder of the 45-minute bike.

Sample Run Training Session: 45 min. Z2 (at 10 min., insert 4 x 6 min. Z4 @ 3 min. jog) Begin your 45-minute run at a pace that will maintain a Z2 heart rate. At 10 minutes into the run, increase your effort enough to maintain a Z4 heart rate for a period of 6 minutes. After the 6 minutes, slow down to an easy 3-minute jog, bringing your heart rate back down to Z1 or Z2. Repeat this sequence four times. After completing four sequences, return to a Z2 heart rate for the remainder of the run.

WU   Easy warm-up.

CD   Easy cooldown.

DR   Swim drills (presented in Chapter 12).

Swim Sessions in Sixteen-Week Training Programs

Perceived Effort

It is suggested you use the following perceived effort levels with the swim sessions:

- Warm-up, drills (see Chapter 12 for swim drills), and cooldown should be at a perceived effort of about 65 to 75 percent.
- Main swim sets should be at a perceived effort of about 80 to 85 percent.
- Main swim sets indicated as "Fast" should be at a perceived effort of about 90 to 95 percent.

How to Read a Swim Workout

Following is an explanation of how to read our notation for a swim session workout:

300wu, 6x50drills@10 sec, 10 x 100@15sec, 5 x 200@20sec, 6x50 drills@10sec, 200cd

1. Start by swimming an easy 300 yards/meters (65 to 75% perceived effort).

2. Then select one or more drills from Chapter 12 and swim it for 50 yards/meters. Rest for 10 seconds at the wall after completing the 50 yard/meter drill and then repeat this entire sequence for a total of six times through, each time swimming 50 yards/meters of the drill and each time taking a 10-second rest after it (65 to 75% perceived effort).

3. Then swim 100 yards/meters and stop at the wall for a 15-second rest. Repeat this entire sequence ten times through (80 to 85% perceived effort).

4. Then swim 200 yards/meters and stop at the wall for a 20-second rest. Repeat this entire sequence for a total of five times through (80 to 85% perceived effort).

5. Then select one or more drills from Chapter 12 and swim it for 50 yards/meters. Rest for 10 seconds at the wall after completing the 50 yard/meter drill, and then repeat this entire sequence for a total of six times through, each time swimming 50 yards/meters of the drill and each time taking a 10-second rest after it (65 to 75% perceived effort).

6. Finish by swimming an easy 200 yards/meters (65 to 75% perceived effort).

Our three sixteen-week training programs are explained below, starting with the Competitive Program.

Competitive Program

The Competitive Program is for the experienced athlete who wants to maximize his potential and has available time to train for an average of about 12.5 hours a week, with several peak weeks of about 15.3 hours each. The total combined training time over the sixteen-week period is approximately 200 hours, so we like to refer to this as the "200-hour plan."

While at first 200 hours may sound overwhelming, the way we like to look at it is that this is really the equivalent of about 8.3 days' worth of training over a sixteen-week period. In other words, over the course of sixteen weeks (112 days), we will train for the equivalent of about eight days. When you look at it that way, it doesn't seem overwhelming at all.

The first eight weeks of the program contain the base-building phase. We start at about eight hours of fully aerobic (Z1 to Z2 heart rates) training in the first week, and then gradually build by about one hour per week, to about fifteen hours in the eighth week. This amount assumes two swims of about one hour per week, but this program also includes an optional third swim, which adds another hour to these totals. If swimming is your weakest area, it will be very helpful to include the third swim if possible.

If you have not already built up to (or close to) eight hours of training per week before starting the Competitive Program, it is suggested that you do so. Depending on your starting point, you should complete four to eight weeks of moderate aerobic exercise to be properly prepared to begin the program.

Our longest sessions in the first eight weeks will be a five-hour transition session and a two-and-a-quarter-hour long run on the last weekend of the eighth week.

Competitive Program: Base-Building Phase, Weeks 1–8

The chart on pages 50–51 details the eight-week base-building phase of the Competitive Program.

Competitive Program: Swim Sessions

Our swims through the first eight weeks will be approximately 3,000 yards or meters in length, which is a workout distance most athletes can complete within one hour. Our suggestion is that if you need to lengthen the session to last a full hour, simply extend the warm-up and/or cooldown portion as needed. If, however, you find you need to shorten the session to make it fit into an hour, reduce the main sets as needed but keep the warm-up, drills, and cooldown the same.

Following are our twenty-four swim sessions for the Competitive Program:

1. 300wu, 6x50drills@10sec, 6 x 50@10sec, 3 x 100@20sec, 3 x 200@30sec, 3 x 100@20sec, 6 x 50@10sec, 6x50 drills@10sec, 200cd

2. 300wu, 6x50drills@10sec, 4 x (100 @10sec, 150@15sec, 200@20sec), 6x50drills@10sec, 200cd

3. 300wu, 6x50 drills@10sec, 7 x (25@5sec, 50@10sec, 75@10sec, 100@20sec), 6x50 drills@10sec, 200cd

4. 300wu, 6x50 drills@10sec, 1x 500@30sec, 2 x 250@20sec, 4 x 125@15sec, 3 x 100@10sec, 6x50drills@10sec, 200cd

5. 300wu, 6x50 drills@10sec, 3 x (100@15sec, 150@20sec, 100@15sec, 250@30sec), 6x50 drills@10sec, 200cd

6. 300wu, 6x50drills@10sec, 8 x 25@5sec, 4 x 50@10sec, 4 x 100@15sec, 3 x 200@20sec, 1 x 400@30sec, 6x50drills@10sec, 200cd

Swim sessions continue on page 52.

COMPETITIVE PROGRAM BASE BUILDING PHASE

WEEK 1	SWIM	BIKE	RUN
M	#1—Optional	Rest Day / Slide Day	Rest Day / Slide Day
Tu	Off	Off	45 min. Z2
W	#2	Trans: 45 min. Z2 (QC)	15 min. Z2
Th	Off	60 min. Z2	Off
F	#3	Off	45 min. Z2
Sat	Off	1:15 Z2	Off
Sun	Off	30 min. Z1 (100+ rpm)	45 min. Z1 to Z2
Totals: 8:00 hrs.	2:00+hrs.	3:30 hrs.	2:30 hrs.

WEEK 2	SWIM	BIKE	RUN
M	# 4—Optional	Rest Day / Slide Day	Rest Day / Slide Day
Tu	Off	Off	45 min. Z2
W	#5	Trans: 45 min. Z2 (QC)	15 min. Z2
Th	Off	60 min. Z2	Off
F	#6	Off	45 min. Z2
Sat	Off	Trans: 1:15 Z2 (QC)	15 min. Z2
Sun	Off	60 min. Z1 (100+ rpm)	60 min. Z1 to Z2
Totals: 9:00 hrs.	2:00+hrs.	4:00 hrs.	3:00 hrs.

WEEK 3	SWIM	BIKE	RUN
M	#7—Optional	Rest Day / Slide Day	Rest Day / Slide Day
Tu	Off	Off	45 min. Z2
W	#8	Trans: 45 min. Z2 (QC)	15 min. Z2
Th	Off	60 min. Z2	Off
F	#9	Off	60 min. Z2
Sat	Off	Trans: 1:45 Z2 (QC)	15 min. Z2
Sun	Off	60 min. Z1 (100+ rpm)	1:15 Z1 to Z2
Totals: 10:00 hrs.	2:00+ hrs.	4:30 hrs.	3:30 hrs.

WEEK 4	SWIM	BIKE	RUN
M	#10—Optional	Rest Day / Slide Day	Rest Day / Slide Day
Tu	Off	Off	45 min. Z2
W	#11	Trans: 45 min. Z2 (QC)	15 min. Z2
Th	Off	60 min. Z2	Off
F	#12	Off	60 min. Z2
Sat	Off	Trans: 2:15 Z2 (QC)	30 min. Z2
Sun	Off	60 min. Z1 (100+ rpm)	1:30 Z1 to Z2
Totals: 11:00 hrs.	2:00+hrs.	5:00 hrs.	4:00 hrs.

WEEK 5	SWIM	BIKE	RUN
M	#2—Optional	Rest Day / Slide Day	Rest Day / Slide Day
Tu	Off	Off	60 min. Z2
W	#1	Trans: 45 min. Z2 (QC)	15 min. Z2
Th	Off	60 min. Z2	Off
F	#3	Off	60 min. Z2
Sat	Off	Trans: 2:45 Z2 (QC)	30 min. Z2
Sun	Off	60 min. Z1 (100+ rpm)	1:45 Z1 to Z2
Totals: 12:00 hrs.	2:00+ hrs.	5:30 hrs.	4:30 hrs.

WEEK 6	SWIM	BIKE	RUN
M	#5—Optional	Rest Day / Slide Day	Rest Day / Slide Day
Tu	Off	Off	60 min. Z2
W	#4	Trans: 45 min. Z2 (QC)	30 min. Z2
Th	Off	60 min. Z2	Off
F	#6	Off	60 min. Z2
Sat	Off	Trans: 3:15 Z2 (QC)	30 min. Z2
Sun	Off	60 min. Z1 (100+ rpm)	2:00 Z1 to Z2
Totals: 13:00 hrs.	2:00+ hrs.	6:00 hrs.	5:00 hrs.

WEEK 7	SWIM	BIKE	RUN
M	#8—Optional	Rest Day / Slide Day	Rest Day / Slide Day
Tu	Off	Off	1:15 Z2
W	#7	Trans: 45 min. Z2 (QC)	30 min. Z2
Th	Off	60 min. Z2	Off
F	#9	Off	1:15 Z2
Sat	Off	Trans: 3:45 Z2 (QC)	45 min. Z2
Sun	Off	60 min. Z1 (100+ rpm)	1:45 Z1 to Z2
Totals: 14:00 hrs.	2:00+ hrs.	6:30 hrs.	5:30 hrs.

WEEK 8	SWIM	BIKE	RUN
M	#11—Optional	Rest Day / Slide Day	Rest Day / Slide Day
Tu	Off	Off	1:15 Z2
W	#10	Trans: 45 min. Z2 (QC)	30 min. Z2
Th	Off	60 min. Z2	Off
F	#12	Off	1:15 Z2
Sat	Off	Trans: 4:15 Z2 (QC)	45 min. Z2
Sun	Off	60 min. Z1 (100+ rpm)	2:15 Z1 to Z2
Totals: 15:00 hrs.	2:00+ hrs.	7:00 hrs.	6:00 hrs.

7. 300wu, 6x50drills@10sec, 3 x (4 x 100@10sec, 1 x 200@20sec), 6x50drills@10sec, 200cd

8. 300wu, 6x50 drills@10sec, 6 x 175@20sec, 6 x 125@10sec, 6x50 drills@10sec, 200cd

9. 300wu, 6x50drills@10sec, 500@35sec, 400@30sec, 300@25sec, 200@20sec, 5 x 100@15sec, 6x50 drills@10sec, 200cd

10. 300wu, 6x50drills@10sec, 4 x (50@5sec, 100@10sec, 150@15sec, 200@20sec), 6x50drills@10sec, 200cd

11. 300wu, 6x50 drills@10sec, 3 x (75@10sec, 125@15sec, 175@20sec, 225@25sec), 6x50 drills@10sec, 200cd

12. 300wu, 6x50 drills@10sec, 6 x 25@5sec, 6 x 75@10sec, 4 x 150@15sec, 6 x 75@10sec, 6 x 25@5sec, 3 x 100@10sec, 6x50drills@10sec, 200cd

13. 300wu, 6x50 drills@10sec, 4 x 200@20sec, 4 x 150@15sec, 4 x 100@10sec, 6x50 drills@10sec, 200cd

14. 300wu, 6x50drills@10sec, 3 x (6 x 75@10sec, 1 x 250@20sec), 6x50drills@10sec, 200cd

15. 300wu, 6x50drills@10sec, 5 x 100@10sec, 6 x 150@15sec, 5 x 100@10sec, 6x50drills@10sec, 200cd

16. 300wu, 6x50drills@10sec, 3 x (1 x 400@30sec, 3 x 100@10sec), 6x50drills@10sec, 200cd

17. 300wu, 6x50drills@10sec, 3x100@10sec, 3x150@15sec, 3x200@20sec, 3x250@25sec, 6x50 drills@10sec, 200cd

18. 300wu, 6x50drills@10sec, 4x75@10sec., 4x125@15sec, 1x 300@20sec, 4x125@15sec, 4x75@10sec, 6x50drills@10sec, 200cd

19. 300wu, 6x50 drills@10sec, 200@20sec, 300@25sec, 400@30sec, 500@35sec, 600@40sec, 6x50 drills@10sec, 200cd

20. 300wu, 6x50 drills@10sec, 12x25@5sec, 8x50@10sec, 5x100@15sec, 8x50@10sec, 12x25@5sec, 6x50drills@10sec, 200cd

21. 300wu, 6x50 drills@10sec, 3 x (75@10sec, 125@15sec, 225@20sec, 275@25sec), 6x50 drills@10sec, 200cd

22. 300wu, 6x50drills@10sec, 8 x 75@10sec, 3x 200@20sec, 8 x 75@10sec, 6x50drills@10sec, 200cd

23. 300wu, 6x50drills@10sec, 3 x (25 Fast@15 sec, 125@15 sec), 3 x (50 Fast@15 sec, 100@15 sec), 3 x (75 Fast@15 sec, 75@10 sec), 3 x (100 Fast@15 sec, 50@10 sec), 6x50 drills@10sec, 200cd

24. 300wu, 6x50drills@10sec, 3 x (200 Fast@30 sec, 500 Pull@30 sec), 6x50 drills, 200cd

Competitive Program: Peak Training and Taper Phase, Weeks 9–16

The second eight weeks (Weeks 9 through 16) of the Competitive Program include both the peak training phase and the taper phase. We start by including Easy Pickups in the ninth week to prepare us to introduce higher-intensity Z4 training. Our quantity of Z4 training will gradually build from there and peak in Week 14. Weeks 10 through 14 will each have four sessions that will include Z4 work, including two bike sessions and two run sessions. With seven bike or run sessions per week during this period, this means that more than half of the sessions (57%) will include Z4 higher-intensity training.

During the second eight weeks we will continue to include two swims of about one hour (3,000 yards/meters) each per week, with an optional third swim, which adds another hour to these totals. Again, if swimming is your weakest area, it will be very helpful to include the third swim if possible.

Just like in the first eight-week base-building phase, our longest sessions in the second eight weeks will be five-hour transition sessions and two-and-a-quarter-hour long runs. This time, however, two of the five-hour transition sessions will be structured as "415-20-45 Bricks," with 20-minute Z4 inserts, and one will be structured with a 40-minute Z3 insert (see Chapter 2).

With nine days to go before our Half Iron-Distance race, we will transition into our crisp taper phase, to have us rested, sharp, and race-ready. Our durations will gradually decrease, and our intensities will be no higher than Z2 during these last nine days. At this point, the hay is in the barn, and it's time to taper smart and become physically and mentally energized.

Following is the eight-week peak training and taper phase of the Competitive Program.

COMPETITIVE PROGRAM
PEAK TRAINING AND TAPER PHASES

WEEK 9	SWIM	BIKE	RUN
M	#13—Optional	Rest Day / Slide Day	Rest Day / Slide Day
Tu	Off	Off	1:15 Z2 (at 10 min. insert 5 x 1 min. PU @ 1 min. jog)
W	#14	Trans: 45 min. Z2 (QC)	30 min. Z2
Th	Off	1:15 Z2 (at 10 min., insert 5 x 1 min. PU @ 1 min. spin)	Off
F	#15	Off	1:15 Z2 (at 60 min. insert 5 min. Z4)
Sat	Off	Trans: 4:15 Z2 (at 4:00 insert 5 min. Z4)(QC)	45 min. Z2
Sun	Off	60 min. Z1 (100+ rpm)	1:45 Z1 to Z2
Totals: 14:45 hrs.	2:00+ hrs.	7:15 hrs.	5:30 hrs.

WEEK 10	SWIM	BIKE	RUN
M	# 16—Optional	Rest Day / Slide Day	Rest Day / Slide Day
Tu	Off	Off	1:15 Z2 (at 10 min. insert 10 x 2 min. Z4 @ 1 min. jog)
W	#17	Trans: 45 min. Z2 (QC)	30 min. Z2
Th	Off	1:15 Z2 (at 10 min., insert 10 x 2 min. Z4 Hill Repeats @ spin back down)	Off
F	#18	Off	1:15 hr. Z2 (at 60 min., insert 10 min. Z4)
Sat	Off	Trans: 4:15 Z2 (at 4:00 hr. insert 10 min. Z4)(QC)	45 min. Z2
Sun	Off	60 min. Z1 (100+ rpm)	2:15 Z1 to Z2
Totals: 15:15 hrs.	2:00+ hrs.	7:15 hrs.	6:00 hrs.

WEEK 11	SWIM	BIKE	RUN
M	#19—Optional	Rest Day / Slide Day	Rest Day / Slide Day
Tu	Off	Off	1:15 Z2 (at 10 min. insert 8 x 3 min. Z4 @ 1.5 min. jog)
W	#20	Trans: 45 min. Z2 (QC)	30 min. Z2
Th	Off	1:15 Z2 (at 10 min., insert 7 x 4 min. Z4@ 2 min. spin)	Off
F	#21	Off	1:15 Z2 (at 55 min., insert 12.5 min. Z4)
Sat	Off	Trans: 4:15 Z2 (at 3:55, insert 15 min. Z4)(QC)	45 min. Z2
Sun	Off	60 min. Z1 (100+ rpm)	1:45 Z1 to Z2
Totals: 14:45 hrs.	2:00+ hrs.	7:15 hrs.	5:30 hrs.

WEEK 12	SWIM	BIKE	RUN
M	#22—Optional	Rest Day / Slide Day	Rest Day / Slide Day
Tu	Off	Off	1:15 Z2 (at 10 min. insert 6 x 4.5 min. Z4 @ 2 min. jog)
W	#23	Trans: 45 min. Z2 (QC)	30 min. Z2
Th	Off	1:15 Z2 (at 10 min., insert 12 x 2.5 min. Z4 Hill Repeats@ spin back down)	Off
F	#24	Off	1:15 Z2 (at 55 min. insert 15 min. Z4)
Sat	Off	Trans: 4:15 Z2 (at 3:50 insert 20 min. Z4)(QC)	45 min. Z2
Sun	Off	60 min. Z1 (100+ rpm)	2:15 Z1 to Z2
Totals: 15:15 hrs.	2:00+ hrs.	7:15 hrs.	6:00 hrs.

COMPETITIVE PROGRAM
PEAK TRAINING AND TAPER PHASES

WEEK 13	SWIM	BIKE	RUN
M	#14—Optional	Rest Day / Slide Day	Rest Day / Slide Day
Tu	Off	Off	1:15 Z2 (at 10 min. insert 5 x 6 min. Z4 @ 3 min. jog)
W	#13	Trans: 45 min. Z2 (QC)	30 min. Z2
Th	Off	1:15 Z2 (at 10 min., insert 6 x 5 min. Z4 @ 2.5 min. spin)	Off
F	#15	Off	1:15 Z2 (at 15 min. insert 15 min. Z4)
Sat	Off	Trans: 4:15 Z2 (at 3:50 insert 20 min. Z4)(QC)	45 min. Z2
Sun	Off	60 min. Z1 (100+ rpm)	1:45 Z1 to Z2
Totals: 14:45 hrs.	2:00+ hrs.	7:15 hrs.	5:30 hrs.

WEEK 14	SWIM	BIKE	RUN
M	# 17—Optional	Rest Day / Slide Day	Rest Day / Slide Day
Tu	Off	Off	1:15 Z2 (at 10 min. insert 4 x 7.5 min. Z4 @ 3.5 min. jog)
W	#16	Trans: 45 min. Z2 (QC)	30 min. Z2
Th	Off	1:15 Z2 (at 10 min. insert 10 x 3 min. Z4 Hill Repeats @ spin back down)	Off
F	#18	Off	1:15 Z2 (at 55 min., insert 15 min. Z4)
Sat	Off	Trans: 4:15 Z2 (at 3:30 insert 40 min. Z3)(QC)	45 min. Z2
Sun	Off	60 min. Z1 (100+ rpm)	2:15 Z1 to Z2
Totals: 15:15 hrs.	2:00+ hrs.	7:15 hrs.	6:00 hrs.

WEEK 15	SWIM	BIKE	RUN
M	#20—Optional	Rest Day / Slide Day	Rest Day / Slide Day
Tu	Off	Off	1:15 Z2 (at 10 min. insert 1 x 10 min. Z4 @ 5 min. jog, then 10 x 2 min. Z4 @ 1 min. jog)
W	#19	Trans: 45 min. Z2 (QC)	30 min. Z2
Th	Off	1:15 Z2 (at 10 min., insert 4 x 7.5 min. Z4 @ 3.5 min. spin)	Off
F	#21	Off	1:15 Z2 (at 60 min. insert 10 min. Z4)
Sat	Off	Trans: 2:15 Z2 (QC)	30 min. Z2
Sun	Off	45 min. Z1 (100+ rpm)	60 min. Z1 to Z2
Totals: 11:30 hrs.	2:00+ hrs.	5:00 hrs.	4:30 hrs.

WEEK 16	SWIM	BIKE	RUN
M	Off	Rest Day / Slide Day	Rest Day / Slide Day
Tu	Off	Off	45 min. Z1 to Z2 (at 10 min. insert 5 x 1 min. PU @ 1 min. jog)
W	30 min. easy	Trans: 45 min. Z1 to Z2 (QC)	15 min. Z1 to Z2
Th	Off	60 min. Z1 (at 10 min. insert 5 x 1 min. PU @ 1 min. spin)	Off
F	30 min. easy	Off	40 min. Z1 (at 10 min., insert 5 x 1 min. PU @ 1 min. jog)
Sat	Off	15 min. Z1—easy bike safety check	20 min. Z1—easy (in a.m.)
Sun	Race!! Half Iron-Distance	Race!! Half Iron-Distance	Race!! Half Iron-Distance
Totals: 5:00 hrs.	1:00 hrs. (+Race)	2:00 hrs. (+Race)	2:00 hrs. (+Race)

The second of our three sixteen-week training programs is the Intermediate Program.

Intermediate Program

The Intermediate Program is for the athlete who fits best in between the Competitive Program and the "Just Finish" Program, both in terms of time available to train and competitive goals. The Intermediate Program athlete needs to have available time to train for an average of about 9.4 hours a week, with several peak weeks of about 11.8 hours. The total combined training time over the sixteen-week period is about 150 hours, so we like to refer to this one as the "150-hour plan."

While at first 150 hours may sound like a challenging amount of training, the way we like to look at it is that this is really the equivalent of about 6.3 days' worth of training over a sixteen-week period. In other words, over the course of sixteen weeks (112 days), we will train for the equivalent of about six days. When you look at it that way, it seems like a much more achievable challenge.

The first eight weeks of the program is the base-building phase. We start at about six hours of fully aerobic (Z1 to Z2 heart rates) training in the first week, and then gradually build by about 45 minutes per week to about eleven hours in the eighth week. This amount assumes two swims of about 45 minutes per week.

If you have not already built up to (or close to) six hours of training per week before starting the Intermediate Program, it is suggested that you do. Depending on your starting point, you should complete four to eight weeks of moderate aerobic exercise in order to be properly prepared to begin the program.

Our longest sessions in the first eight weeks will be a four-and-a-half-hour transition session and a two-and-a-quarter-hour long run on the last weekend of the eighth week.

Intermediate Program: Base-Building Phase, Weeks 1–8

The following chart details the eight-week base-building phase of the Intermediate Program.

INTERMEDIATE PROGRAM
BASE-BUILDING PHASE

WEEK 1	SWIM	BIKE	RUN
M	Off	Rest Day / Slide Day	Rest Day / Slide Day
Tu	#1	Off	45 min. Z2
W	Off	Trans: 30 min. Z2 (QC)	15 min. Z2
Th	#2	45 min. Z2	Off
F	Off	Rest Day / Slide Day	Rest Day / Slide Day
Sat	Off	1:15 Z2	Off
Sun	Off	Off	60 min. Z1 to Z2
Totals: 6:00 hrs.	1:30 hrs.	2:30 hrs.	2:00 hrs.

WEEK 2	SWIM	BIKE	RUN
M	Off	Rest Day / Slide Day	Rest Day / Slide Day
Tu	#3	Off	45 min. Z2
W	Off	Trans: 30 min. Z2 (QC)	15 min. Z2
Th	#4	45 min. Z2	Off
F	Off	Rest Day / Slide Day	Rest Day / Slide Day
Sat	Off	1:45 Z2	Off
Sun	Off	Off	1:15 Z1 to Z2
Totals: 6:45 hrs.	1:30 hrs.	3:00 hrs.	2:15 hrs.

WEEK 3	SWIM	BIKE	RUN
M	Off	Rest Day / Slide Day	Rest Day / Slide Day
Tu	#5	Off	45 min. Z2
W	Off	Trans: 45 min. Z2 (QC)	15 min. Z2
Th	#6	45 min. Z2	Off
F	Off	Rest Day / Slide Day	Rest Day / Slide Day
Sat	Off	Trans: 1:45 Z2 (QC)	15 min. Z2
Sun	Off	Off	1:30 Z1 to Z2
Totals: 7:30 hrs.	1:30 hrs.	3:15 hrs.	2:45 hrs.

INTERMEDIATE PROGRAM
BASE-BUILDING PHASE

WEEK 4	SWIM	BIKE	RUN
M	Off	Rest Day / Slide Day	Rest Day / Slide Day
Tu	#7	Off	45 min. Z2
W	Off	Trans: 45 min. Z2 (QC)	15 min. Z2
Th	#8	60 min. Z2	Off
F	Off	Rest Day / Slide Day	Rest Day / Slide Day
Sat	Off	Trans: 2:15 Z2 (QC)	15 min. Z2
Sun	Off	Off	1:30 Z1 to Z2
Totals: 8:15 hrs.	1:30 hrs.	4:00 hrs.	2:45 hrs.

WEEK 5	SWIM	BIKE	RUN
M	Off	Rest Day / Slide Day	Rest Day / Slide Day
Tu	#1	Off	60 min. Z2
W	Off	Trans: 45 min. Z2 (QC)	15 min. Z2
Th	#2	60 min. Z2	Off
F	Off	Rest Day / Slide Day	Rest Day / Slide Day
Sat	Off	Trans: 2:45 Z2 (QC)	15 min. Z2
Sun	Off	Off	1:30 Z1 to Z2
Totals: 9:00 hrs.	1:30 hrs.	4:30 hrs.	3:00 hrs.

WEEK 6	SWIM	BIKE	RUN
M	Off	Rest Day / Slide Day	Rest Day / Slide Day
Tu	#3	Off	60 min. Z2
W	Off	Trans: 45 min. Z2 (QC)	15 min. Z2
Th	#4	60 min. Z2	Off
F	Off	Rest Day / Slide Day	Rest Day / Slide Day
Sat	Off	Trans: 3:15 Z2 (QC)	15 min. Z2
Sun	Off	Off	1:45 Z1 to Z2
Totals: 9:45 hrs.	1:30 hrs.	5:00 hrs.	3:15 hrs.

WEEK 7	SWIM	BIKE	RUN
M	Off	Rest Day / Slide Day	Rest Day / Slide Day
Tu	#5	Off	60 min. Z2
W	Off	Trans: 45 min. Z2 (QC)	15 min. Z2
Th	#6	60 min. Z2	Off
F	Off	Rest Day / Slide Day	Rest Day / Slide Day
Sat	Off	Trans: 3:45 Z2 (QC)	15 min. Z2
Sun	Off	Off	2:00 Z1 to Z2
Totals: 10:30 hrs.	1:30 hrs.	5:30 hrs.	3:30 hrs.
WEEK 8	SWIM	BIKE	RUN
M	Off	Rest Day / Slide Day	Rest Day / Slide Day
Tu	#7	Off	60 min. Z2
W	Off	Trans: 45 min. Z2 (QC)	15 min. Z2
Th	#8	60 min. Z2	Off
F	Off	Rest Day / Slide Day	Rest Day / Slide Day
Sat	Off	Trans: 4:15 Z2 (QC)	15 min. Z2
Sun	Off	Off	2:15 Z1 to Z2
Totals: 11:15 hrs.	1:30 hrs.	6:00 hrs.	3:45 hrs.

Intermediate Program: Swim Sessions

Our swims through the first eight weeks will all be approximately 2,000 yards or meters in length, which is a workout distance most athletes can complete within 45 minutes. Our suggestion is that if you need to lengthen the session to last a full 45 minutes, simply extend the warm-up or cooldown portion, as needed. If, however, you find that you need to shorten the session to make it fit into 45 minutes, reduce the main sets as needed, but keep the warm-up, drills, and cooldown the same.

Following are our fifteen swim sessions for the Intermediate Program.

1. 200wu, 6x50drills@10sec, 3 x 50@10sec, 2 x 100@20sec, 2 x 150@30sec, 3 x 100@20sec, 3 x 50@10sec, 6x50 drills@10sec, 200cd

2. 200wu, 6x50drills@10sec, 4 x (100 @15sec, 150@20sec), 6x50drills@10sec, 200cd

3. 200wu, 6x50 drills@10sec, 4 x (25@5sec, 50@5sec, 75@10sec, 100@15sec), 6x50 drills@10sec, 200cd

4. 200wu, 6x50 drills@10sec, 2 x 250@30sec, 4 x 125@15sec, 6x50drills@10sec, 200cd

5. 200wu, 6x50 drills@10sec, 3 x (100@15sec, 250@30sec), 6x50 drills@10sec, 200cd

6. 200wu, 6x50drills@10sec, 8 x 25@5sec, 4 x 50@10sec, 2 x 100@15sec, 2 x 200@20sec, 6x50drills@10sec, 200cd

7. 200wu, 6x50drills@10sec, 3 x (150@15sec, 200@20sec), 6x50drills@10sec, 200cd

8. 200wu, 6x50 drills@10sec, 3 x 175@20sec, 3 x 125@10sec, 6x50 drills@10sec, 200cd

9. 200wu, 6x50drills@10sec, 500@35sec, 400@30sec, 300@25sec, 200@20sec, 100@15sec, 6x50 drills@10sec, 200cd

10. 200wu, 6x50drills@10sec, 2 x (50@5sec, 100@10sec, 150@15sec, 200@20sec, 250@25sec), 6x50drills@10sec, 200cd

11. 200wu, 6x50 drills@10sec, 4 x (125@15sec, 225@25sec), 6x50 drills@10sec, 200cd

12. 200wu, 6x50 drills@10sec, 4 x 25@5sec, 3 x 75@10sec, 2 x 125@15sec, 1 x 250@20sec, 2 x 125@15sec, 3 x 75@10sec, 4 x 25@5sec, 6x50drills@10sec, 200cd

13. 200wu, 6x50 drills@10sec, 6 x 150@15sec, 6 x 100@10sec, 6x50 drills@10sec, 200cd

14. 200wu, 6x50drills@10sec, 6 x 250@30sec, 6x50drills@10sec, 200cd

15. 200wu, 6x50drills@10sec, 3 x (25 Fast@15 sec, 125@15 sec), 3 x (50 Fast@15sec, 100@15sec), 3 x (75 Fast@15 sec, 75@10 sec), 6x50 drills@10sec, 200cd

Intermediate Program: Peak Training and Taper Phase, Weeks 9–16

The second eight weeks (Weeks 9 through 16) of the Intermediate Program include both the peak training phase and the taper phase. We start by including Easy Pickups in the ninth week to prepare us to introduce higher-intensity Z4 training. Our quantity of Z4 training will gradually build from there and peak in Week 14. Weeks 10 through 14 will each have three sessions that will include Z4 work, including two bike sessions and one run session. With five bike or run sessions per week during this period, this means that more than half of the sessions (60%) will include Z4 higher-intensity training.

During this phase we will continue to include two swims each week, but each session will now increase to about 2,500 yards/meters.

Our longest sessions in the second eight weeks will be five-hour transition sessions and two-and-a-quarter-hour long runs. This time, however, one of the five-hour transition sessions will be structured as a "415-20-45 Brick," with a 20-minute Z4 insert, and one will be structured with a 40-minute Z3 insert (see Chapter 2).

With nine days to go before our Half Iron-Distance race, we will transition into our crisp taper phase to have us rested, sharp, and race-ready. Our volumes will gradually decrease, and our intensities will be no higher than Z2 during these last nine days. At this point, the hay is in the barn, and it's time to taper smart and become physically and mentally energized.

Following is the eight-week peak training phase and taper phase of the Intermediate Program.

INTERMEDIATE PROGRAM
PEAK TRAINING AND TAPER PHASES

WEEK 9	SWIM	BIKE	RUN
M	Off	Rest Day / Slide Day	Rest Day / Slide Day
Tu	#9	Off	60 min. Z2 (at 10 min., insert 5 x 1 min. PU @ 1 min. jog)
W	Off	Trans: 45 min. Z2 (QC)	15 min. Z2
Th	#10	60 min. Z2 (at 10 min., insert 5 x 1 min. PU @ 1 min. spin)	Off
F	Off	Rest Day / Slide Day	Rest Day / Slide Day
Sat	Off	Trans: 4:15 Z2 (at 4:00 insert 5 min. Z4)(QC)	45 min. Z2
Sun	Off	Off	1:45 Z1 to Z2
Totals: 11:45 hrs.	2:00 hrs.	6:00 hrs.	3:45 hrs.

WEEK 10	SWIM	BIKE	RUN
M	Off	Rest Day / Slide Day	Rest Day / Slide Day
Tu	#11	Off	60 min. Z2 (at 10 min., insert 10 x 2 min. Z4 @ 1 min. jog)
W	Off	Trans: 45 min. Z2 (QC)	15 min. Z2
Th	#12	60 min. Z2 (at 10 min., insert 10 x 2 min. Z4 Hill Repeats @ spin back down)	Off
F	Off	Rest Day / Slide Day	Rest Day / Slide Day
Sat	Off	Trans: 3:15 Z2 (at 3:00 insert 10 min. Z4)(QC)	15 min. Z2
Sun	Off	30 min. Z1 (100+ rpm)	2:15 Z1 to Z2
Totals: 11:15 hrs.	2:00 hrs.	5:30 hrs.	3:45 hrs.

WEEK 11	SWIM	BIKE	RUN
M	Off	Rest Day / Slide Day	Rest Day / Slide Day
Tu	#13	Off	60 min. Z2 (at 45 min., insert 10 min. Z4)
W	Off	Trans: 45 min. Z2 (QC)	15 min. Z2
Th	#14	60 min. Z2 (at 10 min., insert 6 x 4 min. Z4 @ 2 min. spin)	Off
F	Off	Rest Day / Slide Day	Rest Day / Slide Day
Sat	Off	Trans: 4:15 Z2 (at 3:55 insert 15 min. Z4)(QC)	45 min. Z2
Sun	Off	Off	1:45 Z1 to Z2
Totals: 11:45 hrs.	2:00 hrs.	6:00 hrs.	3:45 hrs.

WEEK 12	SWIM	BIKE	RUN
M	Off	Rest Day / Slide Day	Rest Day / Slide Day
Tu	#15	Off	60 min. Z2 (at 10 min., insert 8 x 3 min. Z4 @ 1.5 min. jog)
W	Off	Trans: 45 min. Z2 (QC)	15 min. Z2
Th	#9	60 min. Z2 (at 10 min., insert 10 x 2.5 min. Z4 Hill Repeats @ spin back down)	Off
F	Off	Rest Day / Slide Day	Rest Day / Slide Day
Sat	Off	Trans: 3:15 Z2 (at 2:50 insert 20 min. Z4)(QC)	15 min. Z2
Sun	Off	30 min. Z1 (100+ rpm)	2:15 Z1 to Z2
Totals: 11:15 hrs.	2:00 hrs.	5:30 hrs.	3:45 hrs.

INTERMEDIATE PROGRAM
PEAK TRAINING AND TAPER PHASES

WEEK 13	SWIM	BIKE	RUN
M	Off	Rest Day / Slide Day	Rest Day / Slide Day
Tu	#10	Off	60 min. Z2 (at 40 min., insert 12.5 min. Z4)
W	Off	Trans: 45 min. Z2 (QC)	15 min. Z2
Th	#11	60 min. Z2 (at 10 min., insert 5 x 5 min. Z4 @ 2.5 min. spin)	Off
F	Off	Rest Day / Slide Day	Rest Day / Slide Day
Sat	Off	Trans: 4:15 Z2 (at 3:50 insert 20 min. Z4)(QC)	45 min. Z2
Sun	Off	Off	1:45 Z1 to Z2
Totals: 11:45 hrs.	2:00 hrs.	6:00 hrs.	3:45 hrs.

WEEK 14	SWIM	BIKE	RUN
M	Off	Rest Day / Slide Day	Rest Day / Slide Day
Tu	#12	Off	60 min. Z2 (at 10 min., insert 4 x 6 min. Z4 @ 3 min. jog)
W	Off	Trans: 45 min. Z2 (QC)	15 min. Z2
Th	#13	60 min. Z2 (at 10 min., insert 8 x 3 min. Z4 Hill Repeats @ spin back down)	Off
F	Off	Rest Day / Slide Day	Rest Day / Slide Day
Sat	Off	Trans: 3:15 Z2 (at 2:30 insert 40 min. Z3)(QC)	15 min. Z2
Sun	Off	30 min. Z1 (100+ rpm)	2:15 Z1 to Z2
Totals: 11:15 hrs.	2:00 hrs.	5:30 hrs.	3:45 hrs.

WEEK 15	SWIM	BIKE	RUN
M	Off	Rest Day / Slide Day	Rest Day / Slide Day
Tu	#14	Off	60 min. Z2 (at 40 min., insert 15 min. Z4)
W	Off	Trans: 45 min. Z2 (QC)	15 min. Z2
Th	#15	60 min. Z2 (at 10 min., insert 3 x 7.5 min. Z4 @ 3.5 min. spin)	Off
F	Off	Rest Day / Slide Day	Rest Day / Slide Day
Sat	Off	Trans: 2:15 Z2 (QC)	15 min. Z2
Sun	Off	30 min. Z1 (100+ rpm)	60 min. Z1 to Z2
Totals: 9:00 hrs.	2:00 hrs.	4:30 hrs.	2:30 hrs.

WEEK 16	SWIM	BIKE	RUN
M	Off	Rest Day / Slide Day	Rest Day / Slide Day
Tu	30 min. easy	Off	45 min. Z1 to Z2 (at 10 min., insert 5 x 1 min. PU @ 1 min. jog)
W	Off	Trans: 45 min. Z1 to Z2 (QC)	15 min. Z1 to Z2
Th	30 min. easy	60 min. Z1 (at 10 min., insert 5 x 1 min. PU @ 1 min. spin)	Off
F	Off	Off	40 min. Z1 (at 10 min., insert 5 x 1 min. PU @ 1 min. jog)
Sat	Off	15 min. Z1—easy bike safety check	20 min. Z1—easy (in a.m.)
Sun	Race!! Half Iron-Distance	Race!! Half Iron-Distance	Race!! Half Iron-Distance
Totals: 5:00 hrs.	1:00 hrs. (+Race)	2:00 hrs. (+Race)	2:00 hrs. (+Race)

The final of our three sixteen-week training programs is the "Just Finish" Program.

"Just Finish" Program

The "Just Finish" Program is for the athlete who has limited time available to train, but would like to be able to complete the Half Iron-Distance Triathlon safely, in good health, and in good spirits. The "Just Finish" Program athlete needs to have available time to train for an average of about 6.3 hours a week, with several peak weeks of about 8 hours. The total combined training time over the sixteen-week period is approximately 100 hours, so we like to refer to this as the "100-hour plan."

While 100 hours may sound like a challenging amount of training for some athletes, the way we like to look at it is that this is really the equivalent of about 4.2 days' worth of training over a sixteen-week period. In other words, over the course of sixteen weeks (112 days), we will train for the equivalent of about four days. When you look at it that way, it seems like a very achievable challenge.

The first eight weeks of the program is the base-building phase. We start at about four hours of fully aerobic (Z1 to Z2 heart rates) training in the first week, and then gradually build by about 30 minutes per week to about 7.5 hours in the eighth week. This amount assumes two swims of about 45 minutes each per week.

If you have not already built up to (or close to) four hours of training per week before starting the "Just Finish" Program, it is suggested that you do. Depending on your starting point, you should complete four to eight weeks of moderate aerobic exercise to be properly prepared to begin the program.

Our longest sessions in the first eight weeks will be a two-hour bike session and a one-and-three-quarter-hour long run on the last weekend of the eighth week.

"Just Finish" Program: Base-Building Phase, Weeks 1–8

The following chart details the eight-week base-building phase of the "Just Finish" Program.

"JUST FINISH" PROGRAM
BASE-BUILDING PHASE

WEEK 1	SWIM	BIKE	RUN
M	Off	Rest Day / Slide Day	Rest Day / Slide Day
Tu	#1	Off	30 min. Z2
W	Off	Trans: 15 min. Z2 (QC)	15 min. Z2
Th	#2	30 min. Z2	Off
F	Off	Rest Day / Slide Day	Rest Day / Slide Day
Sat	Off	30 min. Z2	Off
Sun	Off	Off	30 min. Z1 to Z2
Totals: 4:00 hrs.	1:30 hrs.	1:15 hrs.	1:15 hrs.

WEEK 2	SWIM	BIKE	RUN
M	Off	Rest Day / Slide Day	Rest Day / Slide Day
Tu	#3	Off	30 min. Z2
W	Off	Trans: 30 min. Z2 (QC)	15 min. Z2
Th	#4	30 min. Z2	Off
F	Off	Rest Day / Slide Day	Rest Day / Slide Day
Sat	Off	30 min. Z2	Off
Sun	Off	Off	45 min. Z1 to Z2
Totals: 4:30 hrs.	1:30 hrs.	1:30 hrs.	1:30 hrs.

WEEK 3	SWIM	BIKE	RUN
M	Off	Rest Day / Slide Day	Rest Day / Slide Day
Tu	#5	Off	45 min. Z2
W	Off	Trans: 30 min. Z2 (QC)	15 min. Z2
Th	#6	30 min. Z2	Off
F	Off	Rest Day / Slide Day	Rest Day / Slide Day
Sat	Off	45 min. Z2	Off
Sun	Off	Off	45 min. Z1 to Z2
Totals: 5:00 hrs.	1:30 hrs.	1:45 hrs.	1:45 hrs.

"JUST FINISH" PROGRAM
BASE-BUILDING PHASE

WEEK 4	SWIM	BIKE	RUN
M	Off	Rest Day / Slide Day	Rest Day / Slide Day
Tu	#7	Off	45 min. Z2
W	Off	Trans: 30 min. Z2 (QC)	15 min. Z2
Th	#8	30 min. Z2	Off
F	Off	Rest Day / Slide Day	Rest Day / Slide Day
Sat	Off	60 min. Z2	Off
Sun	Off	Off	60 min. Z1 to Z2
Totals: 5:30 hrs.	1:30 hrs.	2:00 hrs.	2:00 hrs.

WEEK 5	SWIM	BIKE	RUN
M	Off	Rest Day / Slide Day	Rest Day / Slide Day
Tu	#1	Off	45 min. Z2
W	Off	Trans: 30 min. Z2 (QC)	15 min. Z2
Th	#2	45 min. Z2	Off
F	Off	Rest Day / Slide Day	Rest Day / Slide Day
Sat	Off	1:15 Z2	Off
Sun	Off	Off	60 min. Z1 to Z2
Totals: 6:00 hrs.	1:30 hrs.	2:30 hrs.	2:00 hrs.

WEEK 6	SWIM	BIKE	RUN
M	Off	Rest Day / Slide Day	Rest Day / Slide Day
Tu	#3	Off	45 min. Z2
W	Off	Trans: 30 min. Z2 (QC)	15 min. Z2
Th	#4	45 min. Z2	Off
F	Off	Rest Day / Slide Day	Rest Day / Slide Day
Sat	Off	1:30 Z2	Off
Sun	Off	Off	1:15 Z1 to Z2
Totals: 6:30 hrs.	1:30 hrs.	2:45 hrs.	2:15 hrs.

WEEK 7	SWIM	BIKE	RUN
M	Off	Rest Day / Slide Day	Rest Day / Slide Day
Tu	#5	Off	45 min. Z2
W	Off	Trans: 30 min. Z2 (QC)	15 min. Z2
Th	#6	45 min. Z2	Off
F	Off	Rest Day / Slide Day	Rest Day / Slide Day
Sat	Off	2:00 Z2	Off
Sun	Off	Off	1:15 Z1 to Z2
Totals: 7:00 hrs.	1:30 hrs.	3:15 hrs.	2:15 hrs.

WEEK 8	SWIM	BIKE	RUN
M	Off	Rest Day / Slide Day	Rest Day / Slide Day
Tu	#7	Off	45 min. Z2
W	Off	Trans: 30 min. Z2 (QC)	15 min. Z2
Th	#8	45 min. Z2	Off
F	Off	Rest Day / Slide Day	Rest Day / Slide Day
Sat	Off	2:00 Z2	Off
Sun	Off	Off	1:45 Z1 to Z2
Totals: 7:30 hrs.	1:30 hrs.	3:15 hrs.	2:45 hrs.

"Just Finish" Program: Swim Sessions

Our swims through the first eight weeks will all be approximately 2,000 yards or meters in length, which is a workout distance most athletes can complete within 45 minutes. Our suggestion is that if you need to lengthen the session to last 45 minutes, simply extend the warm-up or cooldown portion, as needed. If, however, you find that you need to shorten the session to make it fit into 45 minutes, reduce the main sets as needed, but keep the warm-up, drills, and cooldown the same.

Following are our fifteen swim sessions for the "Just Finish" Program:

1. 200wu, 6x50drills@10sec, 3 x 50@10sec, 2 x 100@20sec, 2 x 150@30sec, 3 x 100@20sec, 3 x 50@10sec, 6x50 drills@10sec, 200cd

2. 200wu, 6x50drills@10sec, 4 x (100 @15sec, 150@20sec), 6x50drills@10sec, 200cd

3. 200wu, 6x50 drills@10sec, 4 x (25@5sec, 50@10sec, 75@10sec, 100@15sec), 6x50 drills@10sec, 200cd

4. 200wu, 6x50 drills@10sec, 2 x 250@20sec, 4 x 125@15sec, 6x50drills@10sec, 200cd

5. 200wu, 6x50 drills@10sec, 3 x (100@15sec, 250@30sec), 6x50 drills@10sec, 200cd

6. 200wu, 6x50drills@10sec, 8 x 25@5sec, 4 x 50@10sec, 2 x 100@15sec, 2 x 200@20sec, 6x50drills@10sec, 200cd

7. 200wu, 6x50drills@10sec, 3 x (150@20sec, 200@30sec), 6x50drills@10sec, 200cd

8. 200wu, 6x50 drills@10sec, 3 x 175@20sec, 3 x 125@10sec, 6x50 drills@10sec, 200cd

9. 200wu, 6x50drills@10sec, 400@30sec, 300@25sec, 200@20sec, 100@15sec, 6x50 drills@10sec, 200cd

10. 200wu, 6x50drills@10sec, 2 x (50@5sec, 100@10sec, 150@15sec, 200@20sec), 6x50drills@10sec, 200cd

11. 200wu, 6x50 drills@10sec, 3 x (125@15sec, 225@30sec), 6x50 drills@10sec, 200cd

12. 200wu, 6x50 drills@10sec, 4 x 25@5sec, 4 x 75@10sec, 2 x 150@15sec, 4 x 75@10sec, 4 x 25@5sec, 6x50drills@10sec, 200cd

13. 200wu, 6x50 drills@10sec, 4 x 150@15sec, 4 x 100@10sec, 6x50 drills@10sec, 200cd

14. 200wu, 6x50drills@10sec, 4 x 250@30sec, 6x50drills@10sec, 200cd

15. 200wu, 6x50drills@10sec, 3 x 100@10sec, 2 x 200@15sec, 3 x 100@10sec, 6x50drills@10sec, 200cd

"Just Finish" Program: Peak Training and Taper Phase, Weeks 9–16

The second eight weeks (Weeks 9 through 16) of the "Just Finish" Program include both the peak training and the taper phase. We start by including Easy Pickups in the ninth week to prepare us to introduce higher-intensity Z4 training. Our quantity of Z4 training will gradually build from there, and peak in Week 14. Weeks 10 through 14 will each have three sessions that will include Z4 work, including two bike sessions and one run session. With five bike or run sessions per week during this period, this means that more than half of the sessions (60%) will include Z4 higher-intensity training.

During this phase we will continue to include two swims of about 45 minutes (2,000 yards/meters) each per week.

Our longest sessions in the second eight weeks will be three-and-a-half-hour transition sessions and two-and-a-quarter-hour long runs. One of the three-and-a-half-hour transition sessions will be structured as a shorter version of a "415-20-45 Brick," with a 20-minute Z4 insert (see Chapter 2).

With nine days to go before our Half Iron-Distance race, we will transition into our crisp taper phase to have us rested, sharp, and race-ready. Our volumes will gradually decrease, and our intensities will be no higher than Z2 during these last nine days. At this point, the hay is in the barn, and it's time to taper smart and become physically and mentally energized.

Following is the eight-week peak training and taper phase of the "Just Finish" Program.

"JUST FINISH" PROGRAM
PEAK TRAINING AND TAPER PHASES

WEEK 9	SWIM	BIKE	RUN
M	Off	Rest Day / Slide Day	Rest Day / Slide Day
Tu	#9	Off	45 min. Z2 (at 10 min., insert 5 x 1 min. PU @ 1 min. jog)
W	Off	Trans: 30 min. Z2 (QC)	15 min. Z2
Th	#10	45 min. Z2 (at 10 min., insert 5 x 1 min. PU @ 1 min. spin)	Off
F	Off	Rest Day / Slide Day	Rest Day / Slide Day
Sat	Off	Trans: 2:45 Z2 (at 2:30 insert 5 min. Z4)(QC)	15 min. Z2
Sun	Off	Off	1:15 Z1 to Z2
Totals: 8:00 hrs.	1:30 hrs.	4:00 hrs.	2:30 hrs.
WEEK 10	SWIM	BIKE	RUN
M	Off	Rest Day / Slide Day	Rest Day / Slide Day
Tu	#11	Off	45 min. Z2 (at 10 min., insert 8 x 2 min. Z4 @ 1 min. jog)
W	Off	Trans: 30 min. Z2 (QC)	15 min. Z2
Th	#12	45 min. Z2 (at 10 min., insert 8 x 2 min. Z4 Hill Repeats @ spin back down)	Off
F	Off	Rest Day / Slide Day	Rest Day / Slide Day
Sat	Off	Trans: 60 min. Z2 (at 45 min. insert 10 min. Z4) (QC)	15 min. Z2
Sun	Off	Optional: 30 min. Z1 (100+ rpm)	2:00 Z1 to Z2
Totals: 7:00 hrs.	1:30 hrs.	2:15+ hrs.	3:15 hrs.

WEEK 11	SWIM	BIKE	RUN
M	Off	Rest Day / Slide Day	Rest Day / Slide Day
Tu	#13	Off	45 min. Z2 (at 30 min., insert 10 min. Z4)
W	Off	Trans: 30 min. Z2 (QC)	15 min. Z2
Th	#14	45 min. Z2 (at 10 min., insert 5 x 4 min. Z4 @ 2 min. spin)	Off
F	Off	Rest Day / Slide Day	Rest Day / Slide Day
Sat	Off	Trans: 3:15 Z2 (at 2:55 insert 15 min. Z4)(QC)	15 min. Z2
Sun	Off	Off	45 min. Z1 to Z2
Totals: 8:00 hrs.	1:30 hrs.	4:30 hrs.	2:00 hrs.

WEEK 12	SWIM	BIKE	RUN
M	Off	Rest Day / Slide Day	Rest Day / Slide Day
Tu	#15	Off	45 min. Z2 (at 10 min., insert 5 x 3 min. Z4 @ 1.5 min. jog)
W	Off	Trans: 30 min. Z2 (QC)	15 min. Z2
Th	#9	45 min. Z2 (at 10 min., insert 6 x 2.5 min. Z4 Hill Repeats @ spin back down)	Off
F	Off	Rest Day / Slide Day	Rest Day / Slide Day
Sat	Off	Trans: 45 min. Z2 (at 20 min. insert 20 min. Z4) (QC)	15 min. Z2
Sun	Off	Optional: 30 min. Z1 (100+ rpm)	2:15 Z1 to Z2
Totals: 7:00 hrs.	1:30 hrs.	2:00+ hrs.	3:30 hrs.

"JUST FINISH" PROGRAM
PEAK TRAINING AND TAPER PHASES

WEEK 13	SWIM	BIKE	RUN
M	Off	Rest Day / Slide Day	Rest Day / Slide Day
Tu	#10	Off	45 min. Z2 (at 20 min., insert 12.5 min. Z4)
W	Off	Trans: 30 min. Z2 (QC)	15 min. Z2
Th	#11	45 min. Z2 (at 10 min., insert 4 x 5 min. Z4 @ 3 min. spin)	Off
F	Off	Rest Day / Slide Day	Rest Day / Slide Day
Sat	Off	Trans: 3:15 Z2 (at 2:50 insert 20 min. Z4)(QC)	15 min. Z2
Sun	Off	Off	45 min. Z1 to Z2
Totals: 8:00 hrs.	1:30 hrs.	4:30 hrs.	2:00 hrs.

WEEK 14	SWIM	BIKE	RUN
M	Off	Rest Day / Slide Day	Rest Day / Slide Day
Tu	#12	Off	45 min. Z2 (at 10 min., insert 3 x 6 min. Z4 @ 3 min. jog)
W	Off	Trans: 30 min. Z2 (QC)	15 min. Z2
Th	#13	45 min. Z2 (at 10 min., insert 6 x 3 min. Z4 Hill Repeats @ spin back down)	Off
F	Off	Rest Day / Slide Day	Rest Day / Slide Day
Sat	Off	Trans: 45 min. Z2 (at 20 min. insert 20 min. Z4) (QC)	15 min. Z2
Sun	Off	Optional: 30 min. Z1 (100+ rpm)	2:15 Z1 to Z2
Totals: 7:00 hrs.	1:30 hrs.	2:00+ hrs.	3:30 hrs.

WEEK 15	SWIM	BIKE	RUN
M	Off	Rest Day / Slide Day	Rest Day / Slide Day
Tu	#14	Off	45 min. Z2 (at 25 min., insert 15 min. Z4)
W	Off	Trans: 30 min. Z2 (QC)	15 min. Z2
Th	#15	45 min. Z2 (at 10 min., insert 3 x 7 min. Z4 @ 3.5 min. spin)	Off
F	Off	Rest Day / Slide Day	Rest Day / Slide Day
Sat	Off	Trans: 2:15 Z2 (QC)	15 min. Z2
Sun	Off	Off	1:15 Z1 to Z2
Totals: 7:30 hrs.	1:30 hrs.	3:30 hrs.	2:30 hrs.

WEEK 16	SWIM	BIKE	RUN
M	Off	Rest Day / Slide Day	Rest Day / Slide Day
T	30 min. easy	Off	45 min. Z1 to Z2 (at 10 min., insert 5 x 1 min. PU @ 1 min. jog)
W	Off	Trans: 30 min. Z1 to Z2 (QC)	15 min. Z1 to Z2
Th	30 min. easy	45 min. Z1 (at 10 min., insert 5 x 1 min. PU @ 1 min. spin)	Off
F	Off	Rest Day / Slide Day	Rest Day / Slide Day
Sat	Off	15 min. Z1—easy bike safety check	30 min. Z1—easy (in a.m.)
Sun	Race!! Half Iron-Distance	Race!! Half Iron-Distance	Race!! Half Iron-Distance
Totals: 4:00 hrs.	1:00 hrs. (+Race)	1:30 hrs. (+Race)	1:30 hrs. (+Race)

Guidelines for Adjusting Sixteen-Week Training Programs

In this section we will offer suggestions on how best to make adjustments to the sixteen-week training programs for practice races, missed workouts, and other situations.

Adjusting Training Program for Practice Races

As discussed in Chapter 3, there are up to three optional practice races to include during the three sixteen-week programs. In the following section, we present how best to build the three possible races into your sixteen-week training schedule, should you decide that you want to include any or all of them.

Adjusting Training Program for an Open-Water Swim

As discussed in Chapter 3, an open-water swim practice race is beneficial for most triathletes, especially for those who have not raced in open water recently.

The preferable distance is about 1 mile (or about 1.5 km), and it can be substituted for any of the planned swims. If your Half is going to have a wet suit–legal swim, this is an excellent opportunity to become used to swimming in a wet suit (if you are not already). Preferably, you will wear the same wet suit for your open-water swim as you plan to wear in your Half.

We don't suggest tapering for this particular training race, but instead just using it as a training session. Because open-water swims are typically on Saturday or Sunday mornings, our suggestion is to simply complete it in the morning before your other bike or run training planned for that day, and to count it toward any of your planned swim sessions. Any weekend between Weeks 4 and 15 are fine for this practice race, as long as you are at a point where you feel safe and comfortable in the open water.

Adjusting Training Program for a Sprint or Olympic Distance Triathlon

As discussed in Chapter 3, either a Sprint or Olympic Distance triathlon can serve as a great "dress-rehearsal" for your Half.

The best weeks in the training programs to include a Sprint triathlon (approximately a 0.5-mile swim, a 15-mile bike, and a 3-mile run) or an Olympic Distance triathlon (approximately a 1.5 km swim, a 40 km bike, and a 10 km run) tune-up race are Weeks 10 through 14, and it is suggested that you adjust the days around the race as follows:

- Friday: 30-minute easy swim and 60-minute Z1 to Z2 run (with 5 x 1 min. Easy Pickups @ 1-minute jog).
- Saturday: 30-minute Z1 (easy) run in the morning and 30-minute Z1 (easy) bike safety check anytime later in the day.
- Sunday: Sprint or Olympic Distance race in the morning, then a two- to three-hour Z1 to Z2 bike session anytime later in the day.
- Monday: Complete long run originally planned for Sunday.
- Tuesday: Rejoin training schedule as planned; however, do not include Z4 portion of Tuesday's run. Instead, just cover the time of Tuesday's run in Z2.

Adjusting Training Program for a Half Marathon

As discussed in Chapter 3, a half marathon can be a beneficial practice race for athletes who do not come from a running background, or who have not completed this length distance of a road race in a while.

The best weeks in the training program to include a half marathon (13.1 miles) are during Weeks 10 through 14, and it is suggested that you just substitute this race in for one of your Sunday long runs. The one suggested adjustment to the schedule is not to include the Z4 insert in the bike session on the day before the half marathon. Otherwise, no other adjustments are needed to the schedule. Just treat it as a fast and fun training run.

It is suggested that if you plan to do both a half marathon and a Sprint or Olympic Distance triathlon, that you do not do them on consecutive weekends. Spread them apart by at least two weeks.

AN IRONFIT MOMENT

Should I Train with Watts on the Bike?

The answer to this question depends on several factors, most important your experience level, your level of competitiveness, and how much flexibility you desire in your training.

Various trends sweep the endurance sports world from time to time. Currently, watts-based training for the bike is one of them. Even the most novice athletes seem to think that this is some kind of magic bullet that will instantly put them on the starting line at the 70.3 World Championship.

Athletes often tell us that they "train with power." When we ask them exactly what they mean by this, we come to learn that they basically have power meters on their bikes, and they casually take note of how many watts they are generating during some of their training. Then after telling us this, they usually ask a question like, "I usually do my bike workout around 180 watts; is that good?" Well, the answer to that question is, "It depends." These athletes are not really doing watts-based training; they're really just riding with a power meter and taking note of their wattage, and there's a big difference.

True power training involves proper power testing, setting power levels, and performing very specific training sessions based on these levels. We have been training many of our elite coached athletes using watts-based training for many years, and while these athletes have been very successful with it, we have also learned that true power training is not for everyone. Many find that it is too technical and too restrictive for their liking. While some athletes prefer it, many others prefer the greater flexibility of our approach to heart rate training.

Please also consider that while we have coached many athletes with watts on the bike who have qualified for both the 70.3 World Championship and the Ironman World Championship, we have trained just as many athletes who accomplished the same, but preferred to use our heart rate training system for the bike as well as the run. In fact, we have trained many top elite athletes who have won their age group at the Hawaii Ironman and many other major world-class events training with heart rate zones, not power levels.

We suggest you consider these factors when deciding if you want to invest the money in a power meter and do this type of training.

For "Just Finish" and Intermediate level athletes, we suggest you use the heart rate training system presented in this book. If you are an experienced competitive athlete, you will still be very successful with the heart rate training system in this book. If you do decide you want to try watts-based training, we suggest you do so under the guidance of an experienced coach. In Appendix C, we have a list of suggested books, including some good ones that deal specifically with power training, so you may want to check these out as well.

There is another option for those who already have a power meter. It's what we refer to as the "gateway to power training." Use the heart rate system in this book, but determine what your approximate watts-equivalent ranges are for Z1, Z2, Z3, and Z4. By doing this you can monitor your workouts by both heart rate and watts. Once you have some experience with this, you will be in a much better position to decide if you want to transition into a more-complete watts-based approach on the bike, or stick with a heart rate approach for both the bike and run.

Adjusting Training Program for Missed Workouts

What if you miss a period of training due to an illness, a business trip, or some other reason? After not training for several days, we do not want to risk injury by just jumping back into our program where we left off. We want to ease back in safely at just the right rate of increase to get us back on track to achieving our goals.

Guidelines for Adjusting for Missed Workouts

1. **One to two days of missed training:** If you miss one to two days of training for any reason, and you cannot fit the missed sessions in by using the rest day / slide days, then just skip them. Missing one or two workouts is never going to matter in the long run, but trying to play catch-up and doubling workouts is risky, and could result in setbacks.

2. **Three to four days of missed training:** Rejoin your training program (again, skip the missed days), but when you do, complete only half of the scheduled training on the first day back, and then resume full training on the second day back.

3. **Five to six days of missed training:** Rejoin your training program (again, skip the missed days), but when you do, complete one-third of the scheduled training on the first two days back, and two-thirds of the scheduled training on the next two days back. Resume full training on the fifth day back.

4. **Seven or more days of missed training:** Reconsider the timing of your goal and consider a major redesign of your training program.

You should always first attempt to use the rest day / slide days to prevent missed workouts as discussed earlier. But if that is not possible to account for the missed workouts, please consider the above guidelines.

Other Training Program Adjustment Tips

The "Mom Shift"

Don't forget to consider the "Mom Shift," which we discussed earlier. The sixteen-week programs are designed to best fit athletes who need to do their longest training sessions on Saturday and Sunday. If you find that other days work better for you (e.g., Tuesday and Wednesday), then consider shifting the entire weekly training cycle ahead by three days, so that the longer sessions fall on Tuesday and Wednesday.

Cross-Training through Injury

If you miss training due to a minor injury, check with your doctor to see if a cross-training alternative can be substituted in to keep you on schedule. For example, if your doctor determines that running will aggravate your injury, but the elliptical machine will not, consider substituting elliptical sessions for your runs until you return to 100 percent good health.

Now that we have outlined the three sixteen-week training programs, we will move on to Chapter 6, where we will present the optimal functional strength and core program, warm-up routine, and flexibility program, to complement your swim, bike, and run training.

The Half Iron-Distance Functional Strength and Core Program, Warm-Up Routine, and Flexibility and Stretching Program

Nothing will ever be attempted if all
possible objections must first be overcome.

—Samuel Johnson

n this chapter we will present a functional strength and core program, a warm-up routine, and a flexibility and stretching program, all specially designed for success in the Half.

The Half Iron-Distance Triathlon is what we like to call a middle distance event. To the average onlooker, it may appear to be purely an endurance race. But if you have ever raced one, you know it's much more than that. It not only requires good endurance, but also excellent power and strength. We need to focus on building our functional and core strength, right along with our aerobic capacity.

We can accomplish this fairly easily throughout the year by integrating just one to two weekly functional strength and core training sessions into our sixteen-week training programs (Chapter 5) and our recovery and maintenance training program (Chapter 15). Of course, even two additional workouts per week can be challenging for many busy athletes training for a Half, because they are already stretched for time. So we have developed two very efficient 20- to 30-minute functional strength and core training programs that can be completed following any of your weekly cardio workouts. A consistent and focused functional strength and core program like what we have designed in this chapter will help you to build strength and functional power and remain injury-free throughout the year.

We suggest doing your two functional strength and core training sessions on nonconsecutive days to give your body adequate recovery time between sessions. Working with the sixteen-week training programs in Chapter 5, most athletes find that Tuesday and Thursday work best. But if those days don't fit well for you, any two nonconsecutive days will work fine.

Because your body is already warmed up after a workout, you can save more time by completing these sessions immediately after any of your swim, bike, or run sessions, without having to do any pre-movement exercises. If you do not have the ability to do your strength and functional training after a cardio workout, however, then it is important to ready your body with our pre-movement exercises. We call them the "Easy Eight"—eight easy movements that you can do in as little as five minutes to ready yourself for a functional strength and core training session, or any other workout if you choose.

Another important element in keeping yourself strong and healthy is stretching. Yes, the dreaded stretching! As you get older it becomes much more important as you lose the elasticity and suppleness of your muscles, joints, and tendons. The key to a good stretching program is to do it post-workout after you have raised your core body temperature and your muscles are warmed up. It is most effective then, and helps to prepare your body for the next day's training.

Following are our suggested warm-up routine, functional strength and core program, and flexibility and stretching program, all specially designed for success in the Half.

"Easy Eight" Warm-up Routine

1. Pelvic Circles in Standing Position

Start in a standing position with your feet at about the three o'clock and the nine o'clock positions, slightly beyond shoulder-width apart, with your hands on your hips. Begin with a deep breath in through your nose, exhale, and start by making a circular motion "around the clock" with your hips and pelvis. Go ten slow circles clockwise and then reverse with ten circles counterclockwise.

This will help to increase blood flow and open up the hips and pelvis. (See photo 1.)

2. Chest Openers

Start in a standing position with your feet slightly apart. Inhale, and begin by raising one leg off the ground with your hands at your sides. While exhaling, raise both arms straight out in front of you, with palms facing down, and then open your arms straight out to your sides as you rotate your palms toward the ceiling, simultaneously bringing your leg back so your quad is perpendicular to the floor. Bring arms back to front and repeat the movement five times before switching legs and repeating five more times. Be sure to maintain good posture throughout the movement by drawing your belly in and lifting your chest. (See photos 2a and 2b.)

3. Three-Position Lunge (Front, 45°, Side) with Opposite Arm Raise

Start in a standing position with your hands at your sides. Begin the movement by performing a forward lunge with your left leg while raising your right arm, with palm up over your head. Press off your left foot, return arm to your side, and return to the start position. With your left leg, lunge again but at a forward angle of 45°, raising your right arm palm up over your head.

Press off your left foot and return your arm back to your side as you return to the start position. Again with your left leg, lunge directly to the side while raising your right arm palm up over your head. Press off your left foot and return arm to your side as you return to the start position. Repeat this lunge pattern with your right leg and left arm. (See photos 3a, 3b, and 3c.)

4. Forward Lunge with Elbow inside Knee

Start in a standing position and then lunge forward with your left leg while bringing your left elbow inside your left knee; place your right hand on the

floor, even with left foot. Hold that position for a 30-second count. Your knee should be over your ankle and your quadriceps should be at least parallel to the ground. Then take your left arm outside of your left knee and raise it straight up over your head, look toward the ceiling, and hold for a second. Then return your arm to the start position and repeat the arm raise four more times. Bring your left leg back even with your right foot and stand up. Repeat lunge with right leg and perform movement on that side. (See photos 4a and 4b.)

5. McKenzie Press-up

Start by lying flat on your stomach with your arms bent, palms near your shoulders and toes pointed. Begin the movement by inhaling, then exhale as you press up with your arms while keeping your hips on the floor and letting your stomach and back sag. Extend your arms fully without pulling your hips off the floor, if you can. Repeat this movement ten times. (See photo 5.)

6. Kneeling Stretch

Starting from the up position of the McKenzie Press-up, sit back on your knees, keep your head down, extend your arms in front of you, and hold that stretch for 20 seconds. For an added stretch, allow your hips to drop slightly to one side and then repeat on the other side for a 20-second count. (See photo 6.)

7. Abs and Back Stretch over Stability Ball with Arms Overhead

Start by sitting on the stability ball and walk your feet out from it while your back follows the ball's contour as you lower it to the ball. Keep arms at your sides as you stretch your back and abs over the ball for a 30-second count. Then, extend your arms over your head and roll on the ball while keeping your head, neck, and back in contact with the ball. If you can, allow your hands to touch the floor behind you, hold, and then roll forward, letting your body follow the curve of the ball until you are almost sitting on the floor. At all times your head and back must be in contact with the ball. Roll forward and backward several times. (See photo 7.)

8. Torso Rotation over Stability Ball

Start from the abdominal and back-stretch position in the previous exercise, but roll out on the ball so your head and neck are resting centered on the ball. Raise your arms straight up and bring your palms together. Roll your shoulders and torso to one side and bring your arms with you. Roll from side to side with arms and hips extended, feet apart. Repeat this ten times. (See photo 8.)

Once you get the hang of the pre-movement exercises, you can usually complete them in as little as five minutes, or extend them if you feel you need the extra warm-up.

Functional Strength and Core Training Programs

Now you are ready to begin your one to two 20- to 30-minute functional strength and core training sessions of the week for the off-season, preseason, and competitive season.

We will define our off-season as any time of the year when you are not racing or within a specific training cycle preparing for a race. These exercises are best used during the recovery and maintenance phase, as presented in Chapter 15.

Then, with about four months to go before your first "A Race" of the season, we will move into our preseason exercises. These exercises should be used in conjunction with the eight weeks of the base-building phase of any of the programs in Chapter 5.

Once we enter our competitive season, which is our primary racing season, we will drop to one session a week of only four exercises. These exercises should be used in conjunction with the first seven weeks of the eight-week peak training and taper phase of any of the programs in Chapter 5. Note that we do these exercises for only the first seven weeks of the peak training and taper phase, as we want to discontinue all functional strength and core training during the final week before our Half.

For sets and repetitions that involve weights of some type, you should select the weight that allows you to complete the first set of that exercise within the suggested range of repetitions. For example, if the exercise indicates 8 to 12 repetitions, you should select a weight with which you can complete a maximum of 8 to 12 repetitions in the first set. Please note that if you can complete 8 to 12 reps in the first set, it is likely that you will only be able to complete some lesser number of repetitions in the second and third sets.

Once you find that you have become stronger and can now do more repetitions in the first set than the amount suggested, you should move up to a higher weight that puts you back into the suggested range on the first set. For example, if the exercise indicates 8 to 12 reps, once you can do more than 12 reps in the first set, you should move up in weight to bring you back into the 8- to 12-repetition range. Usually a 5 percent increase in weight will accomplish this.

Off-Season Functional Strength and Core Training Program

There are twelve exercises in total for the off-season. We will split them into two days of six exercises each, as follows. During this period, we will do fewer repetitions but with increased weights.

Off-Season: Day 1	Off-Season: Day 2
1. Squats	7. Back Lunge with Overhead Reach
2. Chest Press	8. Transverse Lunge
3. Dead Lifts	9. Chest Flys
4. Delt Flys	10. One Leg Split/Squat
5. Push-ups	11. Push-ups
6. Abs-Triangles	12. Planks

Preseason Functional Strength and Core Training Program

There are ten exercises in total for the Preseason. We will split them into one day of four exercises and a second day of six exercises as follows. During this period, we will increase our repetitions and maintain at about the same weights.

Preseason: Day 1	Preseason: Day 2
1. Ax Chop	(Same as Exercises of Day 2 in Off-Season)
2. Side Lunge with Front Raise	
3. Jump Squats	
4. Get-ups	

Competitive Season Functional Strength and Core Training Program

There are only four exercises in total for the competitive season. We will complete them one time per week on one day.

Competitive Season: Day 1

1. Squat to Curl and Press
2. Superman
3. Straight Arm Raises
4. Obliques

In the following section we present the functional strength and core training programs for the off-season, preseason, and competitive seasons, including detailed descriptions of the exercises, along with the recommended sets and repetitions. Before you get started, familiarize yourself with the exercises to make sure you understand the proper form and technique required to perform each one.

Off-Season: Day 1

1. Squats with Dumbbells

Purpose: To strengthen glutes, hamstrings, quads, and core.

*Basic: Squats with Dumbbells—
Stability Ball against the Wall*

Start in a standing position with the stability ball against the wall, centered at your lower back. Your feet are about shoulder-width apart and you have a dumbbell in each hand at your sides. Begin by inhaling and shifting your hips back and bending your knees into a squat position, bringing your quadriceps parallel to the floor. Then, exhale as you extend your legs back to the standing position. (See photo 9.)

9

Intermediate: Squats with Dumbbells—on BOSU

Same as the Basic, except you are standing on BOSU, without your back touching a stability ball. Press hips back and avoid arching your back.

Advanced: One-Leg Squat with Dumbbells

Start in a standing position not on the BOSU, holding a dumbbell in each hand. Raise one leg off the ground, and then extend it behind you as you perform a squat on the other leg. Hold, and then return to the start position without placing the foot on the ground. Repeat for the desired number of repetitions. Switch legs and perform the same number of reps on the other leg.

Sets/Reps: Off-Season—three sets of 8 to 12 reps / Advanced: Off-Season—three sets of 8 to 12 reps, each leg

2. Chest Press over Stability Ball with Hip Extension

Purpose: To strengthen pectorals, deltoids, triceps, glutes, hamstrings, abdominals, and balance.

Basic: Chest Press over Stability Ball with Hip Extension

Start by lying with your head and neck centered on top of the stability ball, with your hips extended and knees bent to create a straight line from your knees to your shoulders. With arms bent, elbows out to the sides, and a dumbbell in each hand, held level with your chest, inhale, and then exhale as you press the dumbbells toward the ceiling. Hold at the top, and then return to the start position. Do not relax arms on the stability ball; keep elbows extended out to your sides.

Intermediate: Chest Press over Stability Ball, Alternating Arms

Same position as the Basic, except you will perform the exercise by alternating arms through the movement.

Advanced: One-Arm Chest Press over Stability Ball with Rotation

Same as the Basic, except you will use only one arm with a dumbbell, and press the dumbbell toward the ceiling as you roll onto your

10

opposite shoulder. Hold and repeat for the desired number of repetitions. Then, with dumbbell in the opposite hand, perform the movement with that arm. Rotate torso while you perform this movement and keep other arm straight out to the side. (See photo 10.)

Sets/Reps: Off-Season—three sets of 8 to 12 reps

3. Dead Lifts with Dumbbells

Purpose: To strengthen glutes, hamstrings, quads, ab/adductors, calves, and core.

Basic: Dead Lifts with Dumbbells

Start in a standing position with feet about shoulder-width apart and a dumbbell in each hand. Keep belly drawn in and shoulder blades back and down. Keeping arms straight down the entire time, lower the dumbbells toward the floor, with knees slightly bent and a straight back. Then return to a standing position by pushing through your glutes and hamstrings as you return to the start position. (See photo 11.)

Intermediate: Dead Lifts with Dumbbells to Calf Raise

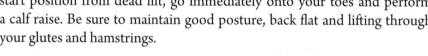

Same as the Basic, except as you return to start position from dead lift, go immediately onto your toes and perform a calf raise. Be sure to maintain good posture, back flat and lifting through your glutes and hamstrings.

Advanced: Dead Lifts with Dumbbells to Calf Raise on One Leg

Same as the Intermediate, except you will perform the dead lift to calf raise while standing on one leg only. Be sure to maintain good posture, drawing your belly in and keeping your shoulders back and down. You can keep your off leg straight or slightly bent.

Sets/Reps: Off-Season—three sets of 8 to 12 reps

4. Rear Deltoid Flys in a Stork Position

Purpose: To strengthen deltoids, rhomboids, hamstrings, quads, core, and balance.

Basic: Rear Deltoid Flys in a Stork Position

Start in a standing position with a dumbbell in each hand. Raise one leg straight behind you and balance on the other leg in a stork position, letting your arms hang straight down. Depress your shoulder blades toward your spine and raise the dumbbells with slightly bent arms out to the sides, but not higher than shoulder height. Hold for a 2-second count and then return arms back to  the start position and repeat. Keep hands soft as you squeeze your shoulder blades together to elevate the weights. Perform half the repetitions on one leg and then switch and perform half the repetitions on the other leg. (See photo 12.)

Intermediate: Rear Deltoid Flys in Stork Position, Alternating Arms

Same as the Basic, except perform this exercise by raising one arm at a time and alternating arms. Perform half of the repetitions on one leg and then switch and perform half of the repetitions on the other leg.

Advanced: Rear Deltoid Flys, with One-Leg Squat in Stork Position

Same as the Basic, except start this exercise from the stork position and begin with a one-leg squat. Then, as you extend from the squat, simultaneously raise the weights as you return to the start position. Perform half of the repetitions on one leg and then switch and perform half of the repetitions on the other leg.

Sets/Reps: Off-Season—three sets of 8 to 12 reps

5. Straight-Leg or Bent-Knee Push-up

Purpose: To strengthen chest, shoulders, triceps, abs, and core.

Basic: Straight-Leg or Bent-Knee Push-up

Start by lying facedown on the floor with your arms bent and hands to the outside of your shoulders. Raise your torso, head, and legs off the floor by extending your arms straight into a plank position to get to the start position. While holding a straight line from your ankles to your shoulders, and keeping your head in alignment with your spine, lower your chest toward the floor and hold for 1 second before pushing your body back into the straight-line position. Breathe in on the way down and exhale on the exertion. Repeat for the desired number of repetitions.

Intermediate: Straight-Leg or Bent-Knee Traveling Push-up

Same as the Basic, except after you perform one push-up and return to the start position (arms extended), one at a time, move one hand 12 inches inward or outward and the other hand 12 inches similarly in or out. Perform another push-up and repeat the traveling motion back toward the other direction (outward or inward). You can also do this by traveling across a step or BOSU. (See photos 13a, 13b, and 13c.)

13a   13b   13c

Advanced: Straight-Leg Push-up with One Leg Raised

Same as the Basic, except in the starting position raise one leg so it is parallel to the ground but not touching; perform half the number of repetitions on one leg, and then raise the other leg and perform the remaining number of repetitions.

Sets/Reps: Off-Season—three sets of 8 to 12 reps / Preseason—three sets of 10 to 12 reps

6. Abs—Open and Close Triangles

Purpose: To strengthen overall core and abdominals.

Basic: Abs—Open and Close Triangles

Start by lying on the floor on your back with legs extended straight, so they are perpendicular to the floor, and your arms extended toward your knees. Your legs, torso, and arms should almost form a right triangle. Simultaneously, lower your legs together toward the floor and your arms straight over your head from your shoulders. Hold your position when you are straight but not quite touching the ground, and then return to the start position and repeat. (See photos 14a and 14b.)

14a   14b

Intermediate: Abs—Stability Ball Pass from Hands to Feet

Same as the Basic, except you start with a stability ball in your hands as you lower your arms overhead and your legs toward the floor. Then, simultaneously, raise your arms and legs together and pass the stability ball from your hands to between your feet and repeat the movement. Continue passing the ball from your hands to your feet at each return to starting point, and make the movement continuous.

Advanced: Abs—Stability Ball Pass from Hands to Feet with Raised Torso

Same as the Intermediate, except raise your torso off the floor every time you raise your arms back to the straight position, with or without the stability ball.

Sets/Reps: Off-Season—three sets of 8 to 12 repetitions

Off-Season: Day 2

7. Back Lunge with Overhead Reach Using Dumbbell

Purpose: To strengthen glutes, hamstrings, quads, obliques, core, and balance.

Basic: Back Lunge with Overhead Reach Using Dumbbell

Start in a standing position with a light dumbbell in one hand. Take a step back with the same side leg as the hand with the dumbbell. As you step back into a lunge position, raise your arm to the side with a slight bend, palm facing up in an arching motion over your head. Then, extend your hips, glutes, and quads to return to the start position and simultaneously return your arm to your side. Repeat repetitions on that leg/arm before switching to the other leg/arm.

15

Intermediate: Back Lunge off Step with Overhead Reach Using Dumbbell

Same as the Basic, except start by standing on a step. (See photo 15.)

Advanced: Back Lunge off BOSU with Overhead Reach Using Dumbbell

Same as Intermediate, except start by standing on a BOSU with one foot more centered on the BOSU and the other just touching lightly next to it.

Sets/Reps: Off-Season—three sets of 8 to 12 reps each leg / Preseason—three sets of 10 to 12 reps each leg

8. Transverse Lunge with Stretch Cord or Cable Row

Purpose: To strengthen glutes, hamstrings, quads, shoulders, back, core, and balance.

Basic: Transverse Lunge with Stretch Cord or Cable Row

Start in a standing position facing forward with the stretch cord or cable in your right hand and arm extended straight, about shoulder height. The stretch cord/band should have sufficient tension on it. Perform a transverse lunge (lunge back at 45° angle) by rotating your entire body to the right, keeping your left foot planted. Simultaneously, pull the cord/band toward your shoulder by bending your elbow back but keeping your arm parallel to the floor with a 1-second hold. Then, return to the start position and repeat for the desired number of repetitions with that arm before switching to the other arm. (See photos 16a and 16b.)

16a

16b

Intermediate: Transverse Lunge onto Step with Stretch Cord or Cable Row

Same as the Basic, except the lunging leg lands on a step.

Advanced: Transverse Lunge onto BOSU with Stretch Cord or Cable Row

Same as the Basic, except the lunging leg lands on a BOSU.

Sets/Reps: Off-Season—three sets of 8 to 12 reps each leg / Preseason—three sets of 10 to 12 reps each leg

9. Chest Flys with Stretch Cords in Lunge Position

Purpose: To strengthen pectorals, shoulders, glutes, hamstrings, abdominals, core, and balance.

Basic: Chest Flys with Stretch Cords in Lunge Position

Start in a standing position, holding the ends of the stretch cord in both hands, facing away from the door/wall with your legs in a lunge position. Extend your slightly bent arms out to the sides about chest level. Inhale, then exhale as you squeeze your chest and bring your arms together in front with palms facing down, hold, then return to the start position while keeping your arms extended from your sides. (See photo 17.)

17

Intermediate: Chest Flys with Stretch Cords, Standing on One Leg

Same as the Basic, except start by standing on one leg. Perform the movement with one leg raised for half of the repetitions, and then repeat with the other leg raised for the other half of the repetitions.

Advanced: Alternating Arm Chest Flys with Stretch Cords, Standing on One Leg

Same as the Intermediate, except with leg raised, perform the movement with alternating arms. Start with both arms extended in front of you and then perform a fly with only one arm. Perform half of the repetitions on one leg and then switch legs and perform the remaining repetitions.

Sets/Reps: Off-Season—three sets of 8 to 12 reps / Preseason—three sets of 10 to 12 reps

10. One-Leg Split/Squat with Elevated Leg

Purpose: To strengthen glutes, hamstrings, quads, abs, core, and balance.

Basic: One-Leg Split/Squat with Elevated Leg

Start in a standing position about 2 feet in front of a bench/chair. Bring one foot behind you and place the top of your foot on the bench/chair. Inhale, then squat down by flexing hip and knee of front leg until knee of rear leg is as close to the floor as possible. Hold, and then extend hip and knee of front leg back to start position. Repeat on that leg through a full set of repetitions and then switch legs.

Intermediate: One-Leg Split/Squat with Elevated Leg and Kettle Bell

Same as the Basic, except you will perform the exercise while holding one kettle bell with both hands at your chest. (See photo 18.)

18

Advanced: One-Leg Split/Squat with Elevated Leg and Two Kettle Bells or Dumbbells

Same as the Intermediate, except hold two kettle bells or dumbbells—one in each hand, at your sides—and perform the exercise.

Sets/Reps: Off-Season—three sets of 8 to 12 reps each leg / Preseason—three sets of 10 to 12 reps each leg

11. Straight-Leg or Bent-Knee Push-up

Purpose: To strengthen chest, shoulders, triceps, abs, and core.

Basic: Straight-Leg or Bent-Knee Push-up

Start by lying facedown on the floor with your arms bent and hands to the outside of your shoulders. Raise your torso, head, and legs off the floor by extending your arms straight into a plank position to get to the start position. While holding a straight line from your ankles to your shoulders and keeping your head in alignment with your spine, lower your chest toward the floor and hold for 1 second before pushing your body back into the straight-line position. Breathe in on the way down and exhale on the exertion. Repeat for the desired number of repetitions.

Intermediate: Straight-Leg or Bent-Knee Traveling Push-up

Same as the Basic, except after you perform one push-up and return to the start position, one at a time, move one hand 12 inches to one side and the other hand 12 inches in the same direction. Perform another push-up and repeat the traveling motion back toward the other direction. You can also do this by traveling across a step or BOSU. (See photos 13a, 13b, and 13c on page 96.)

Advanced: Straight-Leg Push-up with One Leg Raised

Same as the Basic, except in the starting position raise one leg so it is parallel to the ground but not touching. Perform half the number of repetitions on one leg and then raise the other leg and perform the remaining number of repetitions.

Sets/Reps: Off-Season—three sets of 8 to 12 reps / Preseason—three sets of 10 to 12 reps

12. Planks with Rollout on Knees and Forearms on Stability Ball

Purpose: To strengthen shoulders, back, abdominals, and core.

Basic: Planks with Rollout on Knees and Forearms on Stability Ball

Start by kneeling in front of a stability ball with your forearms and hands together on the front part of the ball. Raise your torso in a straight line and slowly roll the ball out from your body with your forearms until you feel your abdominals engaging, without arching your back. Hold for 3 to 5 seconds and then return to the start position. (See photo 19.)

Intermediate: Planks on Toes and Forearms on Stability Ball

Same as the Basic, except start on your toes (not on your knees), and roll the ball out so that your legs are straight and your forearms are on the stability ball, with your body in a straight line from your shoulders to your ankles. Hold this position for 30 to 60 seconds. Then, return to the start position.

Advanced: Planks on Toes with One Leg Raised

Same as the Intermediate, except raise one leg and hold for 15 to 60 seconds and then repeat with the other leg raised.

Sets/Reps: Off-Season—three sets of 8 to 12 reps / Preseason—three sets of 10 to 12 reps / Intermediate and Advanced: Off-Season—three sets of 15 to 30 seconds / Preseason—three sets of 30 to 45 seconds

Preseason: Day 1

1. Squat with Ax Chop on BOSU

Purpose: To strengthen hamstrings, quads, glutes, abdominals, arms, shoulders, back, and core.

Basic: Squat with Ax Chop on BOSU using Medicine Ball

Start by standing on top of the BOSU and holding a medicine ball at shoulder height to one side, with arms bent. As you are performing a squat, and at the same pace as the squat, lower the medicine ball to the opposite side across your body in a chopping motion until you complete the squat. Return to the start position, extending the legs while reversing the chopping motion, and then repeat on the same side before switching to the other side. (See photo 20.)

Intermediate: Squat with Ax Chop on BOSU using Kettle Bell

Same as the Basic, except use a kettle bell to perform the exercise.

Advanced: Side Lunge with Ax Chop on BOSU using Kettle Bell

Start by standing on top of the BOSU and holding a kettle bell at shoulder height to one side, with arms bent. As you are performing a side lunge, swing the kettle bell to the opposite side across your body in a chopping motion, to the outside of your lunging leg, until you complete the lunge. Return to the start position and bring the kettle bell back to the opposite shoulder by reversing the chopping motion. Repeat on the opposite side.

Sets/Reps: Preseason—three sets of 10 to 12 reps on each side

2. Side Lunge with Front Raise

Purpose: To strengthen glutes, hamstrings, quads, ab/adductors, shoulders, and core.

Basic: Side Lunge with Front Raise

Start in a standing position with a dumb-bell in each hand at your sides. Perform a side lunge, keeping your hips back and lunging leg bent while your other leg stays straight. From that position, raise your arms with dumbbells out straight to shoulder height, hold, and then simultaneously bring your arms back to your sides while extending your hips, glutes, and quads back to the start position. Perform half of the repetitions on one leg and then switch and perform half of the repetitions on the other leg. (See photo 21.)

Intermediate: Side Lunge onto Step with Front Raise

Same as the Basic, except side-lunge onto a step.

Advanced: Side Lunge onto BOSU with One-Arm Front Raise

Same as the Intermediate, except side-lunge onto a BOSU so your foot strikes the center of it, and raise the same side arm. Then, repeat with other leg and arm.

Sets/Reps: Preseason—three sets of 10 to 12 reps / Advanced—three sets of 10 to 12 reps, each side

3. Jump Squats onto Step or Box

Purpose: To strengthen glutes, hamstrings, quads, ankles, abs, core, and balance.

Basic: Jump Squats onto Step or Box

Start in a standing position with your feet about shoulder-width apart in front of a step or box. With your arms at your sides, inhale and perform a deep squat. From the deep squat position, exhale and jump onto the step or box with both feet and land in a squat position. Step off step or box and repeat the squat and jump. (See photo 22.)

Intermediate: Jump Squats onto BOSU

Same as the Basic, except you will start by standing in front of a BOSU, jumping onto it, and landing in a squat position. Step off the BOSU and perform the squat and jump again.

22

Advanced: Jump Squats on the BOSU

Start by standing on the BOSU. Perform a deep squat and jump by extending your legs, hips, and glutes straight up, then landing in a deep squat position back on the BOSU.

Sets/Reps: Preseason—three sets of 10 to 12 reps

4. Get-ups off BOSU with Arms at Your Sides

Purpose: To strengthen core and abdominals, glutes, quads, core, and hamstrings.

Basic: Get-ups off the BOSU with Arms at Your Sides

Start by sitting on the BOSU with arms at your sides and bent knees. Extend your torso back so you are completely parallel to the floor and legs are raised off the floor. Then, raise torso and simultaneously put your feet on the floor and stand straight up. Then, return to the start position and repeat. (See photos 23a, 23b, and 23c.)

Intermediate: Get-ups off BOSU with Arms Raised

Same as the Basic, except with both arms extended over your head. Raise torso and simultaneously bring your feet to the floor and stand up, keeping arms extended over your head.

Advanced: Get-ups off Floor with Medicine Ball Overhead

Same as the Intermediate, except start by lying on the floor instead of the BOSU, with knees bent and holding a medicine ball over your head. As you begin to "get up," bring the ball down from over your head to in front of your chest.

Sets/Reps: Preseason—three sets of 10 to 12 reps

Preseason: Day 2

Same as Off-Season, Day 2 (Exercises 7–12, pages 98–103)

Competitive Season: Day 1

1. Squat to Curl and Press

Purpose: To strengthen glutes, hamstrings, biceps, shoulders, and core.

Basic: Squat to Curl and Press

Start in a standing position with a dumbbell in each hand. Begin by inhaling, and then perform a freestanding squat. As you return from the squat position, begin to curl the dumbbells as you get to the start position, and then press the dumbbells over your head. Return the dumbbells to your sides and repeat. (See photos 24a and 24b.)

Intermediate: Squat on BOSU, Curl and Press

Same as the Basic, except start by standing on the BOSU.

Advanced: Squat on One Leg, Curl and Press

Same as the Basic, except start by raising one leg straight up, with knee bent and parallel to the ground. Swing leg back, perform squat with other leg, then curl and press the weights over your head, and then return the weights to your sides. Repeat with same leg through a complete set of repetitions before switching to the other leg.

Sets/Reps: Competitive—three sets of 12 to 15 reps

2. Superman on BOSU

Purpose: To strengthen back, shoulders, glutes, hamstrings, abdominals, and core.

Basic: Superman on BOSU

Start by lying facedown with your hips centered on the BOSU, your legs straight and hip-width apart, and your palms facing up. Extend your shoulder blades back and down toward your spine. Inhale to prepare for the movement and then exhale as you extend your lower back, squeezing your glutes as you extend your torso up while rotating your thumbs toward the ceiling. Hold for 1 second in that position before returning to the start position.

Intermediate: Superman on BOSU with Arms Overhead

Same as the Basic, except raise your arms over your head and perform the movement without rotating your thumbs toward the ceiling.

Advanced: Swimming on BOSU

Start by lying facedown, balanced on your midsection over the BOSU, with legs extended and arms overhead. Raise your arms and legs off the floor, find your balance, and then perform a swimming-type movement (no need to do the crawl stroke, exactly) by fluttering your arms and legs for about 30 to 60 seconds. (See photo 25.)

Sets/Reps: Competitive Season—three sets of 12 to 15 reps / Advanced: Sets/Reps: Competitive Season—three sets of 30 to 60 seconds

3. Overhead Raises with Stretch Cords or Bands

Purpose: To strengthen shoulders, back, lats, abdominals, and core.

Basic: Overhead Raises with Stretch Cords or Bands

Start by holding one end of a stretch cord in both hands and place your foot on the other end of the stretch cord on the floor to hold it in place. Give yourself enough slack so you can extend the stretch cord directly over your head, keeping your arms straight. While keeping your arms straight, raise the stretch cord directly above your shoulders and head; then, lower to start position and repeat.

Intermediate: Overhead Raises with Stretch Cords or Bands in Lunge Position

Same as the Basic, except stagger your feet in a lunge position while raising the stretch cord directly over your head. Split the repetitions between each leg. (See photo 26a.)

Advanced: Squat with Overhead Raises Using Kettle Bell

Start by standing with feet shoulder-width apart, holding one kettle bell with both hands. Begin by squatting back and bringing the kettle bell through your legs. Then, while extending out of the squat and returning to a standing

26a

26b

26c

position, simultaneously swing the kettle bell straight out in front and above your head while keeping your arms straight. Then, slowly lower the kettle bell and return to the start position. (See photos 26b and 26c.)

Sets/Reps: Competitive Season—three sets of 12 to 15 reps

4. Obliques over BOSU

Purpose: To strengthen obliques.

Basic: Obliques over BOSU

27a

Start by lying on the BOSU with the small of your back centered on top, both arms behind your head, and your feet on the floor. Slightly raise your torso off the BOSU while pointing one elbow toward the opposite knee. Hold and return to the start position and then repeat with the opposite elbow toward the other knee. Repeat by alternating sides. (See photo 27a.)

Intermediate: Obliques over BOSU with One Leg Raised

Same as the Basic, except with both hands behind your head, slightly raise your torso while raising the left leg and pointing the right elbow toward the left knee. Outstretched leg should remain off the floor. Repeat on that side and then switch legs and repeat on the other side.

Advanced: Bicycles over BOSU with Legs Raised

27b

Same as the Intermediate, except with both hands behind your head, raise your torso and legs off the floor so you are balanced on the BOSU. Extend one leg straight and keep the other leg bent. Start the movement by bringing the knee of the extended leg to the opposite elbow so they make contact. Repeat this movement with the opposite arm and leg, alternating the movement from one side to the other while maintaining balance on the BOSU. (See photo 27b.)

Sets/Reps: Competitive Season—three sets of 12 to 15 reps

If you are consistent in your training, the exercises in these three programs will help you to build and maintain a strong and healthy body. The next step is to combine these exercises with an efficient and sound stretching program, and you will be one step closer to your Half Iron-Distance goal!

Stretching Program

The following stretches are suggested for post-workout to help facilitate recovery, prevent injury, and ready your body for the next day's workout.

We will start with the foam roller before we progress to some static stretches.

We want to use the foam roller in a full body motion. With your arms crossed at your chest, start by sitting on the foam roller, which is on the floor in a horizontal position. Slowly walk your feet out away from the foam roller as you lie back onto it and roll it up to your neck. Roll back and forth a few times, and then gradually work your way down your back, then to your glutes, hamstrings, and calves, focusing on holding in the positions where you feel the most tightness or pressure.

Then, flip over onto your quadriceps and slowly roll it down to your shins a few times before moving up to your quadriceps. For a better release, bend your legs, bringing your heels toward your glutes as you roll on your shins and quadriceps. From that position, roll onto your side (hip flexors) and roll several times before moving down the side of your leg (the iliotibial band, or IT band), and eventually the sides of your calves/shins. This is a great way to massage and release the muscle fascia or inflammation, to help bring blood flow to needed areas.

If this is all you have time to do, that's okay.

If you have another 5 to 10 minutes, try to incorporate the following additional stretches. Like the "Easy Eight," these exercises flow from one to the other. You should perform these stretches until you feel a gentle stretch in the muscle but not pain. Hold each stretch for at least 30 seconds without a bouncing motion.

Static Stretches

1. Calf Stretch: Start by standing about a foot in front a wall with your feet staggered about 1.5 to 2 feet apart. Place your forearms against the wall by bending your front knee and keeping your back leg straight to stretch your calf. Repeat with the other leg forward. (See illustration 1.)

Illustration 1

2. Squatting Groin Stretch: From the calf stretch, bring your foot next to the other, about 2 feet apart. Slide your hands down the front of your legs to just above your ankles while bending at your knees and bringing your back end toward the floor. You should feel a stretch in your groin area. (See illustration 2.)

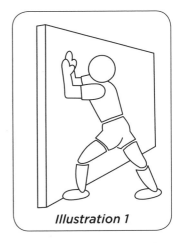

Illustration 2

3. Quad, Psoas, and Hip Flexor: From the groin stretch, stand up straight; take a step forward with one leg with bent knee so your quadricep is parallel to the ground while the other leg is just slightly bent or straight. Then raise the opposite arm straight up toward the ceiling, stretching your psoas. Hold this

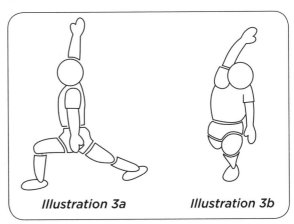

Illustration 3a   *Illustration 3b*

position for 30 seconds. Then, tilt the raised arm over your head and feel a stretch in your hip flexor. Repeat this exercise with the other leg forward. (See illustrations 3a and 3b.)

4. Press-ups: From the last stretch, lie flat on your stomach, facedown, placing your hands next to your shoulders with bent elbows. Begin by pressing up with your arms while keeping your hips on the floor, extending your back. Keep your head in alignment with your spine. Relax your belly and keep your glutes soft during this exercise. Repeat this exercise ten times. (See illustrations 4a and 4b.)

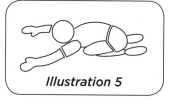

Illustration 4a

Illustration 4b

5. Kneeling Stretch: From the up position of the Press-up, sit back on your knees, keep your head down, extend your arms in front of you, and hold that stretch for 20 to 30 seconds. For an added stretch, allow your hips to drop slightly to one side and then repeat on the other side for a 20- to 30-second count. (See illustration 5.)

Illustration 5

6. Piriformis, Glutes to Hamstring: From the press-up stretch, lie on your back, facing a wall. Bend one knee and place that foot on the wall while bending the other leg and placing your foot at the knee of the foot on the wall. Feel a stretch in your piriformis and glutes. Switch legs and

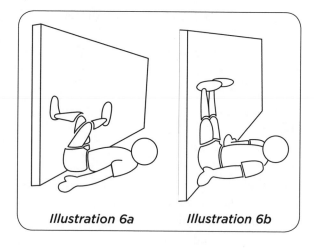

Illustration 6a

Illustration 6b

repeat. Then straighten both legs and bring your body close to the wall to feel a stretch in your hamstrings. (See illustrations 6a and 6b.)

7. Shoulder Stretch: From the glute stretch, stand up a few feet in front of an open door-way. Raise your arms straight out to your sides and back and walk through the doorway. Grab the sides of the doorway with your hands and continue to walk until you feel a stretch in your shoulders. You can do this exercise with one arm at a time to get a better stretch. (See illustration 7.)

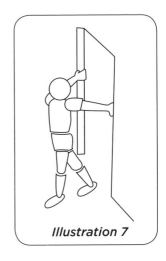

Illustration 7

Now you are done for the day, and have prepared your body to take on the next day's challenges. Be sure to do these pre-movement, foam roller, and post-workout stretches to help maintain a healthy and injury-free body.

Following is the fifth of ten motivating profiles of an inspiring Half Iron-Distance Triathlete.

HALF IRON-DISTANCE SUCCESS STORY:
JEN GONYEA

Jen Gonyea, who has trained and competed in triathlon for over six years, is a full-time, stay-at-home mom with four young children. Jen has established an impressive record of success, and her accomplishments include overall and age-group victories at numerous short-course triathlons, and qualifying for and racing the Boston Marathon.

Jen's husband works away from home on weekdays and does a lot of traveling, so she tries to get all of her longer workouts in during the week. This helps to free up her weekends for her kids' sports and other family activities. Jen also tries to focus on a relatively small number of key races each year, to limit her time away on weekends.

Jen sees the Half Iron-Distance Triathlon as the optimal race for her because while it doesn't require as much training time as the full Iron-Distance, it's still a very great and worthy challenge. Combining this distance with the IronFit training approach has allowed her to be a successful athlete, a great wife and mother, and maintain an overall rewarding lifestyle balance. As Jen puts it, "The Iron-Fit program keeps me laser-focused. I know exactly what I need to do each training day. I've always felt very prepared come race day, after following my program."

Not only does Jen prefer the Half Iron-Distance, but she also enjoys all of the many types of race-course challenges it offers. When asked about her favorite races, Jen said, "I've done completely opposite races. Eagleman 70.3 in Maryland is very flat, and Rev3-Quassy in Connecticut is very hilly; but both were equally satisfying."

The Half Iron-Distance is clearly going to be Jen's race of choice for the future. As Jen puts it, "I'd like to do one full Iron-Distance triathlon at some point, but because of my family, all our commitments, and our busy schedule, the Half Iron-Distance will most definitely be my distance."

CHAPTER 7

Mastering Transitions: "The Fourth Sport"

We are still masters of our fate. We are still captains of our souls.

—Winston Churchill

As experienced triathletes know, the Half Iron-Distance Triathlon has two transition areas. The first is referred to as "T1" and is where the athlete changes from swimming gear to cycling gear, between the swim and bike portions of the race. The second transition area is known as "T2" and is where the athlete changes from cycling gear to running gear, between the bike and run portions of the race.

In the Half, the transitions are among the most important portions of the race. A lot can go wrong during transitions, and inexperienced triathletes can spoil their entire race due to a whole host of easy-to-make "rookie mistakes." Because of the complexity of transitions, they are often referred to as "The Fourth Sport." And as the Fourth Sport, they need to be fully understood and trained for, just like the other three sports.

We are often surprised when we read through the race results and see some extremely long transition times. Long transition times are, of course, absolutely fine if athletes prefer to take their time and soak in the racing experience. Many "Just Finish" athletes approach transitions in exactly this way, and we fully understand and support them.

But for those who want to improve their race times or who are trying to achieve a personal record, this is a major lost opportunity. The transitions are basically packed with "free time," and it's so easy to improve your transition times with just a small amount of effort.

Athletes spend hours and hours working to shave precious minutes off their swim time, but most totally miss the comparably low-hanging fruit of

Suzy Serpico: Pro Triathlete and Half Iron-Distance Competitor
Kimberly Mitchell

transitions. Most athletes can easily shave minutes off their race time with a minimal amount of preparation.

In this chapter we present our proven approach to faster and more efficient transitions—in other words, how to grab some of that low-hanging fruit.

All Transitions Are Not Created Equal

The basic setup and logistics of transition areas varies greatly from one Half Iron-Distance race to another. Sometimes the exact same area is used for T1 and T2. Logistically, this type of transition is usually the simplest, especially if the swim start and race finish are located nearby as well. In other words, everything pretty much starts and ends in the same place.

The other extreme would be to have the swim start in one place, T1 in a second place, T2 in a third place, and the race finish in a fourth place. Most races are somewhere between these two extremes.

In some races, often those with just one transition area for both T1 and T2, the athletes are allowed to set up both their bike and run gear right next to their bike in the transition area. The big advantage of this is that you can set up everything in the exact order you want, and all of your gear will be leaving from and returning to the same place.

Tip: Set your gear up on a brightly colored towel right next to your bike. This will help you to quickly locate it as you enter T1.

Another possibility, especially in larger races, is the use of race gear bags. Prior to the race you put your cycling gear in a designated bike gear bag, and your running gear in another designated run gear bag. The bags are then usually hung on a rack in numerical order. As you enter the transition area from your swim, you grab your cycling gear bag, take it to where your bike is racked, and change from your swimming gear to your cycling gear. Then you proceed with your bike through the designated exit from T1 and out onto the bike course.

Similarly, when you complete the bike portion of the race, you grab your run gear bag off a rack as you enter T2, take it to where you rack your bike, and change from your bike gear to your running gear. You then proceed through the designated exit from T2 and out onto the run course.

Another possible transition area setup is a hybrid of the two. You are allowed to lay out your cycling gear next to your bike in T1, but your running gear is transported to T2 in a run gear bag that you drop off before the race. There are several other possible transition area setups as well.

It doesn't really matter which of the possible transition options you encounter; each one is fun and challenging if you properly prepare. The important thing to understand is that they are all different. It's crucial that you learn in advance what the logistical layout will be so that you can properly prepare for it and know exactly what to expect on race day.

Tip: Note that public nudity is often an automatic disqualification at many races. Be sure to know the rules of your specific race in advance so that you can plan your transition approach accordingly.

Walk-Through Visualization

Once you've set up your gear in the transition area or dropped your gear bags off in the proper place, most athletes then rush down to the swim start.

A better approach is to arrive early enough to allow time for a walk-through of the transition area. Go to the spot at which you will later enter T1 from the swim and do a walk-through of the entire process. Walk to where you will retrieve your gear bag (if the race has gear bags) and then walk to your bike, following the exact same route you will be taking during the race. Count the number of bike racks, or locate an easy landmark that will help you find your bike in the fog and frenzy of the race. Finally, walk to where you will exit T1. While doing your walk-through, visualize what everything will look like during the race, remembering the fact that you will be running, not walking.

Do a similar walk-through of T2 as well. If it's not possible to do a walk-through of one or both transition areas the morning of the race, consider doing them the afternoon of the day before. Whether you do it the day before or the morning of the race, keep in mind that the transition areas are likely to look and feel a lot different during the race. Try your best to visualize what they will actually look and feel like.

The walk-through visualization will save time by eliminating mistakes and give you that great "been there, done that" confidence before the race.

The "Top Down / Bottom Up" Approach to Speedy Transitions

We are often surprised by how many triathletes don't have a transition plan. Once an athlete told us that his transition plan was to "put on my stuff." Okay, that's a start. But for a faster, more error-free transition, we need a plan. Without a plan, mistakes are common, and mistakes almost always result in slower race times.

Many of our coached athletes use our "Top Down / Bottom Up" transition technique. The basic approach is to remove items from your body in the order of top to bottom, and then to put items back on in order from the bottom to the top. This approach provides a nice orderly sequence that is easy to remember.

For example, as you run from the swim finish to T1, remove your goggles and swim cap and unzip your wetsuit. If possible, you can even pull your arms and hands out of the sleeves as you go. When you arrive at your bike in the transition area, remove your wet suit and then begin to put on your cycling gear from the bottom up.

Note that this same approach applies if you are wearing a speed suit instead of a wet suit. We will discuss speed suits later in this chapter and in Chapter 10.

Put your socks on first, if you plan to wear socks. Next, put on your cycling shoes (if you are not attaching your shoes to your pedals in advance). We generally suggest that most athletes wear a one- or two-piece tri suit for the duration of the race, so no change is required. Next comes your race belt if you are wearing one. Next comes your cycling helmet; buckle it right away. (**Tip:** Don't ever forget this one. Besides being extremely important for safety reasons, it's usually an automatic DQ if you forget to buckle!) Finally, put on your sunglasses.

This is a nice, efficient, and easy-to-remember order. Swimming gear comes off from top to bottom, and cycling gear goes on from bottom to top.

Similarly as you enter T2 after the bike ride, remove your cycling gear from the top down and put on your running gear from the bottom up. First, rack your bike (or hand it off to the proper race official) after you safely dismount. Then, as you run toward your bike rack location (or designated changing area), remove your cycling helmet and sunglasses (unless you plan on wearing the same pair of sunglasses on the run). Once you arrive at your bike rack (or designated changing area), remove your cycling shoes and socks, if you are wearing them (unless you plan to wear the same socks for the run). Then, put on your running socks and shoes. Next, make sure that your race number is in place. Finally, put on your race cap and sunglasses.

Tip: Notice how the glasses are last. This means that you will not drip on them while attending to your shoes and other lower-body items. They will be dry, clear, and good to go.

Just like in T1, this T2 approach is a nice, efficient, and easy-to-remember order. Cycling gear came off from top to bottom, and then running gear went on from bottom to top.

This is just one example of an approach that works and has been battle-tested by many athletes over the years. You may have your own plan and approach. This is absolutely fine, as long as you practice it and become efficient with it.

The "Transition Game"

How many minutes a week do most triathletes practice their transitions with their actual race gear (not training gear)? The answer is pretty much zero for most athletes. Again, this is such a missed opportunity.

We encourage our coached athletes to practice their transitions for just 15 minutes per week, and the results have been outstanding. With this minimal time investment, an athlete can take several "free minutes" off their race time.

To really make the point, we have often played the "Transition Game" with several of our coached athletes. We establish two teams of four and set up a transition area with an orange road cone positioned about 50 feet away. The first athlete from each team starts in the transition area dressed in swim gear and runs to the cone, circles it, and runs back to the transition area. The athlete changes from swim to bike gear and again runs to the cone, circles it, and runs back to the transition area. After the change from bike to running gear, the athlete runs to the cone again, circles it, and runs back to the transition area. Once there, the next member of the team repeats the same sequence. All four team members complete the same sequence in this relay-race format. The first team to have all four team members complete the transitions wins.

One of the great benefits of this game is that it provides great transition practice. It simulates the time pressure of an actual race, making it much more real to the athlete.

The second great benefit of the game is that it proves to the athlete the importance of practicing transitions. If the same two teams play several rounds of the game in a row, they almost always become faster with each round. And not just a little faster, they usually become a lot faster. This is simply the result of practice. Each time we repeat steps, we become faster and more efficient at doing them.

If you have an opportunity, get some of your triathlete friends together and play the Transition Game. Besides improving your transition skills, it's also a blast. You will all have fun doing it.

How and When to Practice Your Transitions

Whether or not you have an opportunity to play the Transition Game from time to time, we suggest to all of our coached athletes that they should be practicing their transitions with race gear at least once a week during race season. That's correct—not just the week before your big race, but every week throughout the triathlon season. All you need is about 15 minutes. Get out all of your actual race gear. Put on your swim gear. Then quickly complete the two transitions. Two to three times completely through is all you need. Think robotically. Execute the specific steps of your plan, one after another in sequence, as efficiently as you can.

Sure, we practice T2 in training gear every week during the transition sessions in our sixteen-week training plans, but it's not the same as practicing with the actual race gear and equipment that we will be using on race day. That is why this weekly 15-minute practice session can be so beneficial.

For best results, time yourself for each round. Not only will this simulate the time pressure of the race, but it will also allow you to track your progress. Each time you do it, try to beat your personal record.

Plan your weekly transition practice session for a time immediately following one of your workout sessions, when you are already fatigued and perspiring. This will more closely simulate actual race conditions.

When you practice your transitions, keep in mind the exact setup of the transition area for your next Half Iron-Distance Triathlon and try to mimic the situation as much as possible. For example, if your race allows you to set up your bike gear in T1 next to your bike, that's exactly how you want to do it when you practice. On the other hand, if the race uses gear bags, and you will basically be dumping the contents of your bag on the ground in front of you, then this is exactly how you should practice your transition.

Tip: Consider filming your transition practice sessions periodically—a great way to discover inefficiencies. You can compare the periodic video clips over time to help gauge your progress.

More Time-Saving Transition Tips

Following are several more transition tips for your consideration. Again, if you plan to use any of these in your race, you must first practice them several times to make sure they work for you and are safe and efficient.

1. **Be a minimalist:** Less is usually more. Keep your transitions as simple as possible. The more complicated your plan, the greater the risk of something going wrong.

2. **One- or two-piece tri suit:** Most athletes benefit from racing in either a one- or two-piece tri suit, as opposed to some other type of racing garment. You can wear it right under your wet suit and then just keep it on for the bike and run, greatly simplifying your transitions. There are pros and cons to a one-piece versus a two-piece, so test them both out and see which works best for you. The one-piece has the advantage of providing better sun blockage and being slightly more aerodynamic. The two-piece has the advantage of being a little cooler, and can make bathroom breaks less complicated. We suggest you try them both and use the one that works best for you.

3. **Know the rules:** The transition areas are a great place for receiving penalties and for getting into collisions with other athletes. Know the rules in advance and practice them in training so that on race day you can be safe and penalty-free.

4. **Wet-suit strippers:** Many races offer wet-suit strippers who are volunteers stationed somewhere between the swim exit and T1. Their mission is to assist you in removing your wet suit. Typically, they will ask you to pull your wet suit down to your waist or hips and then sit down on the ground and raise your feet into the air. They then grab hold of your wet suit and pull it off over your feet. It's fine if you want to take advantage of this service; however, most athletes can be faster taking it off themselves with just a little practice.

   Furthermore, rips often occur when someone rapidly pulls your wet suit off in this way. With the high cost of many wet suits, you may be better off learning to remove it yourself.

5. **Socks or no socks:** If you train without socks, then you are fine to race without them. From a transition standpoint, it's one more step to eliminate. But if you don't train this way (and most Half Iron-Distance Triathletes do not), it would be a "rookie mistake" to do it in the race. The risk of blisters and other issues far outweighs the few seconds you may save by not putting on your socks.

6. **Sunscreen:** The best time to apply waterproof sunscreen is before the race, preferably after you have already been marked with your

race number. Be careful not to come in contact with the markings as you apply the sunscreen, however, as this can smear your numbers. If you want to reapply sunscreen during the race, a good time to do it is as you run out of T2 at the start of the 13.1-mile run.

7. **Elastic shoelaces:** Elastic laces in your running shoes allow you to tie your running shoes exactly how you like them in advance and then simply pull your running shoes on in T2 without having to use any time to tie them.

8. **Flying bike mount:** Most pros and some elite age-group athletes do what is called a flying bike mount. Instead of putting one foot into the pedal clip while in a standing position and then pulling the other leg over the top of the bike, these athletes run with their bike and jump onto it, with the first point of contact being the buttocks with the bike saddle. This is a risky approach, and in general we suggest it only for top athletes and those who will practice it weekly in their training. Otherwise, the possibility of gaining a few seconds is not worth the risk of falling and spoiling your entire race.

9. **Shoes on pedals:** Most pros and some elite age-group athletes also attach their bike shoes to their pedals in advance and don't slip their feet into them until their bike is moving. This approach is often used with a flying bike mount, but it can be used with a normal bike mount as well. To keep the shoes from dragging on the ground prior to sliding their feet into them, most athletes will use either a piece of tape or a rubber band to hold the shoe up. This then breaks away once the athlete starts to pedal. This approach also carries with it a much greater risk of a crash, so we only suggest it for pro and elite age-group athletes who commit to practicing it weekly in training and become very safe and proficient with it.

10. **Attaching items to your bike:** The more items you can attach to your bike, the fewer items you'll need to deal with while in transition. This can be a big time-saver. Items athletes typically attach to their bikes in advance are water bottles, bento boxes for

energy gels or energy bars, sunglasses, and bike shoes. This is all fine, as long as it is done well. It is common to see athletes with items falling off their bikes in the middle of a race when they hit a bump in the course, or perhaps when their bike just gets wet and slippery. The key is to test everything out in training and in all possible conditions. If an item falls off your bike, it can easily spoil your entire race.

11. **Run with your bike:** Practice running safely with your bike, with your bike shoes on, so that you are proficient at it on race day. The only time most athletes ever run alongside their bikes is when they do it in T1 of an actual race. Typically, after retrieving your bike from the bike rack, you have to run with it through the transition area and exit at a specific location. Once exiting T1, there is usually a line which, once crossed, you are allowed to mount your bike. Sometimes this is a fairly long run, and it's surprising how many athletes have accidents along the way, crashing into other bikes or other athletes. Practice running with your bike in a controlled and safe way.

We hope the above tips and suggestions help you to find more "free time" in your transitions.

Following is the sixth of ten motivating profiles of an inspiring Half Iron-Distance Triathlete.

HALF IRON-DISTANCE SUCCESS STORY: CRAIG GRUBER

Craig Gruber has been competing in triathlons for over four years; and among his many accomplishments, he raced faster than five and a half hours in just his second Half Iron-Distance Triathlon, and he qualified for the Boston Marathon in only his second marathon.

Craig owns a company that sells electric power. Though the responsibilities of managing his company are great, it does provide him some degree of time flexibility and more control over his schedule, which helps him to be very consistent with his training sessions. Craig values this greatly and sees consistency in training as one of the great determinants of triathlon success. We could not agree more.

Craig has an extremely supportive family, and that is probably his other greatest endurance sports asset. His wife, Brenda, is an accomplished road racer, and it's not unusual for both Brenda and their three sons to be cheering Craig on at his races.

As with many parents who participate in endurance sports, one of Craig's motivations for training and competing is the positive impact he hopes it will have on his family. Evidently this strategy has worked, as all three sons participate in road races in addition to other sports, including soccer, baseball, and tennis. In recent years, the entire family has competed in an informal "Gruber Family Championship" at a local Thanksgiving Day 5K.

Craig credits the IronFit training approach for helping him to stay healthy with the proper mix of training elements and the gradual progressive increases in training volume. Craig jokes that if you are consistent with IronFit training, "Fitness kind of creeps up on you." Craig also finds the rest day / slide day concept essential to providing greater flexibility and keeping him healthy.

While Craig plans to race his first full Iron-Distance triathlon in the coming year, he expects to mostly race the Half Iron-Distance in the future. He cites the many advantages of the Half Iron-Distance, including a lesser overall training time requirement, less race travel time, lower race expense, and also a reduced risk of injury.

Watch for Craig and his family at the races as he continues to lower his Half Iron-Distance times, and his supportive endurance sports family continues to set a positive example for all of us.

CHAPTER 8

Half Iron-Distance Race Strategies, Fueling, and Hydration

Fortune favors the brave.

—Publius Terence

n this chapter we will present several important race strategies for the Half Iron-Distance Triathlon, including targeted race intensity, fueling and hydration strategy, approach to pre-race warm-up, course segmentation strategy, and a special strategy for the "Just Finish" athlete.

We will begin with the two most crucial strategy elements: intensity level and fueling and hydration. More specifically, we will address:

1. Your targeted intensity level during the race, which can be measured in perceived effort, pace, heart rate, watts, or some other indicator; and

2. Your fueling and hydration before and during the race, which includes exactly what you plan to eat and drink, and exactly when you plan to eat and drink it.

Sure, there are many other factors that affect your racing performance, but these are the big ones. If you nail these two, your chances of realizing your potential on race day are infinitely improved. And if you blow any of these factors (e.g., you go out too fast, or you forget to eat and drink properly), your chances of success are greatly diminished. These are the two most important elements around which to build your racing strategy and approach.

So much is written on the topic of race strategy, and so much of it is overly technical and complicated. Having coached hundreds of athletes for many years, we know this is not what most athletes want. What most athletes want

Jen Luebke: Pro Triathlete and Half Iron-Distance Competitor
Tom Robertson Photography

is a clear and sensible approach that they can put right to use and achieve positive results. That is exactly what we will provide in this chapter.

Strategy for Maintaining Proper Intensity Level

Let's start with effort level. Simply put, if we start out racing at too high of an intensity level, we will run out of energy at some point and slow down drastically, thus not maximizing our overall racing performance. Likewise, if we start out racing at too conservative of an intensity level, we may get to the end of the race and realize that we didn't maximize our performance because we still had "a lot left in the tank." This is why it is crucial to have a good strategy for being at the proper intensity level at all times throughout the race.

Many athletes do not realize that the optimal racing approach to the Half Iron-Distance differs from the full Iron-Distance. Maybe it's because they both have the word "Iron" in them, or something like that, but these races are not the same. The full Iron-Distance is basically a "Z2 Race" for most. In other words, most athletes will maximize their performance if they stay somewhere in their Z2 heart rate zone (moderate intensity) for all, or almost all, of the race.

For faster Iron-Distance Triathletes—say, for those completing the race in less than ten hours—this may mean mostly the mid- to higher end of their Z2 heart range. For athletes in the twelve- to fourteen-hour range, this may mean mostly the lower to mid-range of their Z2 heart rate zone. And for athletes needing sixteen to seventeen hours to finish, this may mean mostly high Z1 to low Z2. But, overall, the full Iron-Distance is mostly a Z2 race.

The intensity of the Half Iron-Distance is higher. As discussed in Chapter 4, as the intensity level of the race goes up, the mix of energy systems being utilized becomes more anaerobic, while remaining still a mix of both aerobic and anaerobic. For athletes completing the Half Iron-Distance in over six hours, it may still be partly, or even mostly, a Z2 race, but for those athletes racing faster times, in the four- to six-hour range, it's more likely to be primarily a Z3 race.

Many athletes don't realize this subtle difference between the Half and full Iron-Distances, and because of that, they don't train properly for it or they don't execute the optimal strategy and approach on race day. Not only does our training need to support the proper heart rates associated with correctly racing this distance, but the athlete also needs to know how to be in the right heart rate at the right time throughout the race in order to maximize performance.

Many athletes find that racing the Half Iron-Distance by heart rate can be very difficult. It's usually not as easy as saying "I am an under-five-hour Half Iron-Distance triathlete, so I will maintain a steady Z3 heart rate throughout the race." Or, "Because I am an over-seven-hour Half Iron-Distance athlete, I will maintain a steady Z2 heart rate throughout the race."

Perhaps on some very flat courses it is possible to lock in on the proper heart rate and hold it right there for several hours. But when courses are hilly or windy, as many are, this is much more difficult. When you are going up a hill, your heart rate may shoot up into Z4; then, when you are going downhill, your heart rate may drop into Z1. You might find yourself thinking: "For a Z3 race, I don't seem to be in Z3 very much."

The "90-95-100" Perceived Effort Approach

Years ago, after receiving feedback from many athletes, and based on our own racing experience regarding how hard it is to maintain certain heart rate targets in a Half Iron-Distance, we developed a perceived effort approach to this race. We like to call our battle-tested strategy the "90-95-100" Perceived Effort Approach. While we do sometimes apply this type of approach to other distances as well, there is no better race to use it than the Half. For most athletes, it's the best strategy for maximizing their Half Iron-Distance performance.

Here is how to apply the "90-95-100" Perceived Effort Approach to racing the Half Iron-Distance:

1. Start by racing the 1.2-mile swim portion of the Half at a 90 percent perceived effort of what you would race at if you were only going to do a 1.2-mile swim. In other words, swim as if you were going to stop after the swim. We want to mentally feel like we are backing off this effort level by 10 percent.

2. Then, race the 56-mile bike portion of the Half at a 95 percent perceived effort of what you would race were the race to be over after the bike—in other words, as if you were not going to do the run portion after the bike. We want to mentally feel like we are backing off this effort level by 5 percent.

3. Finally, race the 13.1-mile run portion at an even 100 percent perceived effort of whatever strength and energy you have left at the start of the run; in other words, the maximum level of effort you feel you can maintain straight through to the finish line. While running, continue to reassess and make adjustments as you go. For example: Perhaps you will get halfway through the run and feel that you have more energy than expected. If so, increase your level of effort to one that you now feel you can maintain to the finish.

We have used the "90-95-100" Perceived Effort Approach with many of our coached athletes at all levels for years, and most find that it helps them to maintain the right level of effort at exactly the right time, to maximize overall racing performance. We hope you will give it a try as well.

Now that we have discussed our suggested strategy and approach for our Half Iron-Distance racing intensity level, we will consider our strategy and approach for fueling and hydration.

Optimal Fueling and Hydration Strategy for the Half Iron-Distance Triathlon

The second major strategy we need to have for the Half concerns consuming the proper fluid amounts, calorie requirements, and sodium and other electrolyte replacement; in short, the elements of a complete fueling and hydration plan. As we often tell our coached athletes, after the training itself, the greatest factor to Half Iron-Distance success is proper fueling and hydration. And, as we like to joke, mistakes in fueling and hydration are measured in hours, not minutes.

But here's the secret: A proper race-day fueling and hydration plan is built over many weeks, and even months, before the race. Many athletes don't realize this. They treat it like a last-minute decision. They will read an article about some coach's specific plan the week before the race, or hear what some pro athlete is doing, and try to copy it. This is a big rookie mistake. We are all different, and the optimal fueling and hydration plan is unique to you. It's fine to start with a program you read about somewhere; but only after you have tested it and refined it, over several weeks in training, do you know if it is the best plan for you.

In the following sections, we will explain the secrets of how to develop your optimal fueling and hydration plan.

Determining Race Hydration Needs

If you wait until you are thirsty, you have probably already waited too long. There is a delayed reaction between when we first start to get behind on our hydration and when we actually feel thirsty.

What we want to do is to determine our personal hydration needs and then evenly consume that amount of hydration throughout our race. The easiest way to determine your body's unique hydration needs is through proper testing in training. We have developed a simple "Sweat Rate Test" that we have successfully used over the years with the athletes we coach.

Our Sweat Rate Test protocol is as follows:

Sweat Rate Test

1. Weigh yourself (without clothing) just prior to beginning your endurance activity (e.g., run, cycle, swim, etc.).

2. Do your endurance activity for 60 minutes at a heart rate equal to 75 percent of your maximum heart rate (MHR).

3. During the 60 minutes of activity, very evenly consume 16 ounces of water.

4. Weigh yourself (without clothing) immediately after your 60-minute activity has been completed.

5. Complete the following calculations:

6. Weight Before – Weight After = Net Weight Loss

7. Net Weight Loss + 1.0 pound (16 oz. of water consumed) = Hourly Sweat Loss

Note: 1 pound = 16 ounces

Athlete Example: "Sweat Rate Test"

The following example applies the Sweat Rate Test protocol to Hallie Henderson, a Half Iron-Distance triathlete who finds that she weighs 125 pounds before the test and 124.5 pounds after the test. Following is the calculation:

> Weight before = 125.0 pounds
> Weight after = 124.5 pounds
> Weight Loss: 125.0 – 124.5 = 0.5 pounds (8 ounces)
> Hourly Sweat Rate: 0.5 pound (8 ounces) + 1.0 pound (16 oz. of water consumed) = 1.5 pounds (24 ounces)

Hallie lost 8 ounces, despite replenishing with 16 ounces of fluid. Therefore, she is down a net 24 ounces for the hour. This indicates that under similar conditions (i.e., temperature, heart rate level, and activity), she should replenish her fluids at a rate of about 24 ounces per hour, as one should replenish fluids by as close as possible to 100 percent. Fortunately for her, this is a fairly easy amount to keep track of, especially during the bike portion of the race, as it equates to exactly one 24-ounce bike bottle per hour.

Hallie should begin training with this level of hydration per hour and see how it makes her feel. She should also consider testing slightly higher amounts on hotter days and perhaps slightly lower amounts on cooler days, to adjust for slight changes in sweat rate.

Finally, she should consider testing slightly higher amounts for higher-intensity training sessions, which may more closely simulate actual race-day conditions. Over time, she will fine-tune these amounts and know exactly what her consumption needs will be on race day.

Recently we recorded the following racing hydration data for a sampling of eight of our more elite-level, age-group athletes:

Hydration Racing Data:
- Average fluid oz. per hour: 33.5 oz. (ranging from 24 to 43 oz.)
- Average fluid oz. per hour to weight (lbs.): 0.20 oz. (ranging from 0.15 to 0.24)

Our eight athletes consumed on average 33.5 ounces of fluid per hour while racing, and the range among the eight athletes varied from a low of 24 ounces to a high of 43 ounces. Because size and body mass account for some of this difference, we also looked at this data on the basis of ounces of fluid per pound of body weight. The average ratio for the group was 0.20 ounces of fluid per pound of body weight, with a range of 0.15 to 0.24 ounces per pound of body weight.

This information is valuable when determining your optimal race hydration strategy, and especially your hourly hydration needs. In addition to performing the Sweat Rate Test and testing the results in training, we suggest you also check your results against this sampling of eight experienced athletes on the basis of fluid ounces per hour to body weight.

By simply using the above Sweat Rate Test protocol, comparing the results with the results of this eight-athlete sampling, and then testing and fine-tuning the results in training, you will determine your optimal race hydration replacement plan.

Determining Your Race Fueling Needs

When we talk about "fueling," we are talking about calories. While we suggest consuming straight water for racing and training sessions lasting less than 75 minutes, we find that for races and training sessions of 75 minutes or more, most athletes need to be replacing calories as well, to maximize performance. We refer to this as the "75 Minute Guideline," and while it varies slightly from one athlete to another, most athletes fall right around the 75-minute point. If the workout or race will take more than 75 minutes to complete, you should start fueling (i.e., replacing calories) along with hydrating, right from the start.

How much calorie replacement do we need? We find that most athletes should evenly replace between one-third and one-half of their calories utilized for the Half Iron-Distance Triathlon. The longer it takes the athlete to complete the race, the closer we should typically be to targeting a 50 percent calorie replenishment.

So, for example, if the activity you are doing for over 75 minutes burns calories at a rate of 900 per hour, then you should be replacing your calories at a rate of 300 to 450 calories per hour (i.e., one-third of 900 equals 300, and one-half of 900 equals 450). Half Iron-Distance triathletes should estimate this range and test it in training to determine exactly what calorie amount per hour is optimal for them.

Here's the secret: Our ability to consume higher levels of calories is trainable. In other words, if you find it difficult to take in this many calories at first, by gradually building up to these levels over time, you can train your body to do it. Many athletes make the mistake of giving up too soon when at first they find these higher levels of calories don't agree with them. Yet it is well worth the effort to gradually train your body to be comfortable with consuming sufficient fueling while racing.

In addition to considering your calorie intake based on this range of one-third to one-half of calories used, we suggest you also consider your calories from the standpoint of calories per pounds of body weight. The following fueling data is for the same group of eight elite-level, age-group athletes:

Race Fueling Data:

- Average calories per hour: 404 (ranging from 270 to 537)
- Average calories per hour per body weight (lbs.): 2.6. (ranging from 1.7 to 3.3)

The average calorie intake for these eight elite-level athletes was about 404 calories per hour, and the athletes ranged from 270 to 537 calories per hour. Obviously, the bigger athletes typically had the higher totals and the smaller athletes the lower totals, so to get a better apples-to-apples comparison, we have included the second statistic, which indicates that on average, these athletes consumed 2.6 calories for every pound of body weight.

For example, an athlete who weighs 155 pounds consumed about 400 calories per hour (i.e., 155 x 2.6 = 403). This is very helpful information as you determine the optimal amount of calories per hour in your own fueling plan.

Our suggestion is to use the two above criteria (ratio of calorie intake to calories utilized, and ratio of calorie intake to body weight) to help determine the optimal calories for racing. Once you determine your calorie amount, test it frequently in all of your longer training sessions to see how it makes you feel. Then adjust and fine-tune as you train to arrive at the optimal amount for you.

Calorie Sources

Now that we know how many calories we should be consuming each hour, let's consider what sources we should be getting these calories from. Our best piece of advice on this is the simpler the better. The more complicated you make your race fueling plan, the greater the chance for error during your race. And, of course, errors mean time.

The race fueling of our same group of eight elite athletes has the following nutritional breakdown:

Nutritional Ratio Data (Ranges):

- 93 to 100 percent carbohydrates
- 0 to 5 percent protein
- 0 to 2 percent fat

As you see above, most elite athletes get the vast majority of their calories through carbohydrate sources. Some even get 100 percent from carbohydrates. Simple carbohydrates are quickly digested and go right to work, providing you with energy. The most popular sources include energy drinks and energy gels. Our suggestion is to test these sources first, as they are the easiest to carry and use during the race. In fact, most races provide these items right on the course.

Other possible sources include energy bars, which are often preferred by athletes who like some protein and fat during the race, plus bananas, oranges, pretzels, and other chewy carbohydrate products like GU Chomps.

Athlete Example: Race Fueling and Hydration Plan

The following is an example of a simple race fueling and hydration plan that brings together all of these concepts into one concise and easy-to-use plan:

Hallie Henderson is a Half Iron-Distance Triathlete who weighs 125 pounds. Her simple race fueling and hydration plan for the bike and run portion of her races includes 24 ounces of hydration and 325 calories per hour, as follows:

Hallie Henderson's Race Fueling and Hydration Plan:
- 24 ounces of energy drink (100 percent carbohydrates with 175 calories) per hour, which is sipped gradually throughout each hour.
- 1 GU Energy Gel (100 calories each, or 150 calories per hour) every 40 minutes.

Hallie determined from the IronFit Sweat Rate Test that she needed to replace 24 ounces of fluid per hour. She then tested this in training and confirmed that it was the optimal amount for her in moderate weather conditions.

Hallie then considered that the average ratio for the group of eight athletes discussed above was 0.20 ounces of fluid per pound of body weight, with a range of 0.15 to 0.24 ounces per pound of body weight. She compared her ratio of 0.19 (24 ounces / 125 pounds = 0.19 ounces per pound) and found that it fit nicely into the middle of the range. This made her even more confident that she had determined her proper hourly fluid replacement amount.

Hallie estimated that she uses about 800 calories per hour during the bike and run portions of her races. She calculated the one-third to one-half suggested calorie replacement range to be about 267 to 400 calories (800 x 1/3 = 267 and 800 x 1/2 = 400). She then tested this calorie range in training and found that 325 calories felt best to her.

Hallie then considered the average calories per pound ratio of 2.6 discussed above, and was pleased to find that it fit perfectly (125 pounds x 2.6 = 325 calories per hour). So this became her simple yet extremely effective race fueling and hydration plan.

Hallie determined in advance of her Half Iron-Distance race which energy drink was going to be offered at the race, and she tested it in training. She found that it worked fine for her, so she will use it in her race. This will make her racing logistics simpler, as she will not have to worry about carrying all of her own bottles on the bike course, or wearing a hydration/fuel belt on the run, because she can simply pick up these items on the course.

While the aid stations on the course did offer an energy gel, it was not the brand or flavor she preferred, so she decided to carry her own gels in a bento box on the top tube of her bike, and in the back pocket of her one-piece racing tri suit for the run.

Hallie Henderson's fueling and hydration routine is a great example of how to use the simple approach we have talked about to fine-tune and perfect your own optimal plan.

Pre-Race Fueling and Hydration

A common mistake made by many Half Iron-Distance triathletes is to not fuel and hydrate properly before racing. Insufficient pre-race calories and fluid will significantly affect performance. As the intensity of activity increases, blood flow is redirected from the stomach to fuel the muscles. We race best when we arrive at the starting line properly fueled and hydrated.

Some athletes find this difficult to do because of pre-race nervousness, or, in the case of early-morning training, some athletes prefer just to get out the door and get started. The key is to practice pre-race fueling and hydration regularly in training to allow your body to get used to it.

The same eight elite coached athletes referred to earlier in this chapter have an average of 58.5 ounces of fluids within the three hours leading up to their races, with a range of 45 to 72 ounces. To help adjust for differences in athlete size and body mass, we also consider pre-race hydration on the basis of average fluid per pound of body weight, which is 0.36 ounces per pound of body weight, with a range of 0.28 to 0.43 ounces.

Pre-Race Hydration Data:
- Average fluid oz. consumed: 58.5 (ranging from 45 to 72 oz.)
- Average fluid (oz.) to body weight (lbs.) ratio: 0.36 (ranging from 0.28 to 0.43)

This is valuable information as you determine your optimal pre-race hydration amounts.

The same eight elite coached athletes consume an average of about 951 calories in the three hours before their races, with a range of 690 to 1,212. To help adjust for differences in athlete size and body mass, we also consider pre-race calories on the basis of average calories per pound of body weight, which is 6.6 calories per pound, with a range of 5.7 to 7.3.

Pre-Race Fueling Data:
- Average calories consumed: 951 (ranging from 690 to 1,212)
- Average calories to body weight (lbs.) ratio: 6.6 (ranging from 5.7 to 7.3)

This is also valuable information as you determine your optimal pre-race fueling amounts.

We suggest that your pre-race fueling and hydration exist primarily in the form of easily digested simple carbohydrates, with some lesser amounts of protein and fat. The ratios of carbohydrates, proteins, and fat for the same eight athletes are as follows:

Average Nutritional Ratios:
- 76 percent carbohydrates
- 12 percent protein
- 12 percent fat

Popular food items include energy bars, oatmeal, toast with jelly, and muffins. Popular fluids include energy drinks, water, coffee, tea, and balanced nutritional drinks like Ensure and Boost. The important thing is to test your pre-race fueling and hydration routine regularly in training to fine-tune and perfect it over time.

What works best for one athlete will not necessarily work best for another. Test various items you like, and see what makes you feel the best and perform at your highest level. The best sessions of the week for testing in the Chapter 5 training programs are both the Saturday long transition session and the Sunday long run.

Athlete Example: Pre-Race Fueling and Hydration Plan

The following is an example of a simple pre-race fueling and hydration plan that helps bring together all of these concepts into one concise and easy-to-use plan.

Hallie Henderson, the same 125-pound triathlete in the example above, has a simple pre-race fueling and hydration plan for her Half Iron-Distance Triathlon, which includes consuming 50 ounces of hydration and 820 calories within the three hours prior to her race.

Hallie Henderson's Pre-Race Fueling and Hydration Plan:
- Upon waking three hours before the race starting time, she drinks 6 ounces of coffee and eats two of her favorite energy bars (400 calories).
- Over the next two and a half hours, she gradually drinks two 20-ounce bottles of her favorite energy drink (320 calories).
- Then, 10 minutes before the start of the race, she consumes one energy gel (100 calories) with about 4 ounces of water.

Hallie has practiced and fine-tuned this exact pre-race fueling and hydration plan during the couple of months prior to the race, in all of her longer weekend training sessions. In addition to making her feel strong and energized, she is confident in her specific amounts, as they compare well with the data on the eight athletes above. Hallie's fluid ounces per pound of body weight is 0.40 (50 ounces / 125 pounds = 0.40), and her calories per pound

AN IRONFIT MOMENT

Carbohydrate Loading

Athletes frequently ask us about carbohydrate loading, and whether or not it is something they should consider. We typically find that a lot of confusion exists over what is meant by carbohydrate loading. Today, what it means to most athletes is to eat a lot of carbohydrate-rich foods the day before the race, usually in the form of a big pasta dinner.

Technically, true carbohydrate loading has to do with strategies involving the theory that if you deplete your body of carbohydrates for a period of time (usually a few days) by eating a low-carbohydrate diet, you can then set your body up to store more carbohydrates than usual when you switch to a diet rich in carbohydrates for a period of time—usually a few days just prior to the race. True carbohydrate loading also includes a hard training session right before the athlete begins the few days of low-carbohydrate eating, which is believed to further enhance the depletion process.

Carbohydrates are stored as glycogen, which is a key element for endurance sports success. The theory goes that if you starve yourself from carbohydrates, you then increase your ability to store more glycogen once you switch back to a diet heavy in carbohydrates. There are pros and cons with this approach; while it may be worth considering for some athletes, it may not be for others.

So while we would not discourage you from testing a true carbo-loading approach in training to see if it's something that works for you, we are more comfortable with suggesting that athletes consider an approach called "topping off your glycogen."

Instead of going through the carbohydrate-depletion phase discussed above, simply stick with your normal diet at the start of race week. Once you enter the last forty-eight to seventy-two hours before the race, start to switch your calorie sources over to more carbohydrate-rich foods (preferably low-fiber). Don't try new carbohydrate sources at this point, however; stick with ones that you are used to in your diet. All we will be doing here is increasing the percentage of carbohydrates that make up your diet, as opposed to switching over to any unfamiliar foods.

This approach is less risky, and not only will you probably feel better during race week, but, more important, you will also feel energized and strong on race morning when you step up to the starting line.

of body weight are 6.6 (820 calories / 125 pounds = 6.6). Both of these ratios are well within the range for the eight athletes.

Hallie Henderson's pre-race fueling and hydration routine is a great example of how to use the simple approach we have talked about to fine-tune and perfect your own optimal plan.

Sodium and Electrolyte Replacement

We are frequently asked by athletes if they should take salt tablets or electrolyte tablets to improve their racing performance. Electrolytes are needed by our cells to function properly and to keep our body's fluid in balance. Common examples of electrolytes are sodium, potassium, chloride, and carbon dioxide. Sodium (salt), one of the most important electrolytes, can be lost through exercise and perspiration.

The quick answer is, yes, if you truly need additional electrolytes and sodium, you may want to consider these supplements. But first you must make that determination. The reality is that most of the best endurance energy drinks and energy gels already provide significant levels of sodium and electrolytes.

The majority of athletes can receive the electrolytes they need through a proper fueling and hydration routine; adding salt tablets on top of this may just be overkill, while also adding another layer of complication. Some popular energy drinks have up to 200 milligrams of sodium per 8 ounces, and some energy gels have 100 milligrams or more per serving. This is plenty for the vast majority of athletes.

If your favorite energy drink or energy gel does not have sufficient amounts of electrolytes and sodium, however, and you have reasons why you do not want to change to another brand, you may want to experiment with adding salt or electrolyte tablets to the mix. First, clear it with your doctor, and then safely test it in training, starting with very modest, safe levels. When taking salt or electrolyte tablets, always do so with water.

Please remember, however, that salt and electrolyte tablets are not magical performance pills like some people seem to think they are. If you don't really need them, they are just adding another complication to your race, giving you one more item to carry and remember to take. Furthermore, putting more items in your stomach during the intensity of competition may lead to stomach upset. Our suggestion would be to first try to get what you need from your energy drink and energy gels. Read the labels and calculate how much sodium and other electrolytes you are already receiving. Then only consider tablets as a last resort.

Remember, salt and electrolyte tablets may help, but they are not a replacement for a proper fueling and hydration routine.

AN IRONFIT MOMENT

To Pee or Not to Pee?

If you are a veteran triathlete, you already know that you will (and should!) have to pee at some point during a Half. If you have fueled and hydrated properly, your bladder will need to be emptied at least once during the race. For the novice athlete, this may come as a surprise. But if you are following one of our fueling and hydration plans, you will more than likely have to pee during the swim, bike, or run. The question is, how do you do that?

If it's the swim, that's easy; just go ahead and pee (even in your wet suit). That's a no-brainer. When it comes to the bike, however, that can be a bit more challenging. Either you have to figure out how to pee while biking through your tri suit, or hop off at a port-a-john and get the job done. The same goes for the run. Fortunately, most races have port-a-johns at all of the aid stations for your convenience.

A big mistake is holding it! It can and will probably cause cramping—not something we want during the race. As we have said with many elements of the race, you have to practice in training so you have a plan and can execute it during the race. Peeing is no exception.

Race Warm-Up Strategy and Approach

Another important part of our race-day strategy is how we plan to warm up before the race begins. Because the Half starts with a swim, we suggest a swim warm-up on race morning. Some suggest cycling and running, but depending on your race, it may be too difficult logistically to actually do these activities on race morning.

Others go with no warm-up at all. The issue with this is that the abruptness of the early-morning swim start can really be a shock to both your body and your mind. Our suggestion is to get into the water early for a sensible swimming warm-up routine.

The following suggested routine takes only 9 minutes to complete:

- Swim easy for 3 minutes (suggestion: swim back and forth in the same area to keep from straying too far).
- Swim 3 x 30-second Easy Pickups @ 30 seconds very easy swim.
- Swim again easy for 3 minutes.

Some races clear the water for a significant amount of time prior to the race. Check with race officials ahead of time to know how long in advance you will need to enter the water to complete your 9-minute warm-up routine.

What if they don't allow access to the water, or you just arrive too late to take advantage of it? Our suggestion is to do either the "Easy Eight" warm-up routine in Chapter 6, which takes about 5 minutes to complete, or go for a very easy jog of up to 9 minutes in duration.

Course Segmentation Strategy and Approach

One of the best techniques for making the 70.3 miles of the Half Iron-Distance race seem more manageable and less intimidating, and to allow for better mental focus, is to segment the course in your mind before the race.

Mentally break the course into smaller, more digestible pieces. Then on race day, instead of visualizing the enormity of the entire course, just focus on the section you are currently doing. This is so much easier on your mind and attitude.

When you complete one of your segments, just put it behind you, and mentally move on to the next segment. Focus on completing the current segment instead of dwelling on getting to the finish line, which could be several hours away. In other words, live in the moment.

For example, if the swim course has three or four turn buoys, then it's easy to mentally segment the swim into three or four sections. This same approach can be applied to the bike and run courses. Course locations where turns exist often serve as great transition points between one segment and another. Our suggestion is to mentally break the entire Half Iron-Distance racecourse up into between six and twelve segments, depending on whether you personally prefer a smaller number of longer segments or a larger number of shorter segments.

When you drive the course before the race, pick out some easily definable sections along the course, or some easily located landmarks or mile markers, to mark your segments. Learn the approximate distances between each, and think about how long it will take you to get through each section. If possible, try to keep each of these segments to less than one hour to complete.

Remember: While racing in one particular segment, try to focus only on completing that segment, and don't allow yourself to dwell on any past or future segments. We encourage you to give this race strategy a try. It will help you to maintain your focus and maximize your racing performance.

Special Race Strategy Tips for "Just Finish" Athletes

If your Half Iron-Distance goal is to "Just Finish," then you are probably one of the wiser people reading this book. You surely appreciate that the journey and the accomplishment of completing a Half Iron-Distance Triathlon is the true victory.

On a lighter note, you are probably a lot more economical, too. Do you realize that if the fastest age-grouper in the race completes it in less than half your time, he or she will be paying more than twice as much per mile as you? And that doesn't even include the fact that he or she will have much less time out on the course to enjoy the free, all-you-can-eat catering (aka, aid stations). But seriously, at some level, all of us should have as one of our goals to finish the race in good health and in good spirits.

We have coached many "Just Finish" athletes over the years, and the following are five helpful strategy tips on how to both accomplish your goal on race day and enjoy the experience even more.

1. **Smile and Make Friends**
   It's all about positive mental energy. One of the greatest challenges for the "Just Finish" athlete is to stay mentally positive hour after

hour. The best way to do this for most athletes is to focus on being outwardly positive. Keep a smile on your face as much as possible. Encourage other athletes as you see them out on the course. Thank the aid station volunteers for their help. Projecting this good outward cheer will help to keep you mentally positive and right on track from start to finish.

2. **Swim Buoy to Buoy**

   The swim buoys are usually placed about every 100 meters on the swim course. If you are finding it mentally overwhelming to swim 1.2 miles, divide the swim up into several smaller segments and just focus on swimming from buoy to buoy. Stop briefly and tread water at each buoy (this is especially easy to do in a wet suit), catch your breath, relax, and then swim to the next buoy. You don't need to swim 1.2 miles; you only need to swim about 100 meters at a time. If the swim distance is a concern for you, try this approach in training and see if it works for you.

3. **Planned Bike Course Breaks**

   If the 56-mile bike portion seems overwhelming to you, consider planning to take scheduled bike breaks as well. If your goal is to "Just Finish," you don't need to worry about a quick food and bottle handoff as you speed through the aid station. Instead, plan to safely dismount your bike at some or all of the aid stations, put your feet on the ground for a moment, calmly get the food and drink you want, thank the aid station volunteers, and then safely mount your bike and be on your way. These short stops serve to break up the bike race nicely, and provide for a much more enjoyable ride.

   Prior to the race, determine how many aid stations there will be on the course and approximately how far apart they will be located. Then plan a strategy for which of those you will stop at. We suggest a maximum of three stops depending on the athlete, so if the course happens to have three aid stations fairly evenly located along the course, you are good to go.

   Tip: Planned bike course breaks at aid stations are also good opportunities for bathroom breaks as well.

4. **Run/Walk Approach**

   Elite marathoner, coach, and author Jeff Galloway has popularized the run/walk approach to marathons. This strategy is simply to take short periodic walk breaks throughout the marathon to freshen up the legs and then return to running. While this approach is mostly applied to marathons, it also works especially well for the "Just Finish" athlete in the Half Iron-Distance triathlon.

   One common run/walk strategy is to walk briefly for 10 seconds, or some other brief, predetermined amount of time, at each aid station. Not only does this accomplish the goal of briefly freshening up the legs, but it also makes it easier to accomplish your fueling and hydration plan at the aid station, without spilling or dropping anything.

   Another common approach is to walk briefly for a predetermined amount of time at each mile marker. For example, each time you reach a mile marker, walk for 30 seconds.

   Our favorite run/walk approach is to do it based on time. For example, on a 12-minute cycle you run for 11 minutes and then walk for 1 minute. This organizes each hour into five specific cycles of 12 minutes.

   If you think you would like to use this approach, we encourage you to first test it out in training. Try different amounts of time for your walking breaks, from 10 to 60 seconds, and see if it helps you to experience higher energy levels and maintain a more consistent pace overall. Just be sure to keep your walk breaks on the same time schedule throughout the run and to start taking them right from the start (i.e., don't wait until you are tired to start them). This may or may not be the right approach for you, but you won't know for sure unless you give it a try in training.

5. **Time Segmentation for Finishing Under the Cutoff Time**

   Is your biggest concern that you may not make the cutoff times? It's important to know that the cutoff times vary from race to race, so if this is a concern for you, you should determine well in advance what the cutoff times are for your specific race and plan accordingly. Some races have a total cutoff time of eight hours from the start of the last swim wave; some have a total cutoff of eight and a half hours from the start of the last swim wave; and others may have a cutoff time based on something else altogether. Obviously, if it's based on the start of the last swim wave, and you are going to be in an earlier swim wave, then you may get a little extra time depending on how far apart the waves are spaced.

The most common two scenarios for Half Iron-Distance races is a swim cutoff time of 70 minutes after the start of the last swim wave, a bike cutoff of five or five and a half hours after the last swim wave, and a final race cutoff time of eight or eight and a half hours after the start of the last swim wave.

After determining exactly what the cutoff times are for your race, take a realistic look at these times and see if you can expect to have any tight spots. Because the swim is first and you don't have an opportunity to accumulate any time cushion before the swim, as you do for the bike and run, this is usually the most important cutoff time to consider—especially if this is your weakest of the three sports.

As an example, consider the following scenario for an athlete who is in the last swim wave of a race in which the cutoff times are 70 minutes, five and a half hours, and eight and a half hours, after the final swim wave:

> To finish the 1,900-meter swim in 70 minutes, you need to swim at a pace of about 3 minutes and 40 seconds per 100 meters, or about 3 minutes and 20 seconds per 100 yards. Even though there will be plenty of other factors on race day (i.e., current, chop, other swimmers, etc.), by doing the swim workouts in Chapter 5, you will have a very good idea of whether this pace will be an issue for you or not.
>
> As coaches of a large Masters Swimming program, we find that the average adult swimmer is going to be much closer to 2 minutes per 100 yards than 3 minutes, so this time is very doable for the vast majority of swimmers.
>
> But even if you require the entire 70 minutes to complete the swim, and then require 10 minutes in T1 to prepare to start the bike portion, you would still have about 4 hours and 10 minutes until the bike cutoff time. This means that

all you need to average to complete the bike portion before the cutoff is a little less than 14 miles per hour (about 22.5 km/hour). Again, the cycling training sessions in Chapter 5, especially the longer brick sessions, will give you a good idea if you will be able to maintain this pace for 56 miles (90 km).

Even if you arrived in T2 just seconds before the cutoff time and needed 10 minutes to get ready for the run portion, you would still have 2 hours and 50 minutes to complete the 13.1-mile (21.1 km) run course. This requires a pace of just a little faster than 13 minutes per mile (about 8 minutes per km). Again, the run training sessions in Chapter 5, especially the longer transition sessions and long runs, will give you a good idea if you will be able to maintain this pace for 13.1 miles.

So, there you have it! If you can swim at close to a 3-minute-per-100-yard pace, cycle at about 14 mph (22.5 km/hour), and run at about 13 minutes per mile (8 minutes/km) pace, and keep your total transitions to about 20 minutes or less, you can accomplish the Half Iron-Distance Dream!

If you are a "Just Finish" athlete, we hope the above tips will help you to have a safer, more enjoyable, and successful racing experience.

Following is the seventh of ten motivating profiles of an inspiring Half Iron-Distance Triathlete.

HALF IRON-DISTANCE SUCCESS STORY:
PATIENCE COGAR

Patience Cogar, who has been training for and competing in triathlon for over fourteen years, has what many endurance sports enthusiasts would consider the perfect job: She is an independent Pilates instructor and swim coach.

Patience's career is ideal for many reasons. Being an independent instructor allows her to create her own work schedule. She is able to coordinate her workdays very efficiently with her training schedule. Being a swim instructor, and frequently being around the pool, certainly helps her to keep her strong swim up, too. Also, just being around other athletes and helping them to achieve their goals is very positive energy for her, and it is highly motivational.

So far, Patience has raced eight Half and six full Iron-Distance races. Her favorite Half is the Austin 70.3, which is held in October. She enjoys the cooler, late-season temperatures and the challenge of the course with its rolling hills. It also helps that this is where Patience has had her best Half Iron-Distance performance so far.

While Patience plans to continue to race both the Half and full Iron-Distances, for many reasons she is likely to focus more on the Half. As Patience points out, "Time allows for more of everything when training for a Half. Time is also on your side when it comes to recovering from training for and racing this distance. I do find that it is not as taxing on the body as it is when training for the full Iron-Distance."

Patience also cites the cost and logistical advantages: "The cost of participating in triathlons can add up very quickly. This is a very addictive sport with a high price tag. There is an advantage when only racing the Half Iron-Distance as opposed to the Full. We can do more racing with the lower cost of registration fees, and usually there are many Halfs that are within driving distance, which will cut down on the cost associated with the sport." Patience concludes, "All of this adds up to having a balanced lifestyle, not only physically but mentally."

Even after competing in the sport for fourteen years, Patience switched to the IronFit training approach and immediately set a new personal best at the full Iron-Distance. She is sure to do the same next time she races the Half Iron-Distance. Patience enjoys the balanced training plan, which not only results in better performances, but also allows for better planning and a more balanced lifestyle.

Watch for Patience at the races this coming season as she continues to improve her race times and enjoy the endurance sports lifestyle.

CHAPTER 9

Effective Goal Setting and Race Selection

Nothing great was ever achieved without
enthusiasm.

—Ralph Waldo Emerson

There is nothing that can help to drive us more toward success than highly effective and motivating goals. Goal setting and race selection both need to be addressed fairly early in your Half Iron-Distance journey. Optimizing the entire experience begins with setting the proper type of motivating goals and selecting an exciting race that fits you perfectly.

We suggest both primary goals and stretch goals for athletes preparing for the Half Iron-Distance experience. We discuss both below.

Primary Goals

We define a *primary goal* as the minimum goal in your mind that will constitute success. In the broadest sense, we feel that practically every race is a success. Even when things go terribly wrong, there are always many lessons that can be learned and valuable information to be taken away. But what we are talking about with a primary goal is one that prior to the race you would consider to be the minimum level of positive outcome.

Primary goals vary from athlete to athlete and race to race. For example, a very common primary goal is to set a new personal best time for the Half Iron-Distance. You simply want to finish faster than you have before. Ten minutes faster would be absolutely wonderful, but as long as you cross the finish line even a minute faster, your primary goal has been achieved, and you would consider this to be a successful result.

Another common primary goal is to achieve a certain placing in your age group (e.g., finishing in the first three podium positions) or a certain top percentage in your age group (e.g., top 10 percent). These are all good primary goals depending on the athlete.

For "Just Finish" athletes, we often suggest the primary goal of simply "finishing in good health and good spirits." In a way, this should be at least one of the top goals for any competition any of us ever take part in, but this is what typically constitutes the "Just finish" athlete's primary goal.

Lynn Kellogg (www.trilifephotos.com)

Good primary goals are not easy to achieve, but they are definitely achievable, and they motivate us to a new level of performance.

Stretch Goals

We define a *stretch goal* as something that is possible, but is in fact so challenging that it is not probable. Almost everything has to work out perfectly for us to achieve them. Perhaps stretch goals don't require a miracle, but the stars definitely need to fall into alignment.

A good example of a stretch goal for an athlete may be to win her age group for the first time. Perhaps she has finished in the top ten or the top five in the past, but now she has a new sixteen-week training plan and more motivation than ever before, so her stretch goal is to take first place. She knows it's not necessarily probable, but she also knows that it *is* possible, and if all goes well throughout her training and preparation, she has a fair shot at achieving her goal on race day.

Maximizing the Motivational Power of Your Goals

We want to use our goals as a powerful source of ongoing motivation. We want them to excite us and help to mentally drive us through our sixteen-week training program.

In the monthly training plans we design for our coached athletes, we list the athlete's goals in the very first section at the top of the page. We always want to have our goals front and center to motivate us each time we look at our training schedule. To really enhance the power of these goals, we often encourage our athletes to include both a primary and a stretch goal for the Half.

An example of such an approach to goals and how they might appear on the training schedule is as follows:

Goals:
1. Primary: Achieve new personal best time @ Wildflower.
2. Stretch: Win age group @ Wildflower.
3. Finish Wildflower in good health and good spirits.

In the above example, this athlete's three goals concern her performance at the Wildflower Triathlon, which is in California, and one of the classic races at the Half Iron-Distance level. The athlete's primary goal is to set a new personal best time for the Half Iron-Distance, and her stretch goal is to win her age group. Her third goal is to finish in good health and in good spirits.

If these goals are properly set in advance, they will help to motivate the athlete through the training process. How he feels about his performance after the fact will be good information to take into account when he sets goals for his next major race. If he wins his age group with a substantially faster time, of course he will consider it a total success. If, however, he does not win his age group this time, but still improves his overall time by 5 or 10 minutes, he will still feel the race was a significant success, and it will serve as a great source of continued motivation going forward.

In addition to prominently listing our coached athletes' goals at the top of their training schedule, we also encourage them to "post" their goals. This is a highly motivating approach we will discuss further in Chapter 13 (see pages 202–203).

An important part of setting motivating goals is to select the optimal race. We want both our goals and the race itself to work together to motivate and excite us. Next we will consider the criteria for selecting the optimal race for you.

Race Selection Criteria

There are four main criteria for selecting your Half Iron-Distance Triathlon: race date, experience level, strengths and weaknesses, and time and expense. Following is a discussion of each.

1. **Race Date**
    The first consideration is the race date. Obviously, it needs to be a date that gives you the proper amount of time to prepare, fits in with your work schedule, and, most important, fits in with your family schedule. All of the training programs in Chapter 5 are sixteen weeks in duration. If you are starting from scratch, you will need additional time to build your base fitness up to a proper level to begin the program. This timing all needs to be taken into account when selecting your race.

    Another important reason for selecting your race date early is the fact that because this race distance has become so popular, many of these races sell out months in advance. This is all especially true if you have your eye on one of the more popular classic races in our sport.

2. **Experience Level**
    Is this your first Half, or are you a veteran, with many races under your belt? If it's your first Half Iron-Distance Triathlon, or if you're a relative newcomer to triathlon, we suggest keeping it as simple as possible. You will need to concentrate on the task at hand; the more distractions and complications you have, the greater the chance of something going wrong and spoiling the experience.

    In general, if this is going to be your first Half Iron-Distance race, we suggest you consider a race that has a simple setup without a lot of complicated logistics (e.g., a race where the start, T1, T2, and the finish are all possibly in the same general area), a less-challenging racecourse, and a location relatively nearby to reduce travel complications (e.g., having to ship your bike in advance). In short, keep the first one simple; after you have that one under your belt, you can expand from there.

Tip: Another advantage of selecting a nearby race is that you may be able to visit the site weeks before the race, and do some of your training right on the course. This will greatly help in your preparation and confidence, as well as making this race feel like your "home course."

3. **Strengths and Weaknesses**

   Your specific personal strengths and weaknesses should be considered when selecting your race. This is especially important if one of your goals concerns your finishing place relative to your competitors. If so, select a course that favors you.

   If you are a stronger swimmer, consider a race with a rougher swim course and perhaps where wet suits are not allowed. If you are a weaker swimmer, select a race with a calm lake swim, where wet suits are permitted. If you are a strong cyclist, select a course that is very hilly and challenging. If not, consider a race with a flatter bike course. If you do well in heat and humidity, consider a course in a more tropical climate. If not, you may want to select a race in a more moderate climate.

   Also, if you live at sea level, consider selecting a race that is also at sea level, as opposed to one at altitude, where you will likely be at a disadvantage.

   Depending on your goals for the race, consider the features of the race as they compare with your strengths and weaknesses.

4. **Time and Expense**

   The time and expense can vary greatly from one Half Iron-Distance race to another. It may be a local race, with a reasonable $200 entry fee, close enough to drive to on race morning. On the other hand, a North American–based athlete can do a race in Australia that requires thousands of dollars in time and expense when you add up the race fee, airfare, hotel, meals out, and time away from work. Between these two extremes is a wide range of price points. We suggest calculating exactly what each race option will cost and weigh that with the other factors already discussed.

Tip: Sometimes a great way to do a destination race is to combine it with a family vacation. While there are definite pros and cons to this, it may be a good option for you and your family.

We hope the above criteria and suggestions will help you to select the optimal race for you.

Following is the eighth of ten motivating profiles of an inspiring Half Iron-Distance Triathlete.

HALF IRON-DISTANCE SUCCESS STORY:
CARL WERNICKE

Carl Wernicke has been successfully competing in triathlons for over ten years. Among his many accomplishments in the sport, he won his age group in the Executive Challenge Division of the 2012 Ironman 70.3 World Championship in Henderson, Nevada.

Carl started with Sprint and Olympic Distance races back in 2003, but then quickly completed his first full Iron-Distance triathlon the following year. While still racing at all distances, Carl now competes most often at the Half Iron-Distance.

Like most triathletes, Carl Wernicke is hard-pressed for time. He is a partner at a hedge fund and needs to commute on the morning train to his office. Because of this, he usually completes his cycling and running sessions during weekdays between 4:30 and 6:00 a.m. He participates in Masters Swimming a couple of evenings during the week, but he often needs to work late on the evenings when he doesn't swim. Sometimes Carl even needs to squeeze in more work over the weekend, around his longer cycling and running sessions. In short, time management is always a challenge.

Carl cites the many advantages of the Half Iron-Distance, including a shorter race day, less training time, less traveling time away from work, less potential for mental and physical burnout, less cost, and the ability to enjoy more balance to life. Since using the IronFit training methods, Carl comments, "I have become a more confident competitor, as I can now approach this distance as a race."

Carl's favorite races include Oceanside California in the early part of the year, for its challenging course and strong field. Another favorite is the also challenging Toughman Triathlon in Westchester, New York, in the latter part of the season.

While Carl plans to continue to race all triathlon distances, for the many reasons we have talked about here, he expects to continue to race the Half Iron-Distance most often.

CHAPTER 10

Half Iron-Distance Equipment from A to Z

The best way out is always through.

—Robert Frost

This chapter details all of the equipment needed for the Half Iron-Distance Triathlon and provides tips on how to select the best equipment for you. A lot of hype exists in the triathlon world about how some very expensive products can improve an athlete's race times. Many of these claims are exaggerated, if not outright misleading. We will help you to sort through the noise, avoid wasting money, and find the best equipment for each sport.

But first, we will present our tips for how to "buy speed."

Top Five List for "Buying Speed"

In this section we present the five products that we consider the most worthwhile, because they can directly contribute to an athlete's performance on the racecourse.

1. **Heart Rate Monitor**
    This is such a simple training tool, but if used correctly, it will have an amazing impact on your rate of improvement, reduction of injury and stagnation, and general enjoyment of the sport. And unlike some of the other items on this list, a basic heart rate monitor is inexpensive. Sure, there are fancier models with GPS and other features, which may be fun to have, but bottom line, all you really need to greatly enhance the quality of your training is a basic heart monitor selling for less than $100.

2. **Professional Bike Fit**

   A quality bike fit will make you safer on your bike, less prone to injury, and will improve your power transfer to the pedals. Many triathletes completely overlook this important investment. We are not talking about that nice kid working at the local bike shop for a summer job; we are talking about a certified bike-fitting professional. Get your new bike fit early in the off-season or preseason, so your body has plenty of time to adapt to the new position. Prices for this vary greatly, but you can probably expect to pay $200 or more. A good bike fit will save you many times that amount in time and money.

Lynn Kellogg (www.trilifephotos.com)

3. **CompuTrainer**

   Normally we do not like to suggest a specific brand of product, but in this instance we will make an exception. This is because we have seen no other product have a greater impact on the cycling performance improvement of triathletes than the CompuTrainer. It's a little expensive, but, for most, it is well worth the investment. It makes indoor training much more productive and interesting; and, if you live in a colder climate, it is almost a must. Currently, new CompuTrainer models are priced roughly in the $1,600+ range.

4. **High-End Wet Suit**

   If the race you are doing permits wet suits, definitely consider wearing one. They make almost all swimmers faster. Wet-suit technology has greatly improved over the past twenty years. As a result, most of the major brands offer a top-of-the-line model that includes both the latest technology and the highest legal limit of flotation material. While these wet suits are more expensive, they are worth it. And the weaker a swimmer you are, the more it is worth it. Get the best wet suit you can. This is one top-of-the-line product worth investing in. Currently, new top-rated wet suits are priced roughly in the $500+ range.

5. **Aero Bike Helmet**

This is an easy one, because in the very expensive world of triathlon, this is a relatively inexpensive item. Aero bike helmets are faster than regular bike helmets and will help you to shave time. Years ago aero bike helmets were not well ventilated, and that was the rap on them for use in triathlon. This is no longer the case. Today, there are many great aero bike helmets that are well ventilated and cost only marginally more than regular bike helmets. Currently, new aero bike helmets are priced roughly in the $150+ range.

The Top Three "Think First Before Getting Out Your Credit Card" List

In this section we will present the three products that may be appropriate for some triathletes, but for many may be a waste of money.

1. **Deep Rim or Disc Racing Wheels**

Faster riders can definitely benefit from high-end deep rim or disc racing wheels; they will make a fast rider even faster. But the reality is that they don't help nearly as much for slower riders. If your average race pace is below 18 mph, you may not benefit much at all. For you, these wheels end up being more for show and not for go. This is something to definitely consider, as a new pair of these wheels can easily sell for an amount in excess of $2,000.

2. **Top-of-the-Line Bike Frame**

There are many very fast bike frames available today that cost under $1,000. Sure, you can purchase frames made of very

AN IRONFIT MOMENT

The Best Triathlon Product Is Not Even a Product

There is nothing that will help you more toward achieving your Half Iron-Distance dream than a good coach. As coaches ourselves, of course we may appear biased on this subject, but it's what we honestly believe, and what we have experienced over many years in endurance sports.

By choosing triathlon, and the Half Iron-Distance in particular, you have selected a sport with an almost unquantifiable number of variables. And as complicated as it is, many of the correct answers and approaches are counterintuitive. You will achieve your goals faster, safer, and with greater satisfaction with the benefit of a good coach's "been there, done that" knowledge.

A good coach will keep you on track by helping you to know exactly what you should be doing each day. And, equally as important, sometimes you need a coach to tell you what *not* to do. Whatever your level, beginner to advanced, the right coach will help you to jump the learning curve and avoid costly mistakes.

Coaching can be expensive, and it's not for everyone. Fortunately, there are online options that make good coaching much more accessible.

expensive materials for three times that, or more, but the difference for most riders is negligible. Okay, if you happen to be using your dad's rusted steel frame from the 1970s and you are considering an upgrade, please do so . . . and quickly. But if you already have a good, modern aero bike frame, there is very little, if anything, to be gained by buying a much more expensive model. You would probably be much better served by putting that money toward an aero bike helmet or a great training tool like a CompuTrainer, to improve your bike times.

3. **Anything with the "Cool Factor"**

   Generally, be aware of anything that is the cool new product of the week. We have seen it countless times. Some new product comes out and gets an amazing amount of hype and buzz. Along with it comes a big price tag. But the product doesn't live up to the hype; in fact, over time it proves to not even be as good as what was already in wide use.

   If you have money burning a hole in your pocket, or if you just really enjoy having the "latest and greatest," then go for it. Otherwise, keep it simple. Be skeptical of hype. Keep your goals in mind and make sure that the products you purchase give you a good return on your investment.

In the following sections we will provide tips and suggestions for all equipment used in the Half Iron-Distance Triathlon.

Tips on Swim Gear

One- or two-piece tri suit: As discussed in Chapter 7, for most athletes we suggest a one- or two-piece tri suit, as opposed to some alternative type of race clothing. You can wear it right under your wet suit, and then just keep it on for the bike and run, greatly simplifying your race. There are pros and cons to a one-piece versus a two-piece, so test them both out to see which works best for you. The one-piece has the advantage of providing better sun blockage and being slightly more aerodynamic. The two-piece has the advantage of being a little cooler, and can make bathroom breaks less complicated. We suggest you try them both and use what works best for you.

Additional Tip: Some "Just Finish" athletes like to completely change their race clothing in each transition area. They are not concerned with time, and it feels great to put on fresh, dry clothing just before you start the next leg of the race. If you think you would like to do this, check in advance to make sure that a changing tent is even available. Most races at the Half Iron-Distance do not offer changing tents, and public nudity is usually not permitted.

Wet suit or speed suit: If your race allows wet suits, you should seriously consider wearing one. As discussed above, they will almost certainly make you faster in the water. It may differ for some races, but in North America, for example, an athlete is usually allowed to wear a wet suit and count in the finishing standings if the water temperature is about 76.1 degrees F (24.5 degrees C) or less.

Most athletes find that they are faster in full-length wet suits as opposed to sleeveless wet suits. Yet if you find that your arms and shoulders just don't feel comfortable in a full wet suit, or you get too hot in one, then you may want to consider a sleeveless model.

Consider putting body lubricant on your arms from the elbows down, and your legs from the knees down, to help make it easier to get your wet suit on and off. But make sure you wash the lubricant off your hands before touching your swim goggles. There's nothing as irritating as trying to see through smudged goggles.

If the race does not permit wet suits, you may want to consider a speed suit, which are usually legal in that situation. Be sure to practice your T1s with your speed suit, however, as you don't want added transition time to negate the added benefit of the speed suit.

Elite age-group triathlete Kellie Brown is a good example of an athlete who very effectively uses a speed suit in her non-wet-suit races. Kellie wears it over her tri suit, and thanks to her experience and consistent practice with it, she can remove it extremely quickly in T1—much faster than she can with a wet suit. The time she picks up on the swim more than makes up for the few seconds it may add to her transition.

Additional Tip: It goes without saying that you should try products on for size before you purchase them, but this is especially true when it comes to wet suits. Once you get it wet, it's unlikely to be accepted as an exchange. A wet suit should fit snugly, but should not feel like it is restricting your breathing.

Swim goggles: You may have to try several types of goggles before you find a type that fits your face comfortably and doesn't leak. They all fit a little differently, so take the time to find the type that works best for you. To test the fit of your swim goggles, press the goggles to your face without putting the straps around your head. If they stick without falling off, then they fit.

Consider whether you want to wear goggles with clear or shaded lenses. Some goggles specifically designed for outdoor use also provide greater peripheral vision. Also consider bringing two pairs to the race start, as goggle straps are known to snap at the worst possible time (like 5 minutes before the swim start). If your Half is going to be at a venue that often has bright morning sun, you may want to go with shaded goggles. If possible, have both options available to you, as your race morning may be bright and sunny or dark and rainy.

Additional Tip: Practice swimming with your cap over your goggle straps, instead of the other way around, so you become comfortable racing this way. By wearing your cap on top of your goggle straps, it makes it much more difficult for your goggles to become dislodged during the frenzy of the swim start.

Swim cap: Swim caps are almost always provided by the race. They are typically color-coded by swim wave and start time, and also usually bright-colored for safety reasons. Even though caps are provided by the race, we suggest that you wear a swim cap regularly in your swim training. It will help you become accustomed to wearing one so it won't feel awkward on race day. Furthermore, it's safer wearing a brighter-colored swim cap when you train in open water, and more courteous to others when you swim in a public pool.

Additional Tip: If conditions are extremely cold, you may want to consider wearing a neoprene swim cap. But if conditions are just somewhat cold and not extremely so, consider wearing two swim caps to help retain your body heat. Put your regular swim cap on first, then put your goggles on over it, and then put the race swim cap on over your goggles. Not only will this keep you warmer, but it will also hold your goggles nicely in place.

Tips on Bike Gear

Bike: While most athletes use a tri bike, either a road bike or a tri bike is fine for the Half. It really comes down to personal preference. Some athletes prefer a road bike on hilly courses, but either will work fine on the vast majority of Half Iron-Distance racecourses. Have your bike tuned up and checked over frequently to ensure its safety, and, as discussed above, have a professional bike fit in either the off-season or the preseason to get you at your safest, most efficient, and most powerful on your bike.

Helmet: Make sure that your helmet is safe and legal. Inspect it for any cracks or anything else that may compromise its integrity. As discussed above, while any quality cycling helmet will do, consider getting an aero helmet, which will save you time and cost only marginally more than a regular bike helmet.

Bike shoes: Obviously a good shoe fit is very important. Bike shoes should be a snug fit, but not so tight that they cause discomfort. Try many different types of shoes and find ones that fit you comfortably in terms of length and width. Consider the triathlon style with one Velcro strap to help with speedy transitions.

Additional Tip: Change your bike cleats at least once a year, or as they get worn.

Bike pedals: Consider lighter-weight pedals (e.g., those made of materials like carbon fiber or titanium). Also, compare various pedal types to see what you prefer. Some athletes prefer more fixed-motion pedals, while others prefer pedals with more play in them.

Bike seat: It's very important to get a seat that works comfortably for you. With all of the bike training we will be doing, you don't want to be suffering on a seat that doesn't fit you well. We are all different, and what fits your tri buddy well may not fit you at all. Most riders find the newer-style seats with the cutout portion in the middle to be much more comfortable, so give these a try. Test a variety of seats and see what works best for you. Also, wear chamois cream to add to your cycling seat comfort.

Drinking system and bike bottles: We suggest a combination of an aero drinking system and bottle cages. We prefer the type of aero drinking system that attaches between the aero bars and has a straw that comes up close to your face. This allows you to stay in the aero position longer, and having the straw right there helps to remind you to keep hydrating. Even though you have the opportunity to receive more bottles at aid stations along the way to refill your aero drinking system, we suggest always carrying an extra bottle while racing, just in case you drop one at the aid station or along the way.

For doing your long rides in training, you will want to have room for more bottles on your bike, in addition to your aero system. The most popular places to put additional bike-bottle cages are on the down tube and behind the seat.

Aero bars: Aero bars greatly increase the aerodynamics and can shave significant time in your race. Getting into the aero position does make us less stable, however, so you should practice with your aero bars and become safe and proficient with them before racing with them. Once you are accustomed to riding safely with aero bars, we don't recommend doing all of your rides with them, as they do tend to stress the back. The best place in the training programs in Chapter 5 to practice with your aero bars are in the Z4 higher-intensity portions and in the lower-intensity, high-rpm sessions.

Race wheels: Above we discussed how deep rimmed wheels and discs can be very expensive and really only benefit the faster riders. If you are competitive, then you should seriously consider the investment. If not, however, you may be better off using a good and reliable pair of training wheels.

Tire-changing gear: Learn how to change your tires. We are often horrified by the number of athletes we meet who do not know how to change a flat tire. General bike safety includes knowing how to change a flat tire and properly maintain your bike. If you don't know how, have someone show you right away, and then practice it so you can do it efficiently on your own when you need to.

The Half Iron-Distance race is long enough that a flat tire does not mean the end of your race. If you are prepared to change your tire efficiently, you can do it and get back into the race without losing more than a couple of minutes. To help you get to this level, practice changing a tire with your stopwatch and see how fast you can become at it. Better yet, have tire-changing races. Race one of your tri buddies head-to-head to see who can do it faster. This is a great way to learn to change tires quickly under pressure.

We suggest you race with a small tire-gear pouch behind your seat with two tubes, two tire levers, three CO_2 cartridges (the extra is in case one misfires), and a CO_2 cartridge adapter that fits the specific wheels you are racing with. If you are using tubular tires instead of clinchers, substitute one tire for the two tubes.

Sunglasses: Sunglasses are not necessary, especially on cloudy or rainy days, but many riders prefer them under any conditions to protect their eyes from wind and debris, especially those who wear contact lenses. Most good sunglasses come with different shaded lenses for different weather conditions.

Depending on your aero drinking system, you may be able to attach your sunglasses to it and eliminate one of the steps in T1. If you want to do this, it's important to practice it in training to make sure that you can do it safely and without dropping them.

Socks or no socks: Going sockless can be a big time-saver if you can become accustomed to riding without socks. But you should only race this way if you train this way; race day is not the time to experiment with going sockless.

Tips on Run Gear

Running shoes: The best type of running shoes to wear when racing the Half are light trainers. The very fastest elite runners in the race can probably benefit from racing flats, but the majority of triathletes will do the best with light trainers. These will give them the proper balance between lightness and the ability to absorb road shock. If you are a "Just Finish" athlete, or if you expect to be out there for seven or eight hours, you may be best served by your comfortable and reliable training shoes.

A common rookie mistake is to get new shoes right before the race and then have the race ruined by blisters. Or, some athletes have shoes that they only race in, and don't wear enough to keep properly broken in. We suggest wearing your race shoes in one of the shorter run sessions each week, in the last few weeks leading up to the race, to keep them broken in and ready to go.

While racing, try to avoid getting your shoes wet if possible, as this will greatly increase the chance of blisters. You may also want to put a little lubrication or Vaseline on your toes and heels before putting your running shoes on, to further decrease the risk of blisters. A triathlon secret is to put a little Vaseline into the toe and heel areas of your running shoes in advance. Then, when you put them on in T2, the motion of your running spreads the Vaseline around on your toes and heels and puts up a nice barrier for blisters.

Additional Tips: Replace your shoes as soon as they lose their bounce and good feel. Worn-out running shoes are an injury waiting to happen. A general guideline is to replace running shoes (both training and racing shoes) after about 500 miles of use. Depending on your running speed, this equates to about 60 to 80 hours of running. Note that the Competitive, Intermediate, and "Just Finish" training programs in Chapter 5 have roughly about 75, 50, and 35 hours of running, respectively. Some athletes prefer to buy two pairs of the same shoes and rotate them every other run. This helps to prolong their useful life.

Socks or no socks, part two: This is the same as for cycling above, but probably even more important, because blisters are more common on the run. Going sockless can be a big time-saver if you can become accustomed to running without socks. But you should only race this way if you train this way; race day is not the time to experiment with going sockless.

One- or two-piece tri suit: As discussed above (and also in Chapter 7), for most athletes we suggest a one- or two-piece tri suit as opposed to some alternative type of race clothing. You can wear it right under your wet suit or speed suit and then just keep it on for the bike and run, greatly simplifying your race.

Additional Tip: If you decide to use a tri suit, find one with a convenient back pocket, which is great for carrying energy gels or other items during the bike and especially during the run.

Running cap: A running cap is suggested for most athletes to help ward off the hot sun or cold rain, depending on the conditions. Some prefer a visor-only type cap, as it keeps the sun out of the eyes but allows more heat to escape.

Additional Tip: A great secret for staying cool on the run is to get some ice at the aid station and put it into your cap. The ice slowly melts and has a nice cooling effect.

Sunblock: Unless it's going to be a cloudy or rainy day, we suggest applying sunblock. This should be done at a minimum prior to the swim, and then again before the run. We have seen some pretty nasty sunburns over the years at Half Iron-Distance races, and skin cancer is unfortunately common among endurance athletes. Sunblock will protect your health and make the days after the race much more pleasant. Consider putting a small container of it in your transition bag. Also check with your race staff in advance, as many have it available at T1 and T2, and sometimes even out on the course at the aid stations.

Additional Tip: Do not apply sunblock until you have been marked with your race numbers prior to the swim. Then, while applying it, be careful not to go over the numbers with the sunblock, as it will smudge them and make a mess.

Please consider all of the equipment tips and suggestions above. Hopefully they will help you to have a safer, faster, and more enjoyable racing experience.

Following is the ninth of ten motivating profiles of an inspiring Half Iron-Distance Triathlete:

HALF IRON-DISTANCE SUCCESS STORY:
ROBERT SERLING

Robert Serling was a fairly late arrival to the triathlon party. Though he ran his first road race just prior to turning forty, he didn't find his way to triathlons until closer to age fifty. Since then, however, he has become an accomplished triathlete at all distances, from the Sprint to the full Iron-Distance.

In fact, now fifty-two, and working with the IronFit training approach, he has recorded substantial new personal records at both the Half and full Iron-Distance, as well as qualifying for the Sprint and Olympic Distance USA National Championships. He has also set new personal records at half and full marathons. Amazingly, Robert doesn't train any more than he used to; he just trains smarter.

Robert Serling has a demanding career working in the fashion industry, which requires a daily two-hour commute via train into New York City. A triathlete with this long of a workday requires exceptional time management skills, and that is exactly how Robert makes it all work. He utilizes several of the "Big 10" time management techniques presented in Chapter 1, including early-morning training sessions. While Robert gets most of his key bike and run sessions in before work, he can also squeeze them in during the evening if necessary, on nights other than Tuesday, when he swims with the local Masters Swimming group. Robert manages it all very well and is very consistent with his training.

Robert's job responsibilities require a fair amount of international travel, but he plans his trips well ahead of time, always trying to locate hotels with proper fitness facilities to maintain consistent training.

Robert enjoys the Half Iron-Distance for many of the reasons we have discussed throughout this book. While still a very challenging and worthy event, Robert describes the Half as "a more reasonable event to train for," noting that it doesn't "take over your life" like the full Iron-Distance often seems to do.

Robert and his supportive wife have two teenage sons. Though the oldest is away at college now and the youngest requires less time, Robert still prefers to train early on weekends so that he can spend more time with his family. Robert almost always completes his training before noon on weekends so he can free up the majority of the day.

As often happens, people like Robert—who are living the positive, healthy, endurance sports lifestyle—have an impact on those around them. Not surprisingly, Robert's wife gave triathlon a try a couple of years ago, and now she loves it too. These days, they both enjoy supporting each other in their training and racing.

How can this not have a positive impact on their two sons? Seeing their parents setting challenging goals and then working hard and making sacrifices to accomplish them is very powerful in our typically "do as I say, not as I do" culture.

Watch for Robert and his family at the races this year as they set a great example for all.

CHAPTER 11

Healthy Eating for Ultimate Fitness

The spirit cannot endure the body when overfed, but, if underfed, the body cannot endure the spirit.

—*St. Frances de Sales*

This chapter presents you with the tools you need to reach and maintain your optimal weight to support a high level of training and racing. We will discuss the concept of power-to-weight ratio and how your leanest healthy body weight is usually your fastest. We'll also provide nutritional strategies to optimize your training and recovery.

Optimal Body Weight

This is a topic we address head-on with our coached athletes. If you want to maximize your performance, you need to minimize your weight in an effort to produce your optimal power-to-weight ratio. We have many athletes who embrace the concept, but we also understand that, for many, this is not of utmost importance. They want to race well, but they aren't willing to sacrifice to quite that extent, and that's fine.

How do we determine our optimal body weight to maximize our power-to-weight ratio? A good starting point is to determine your current body mass index (BMI).

Body Mass Index

BMI is a relative measure of body height to body weight for purposes of determining a healthy weight. In metric terms, it is defined as the ratio of the weight of your body in kilograms divided by the square of your height in meters (kg/m^2). If you are not comfortable making this calculation manually, you can find many online calculators that will calculate it for you by just entering your height and weight.

The National Institutes of Health have issued BMI standards and classifications as follows, and you can use these classifications once you have determined your current BMI:

BMI	CLASSIFICATION
18.5 and under	Underweight
18.5 to 24.9	Normal weight
25 to 29.9	Overweight
30 to 39.9	Obese
40+	Morbidly obese

An endurance athlete wants to be in the 18.5 to 24.9 range at minimum, which is considered a normal healthy weight. The flaw in this index is that it uses total body weight in the calculation, and does not discriminate between fat weight and lean muscle. However, most successful endurance athletes, who usually have plenty of lean muscle mass, tend to be in the lower to middle end of the normal weight BMI range, which is a BMI in the range of about 18.5 to 22.0. Ultimately, this is a good range for competitive triathletes to target.

Athlete Example: Cary Cambridge

Half Iron-Distance competitor Cary Cambridge currently weighs 200 pounds (91 kg) and is 6 feet tall (183 cm, or 1.83 meters). His current BMI is determined to be about 27, as follows:

$$BMI = kg/m^2$$
$$Kg \text{ (kilograms)} = 91$$
$$M \text{ (meters)} = 1.83$$
$$m^2 = 1.83 \text{ meters} \times 1.83 \text{ meters} = 3.3489$$
$$\text{Therefore, BMI} = 91 \text{ kg} / 3.3489 = 27.1$$

Unfortunately, Cary is not even within the normal weight range, let alone the lower half of the normal weight range. To at least get down to the normal weight and BMI of 24.9 or less, Cary needs to decrease his weight into at least the low 180s (lbs.):

$$Kg = BMI \times m^2$$
$$BMI = 24.9$$
$$m^2 = 1.83 \text{ meters} \times 1.83 \text{ meters} = 3.3489$$
$$\text{Therefore, } kg = 24.9 \times 3.3489 = 83.3 \text{ kg} = 183 \text{ lbs.}$$
$$\text{Note: 1 lb.} = 0.453592 \text{ kg}$$

Again, if you don't feel comfortable making the above calculations, you can easily find several online BMI calculators that will do the number-crunching for you.

So now that we know how to determine our BMI, and we know that we want to strive to be in at least the normal weight range (if not the lower half of the normal weight range), what is our next step?

Our next step is to understand the calories required just to fuel our bodily functions without consideration of exercise. To do this, we start with determining our basal metabolic rate (BMR).

Basal Metabolic Rate (BMR)

Our current BMR is the unique number of calories that our body requires to simply maintain its normal bodily functions without regard for exercise or even minor activity. Think in terms of a totally sedentary person who basically lies on the couch all day.

One of the most generally accepted formulas for determining BMR is the Harris-Benedict Equation (originally published by James Arthur Harris and Francis Gano Benedict in 1919):

- The formula to calculate BMR for women: 655 + (4.35 x weight in pounds) + (4.7 x height in inches) – (4.7 x age in years).
- The formula to calculate BMR for men: 66 + (6.23 x weight in pounds) + (12.7 x height in inches) – (6.8 x age in years).

However, for endurance athletes we take this formula one step further, because, obviously, most athletes are not sedentary individuals. They are typically very active people with busy lives. Having worked with many athletes for many years, we have determined a much better approach—what we call "Active BMR."

Active BMR

To calculate your active BMR, simply take your BMR and increase it by 30 percent. This is a more accurate calculation for anyone with an active lifestyle.

Athlete Example: Lisa Lubbock

Half Iron-Distance competitor Lisa Lubbock is thirty-five years old, weighs 130 pounds, and is 5 feet, 6 inches tall. Using the formula above, her BMR is 1,366 calories, as follows:

$$\text{BMR} = (655 + (4.35 \times 130 \text{ lbs.}) + (4.7 \times 66 \text{ inches}) - (4.7 \times 35 \text{ years of age}) = 1,366$$

Lisa has an active lifestyle, so she determines her active BMR, which is 1,776 (1,366 x 130 percent = 1,776). If Lisa wants to maintain her current weight of 130 pounds, she should try to consume approximately 1,776 net calories on a daily basis.

Alternatively, another simpler method to determine your optimal calories to maintain your weight is the "14 Calories per Body Pound" formula.

14 Calories per Body Pound

To determine your optimal calories using the 14 calories per body pound approach, simply take your current body weight in pounds and multiply it by 14 calories (if using kilograms, multiply your weight in kg by 30.8 calories). For Lisa, that would be approximately 1,820 calories daily (130 lbs. x 14 = 1,820 calories). Note how this "shortcut" method yielded a very similar result to the more-complicated calculation for "Active BMR."

Together, these two approaches give us a very good idea of how many net calories we need daily to maintain our current weight.

Net Calories after Exercise

As athletes, we not only need to be concerned with our total calorie intake, but we must also consider the calories we expend during exercise. The net result of your total calories consumed less your total calories expended in training is what we call our "net calories after exercise." Our net calories after exercise is the number of calories remaining after we have considered our exercise for the day. Remember that the 30 percent increase of our BMR to calculate our active BMR is only to account for an active lifestyle, not for the additional calories utilized in training.

For instance, let's say you ran for one hour at an aerobic (Z2) heart rate. In the case of Lisa Lubbock, we would estimate her calorie expenditure for a one-hour run to be about 600 calories.

Therefore, using the 14 calories per body pound approach to maintain her current weight, she should eat a total of about 2,420 calories for that day. By doing so, she would arrive at her desirable net calories of 1,820 per day (2,420 calories consumed – 600 calories expended during exercise = 1,820 net calories after exercise). If she does this, she will maintain her current weight.

To help you estimate your calorie expenditure based on various types of exercise and intensity, below are the estimated calorie ranges we suggest for most athletes:

EXERCISE ACTIVITY	ESTIMATED CALORIE EXPENDITURE PER HOUR
Running	600 to 1,000
Cycling	500 to 900
Swimming	400 to 800
Strength Training	200 to 400

Most training sessions will fall within these ranges; however, exactly where you fall depends primarily on your body mass and the level of intensity for the session. The higher your body mass and the higher the intensity, the higher within the range you will be. This is only an estimate, but by using these tools, many athletes can become pretty good at estimating the calories they utilize in training.

Alternatively, there are many online tools (e.g., www.healthstatus.com, www.livestrong.com, www.myfitnesspal.com, www.loseit.com, etc.) and gadgets (like the Garmin, Polar, and other assorted training devices) that will provide you with an estimate of the calories expended for any particular exercise activity, based on the stats you input at the start (e.g., height, weight, age, etc.).

Optimal Daily Calories to Lose Weight

Now that we know how to maintain our weight, how do we determine the optimal number of daily calories required to lose weight? There are two very helpful approaches for accomplishing this.

500 Calories per Day Reduction

The most common method is to reduce your daily calorie intake by 500 calories per day. The 500 calories per day equates to 3,500 calories per week, which is equivalent to one pound a week. This simple approach works well for most athletes if you start with your active BMR and reduce it by 500 calories per day.

For example, you set a new personal best time at the Half last summer when your weight was 150 pounds, but now, heading into the new season, you currently find yourself at a weight of 162 pounds. Using the Harris-Benedict formula above and the 30 percent adjustment, you have calculated your current active BMR to be 2,136 calories. To lose a pound a week, you would need to net about 1,636 calories a day (2,136 calories – 500 calories = 1,636 calories). All else being equal, this will result in reducing your weight to 150 pounds over twelve weeks, at a rate of 1 pound per week.

11 Calories per Body Pound

Another calorie-reduction method is the "11 Calories per Body Pound" approach. Simply take your current body weight in pounds and multiply it by 11 calories (in kilograms, multiply your current weight by 24.2 calories). Using the same example above, an athlete weighing 162 pounds would need to net approximately 1,782 calories per day (162 lbs. x 11 calories =1,782 calories).

We prefer this simpler approach for most athletes because it applies a constant percentage of calorie reduction across all body weight levels, whereas the "minus 500 calorie" approach applies a bigger percentage amount to smaller athletes, and a smaller percentage amount to larger athletes.

If your goal is to lose weight, we encourage you to try one of these approaches to achieve your optimal body weight in a healthy and sustainable way.

AN IRONFIT MOMENT

VO2 Max and "Leaner is Faster"

The easiest way for most age-group triathletes to become faster is to simply lose weight. We have found that most triathletes either don't know this, or they know it, but don't appreciate how significant it truly is. The simple truth is this: Your leanest healthy weight is also your fastest weight.

The best illustration of this can be seen when you look at an athlete's VO2 max (or maximal oxygen uptake). This is a popular test that determines an athlete's ability to process oxygen and convert it to energy. While having a high VO2 max is partially genetic, proper training increases it. As you would expect, the top endurance athletes test very high for VO2 max.

But while proper training will increase an athlete's VO2 max, the fastest way for the majority of athletes to increase theirs is simply to lose weight. If you hold all other factors constant, and your VO2 max increases, you will be faster. Please keep this fact in mind; it may very well give you the willpower to skip dessert tonight.

Strategy to Obtain and Maintain Optimal Weight

If there is one thing we have learned from our many coached athletes, it is that to lose or maintain your optimal weight, you must record everything you eat and drink every day. Even if you are super-disciplined, this is really the only sure way of determining how much you are taking in and expending on a daily basis. As we like to say, "If you aren't willing to record your calories, then you're not serious about losing weight."

In this high-tech age, it's very easy to do this. Following are a few good online calorie-tracking applications that can help you:

- My Fitness Pal: www.myfitnesspal.com
- Live Strong: www.livestrong.com
- Lose It: www.loseit.com
- Weight Watchers: www.weightwatchers.com

Once you begin the process of tracking your daily nutrition, you can determine very quickly where you need to control your portion sizes, snacking, and overeating. The beauty in these applications is that they also tell you where you are falling short in terms of protein, fat, carbohydrates, fiber, and daily vitamins. It is an excellent way to determine what foods you need to replace with more nutrient-rich foods, and how to supplement your traditional three meals a day to support the extra calories your body requires for training.

The Grazing Concept

One of the most effective ways to maximize your daily nutrition and support your training is through something called the "The Grazing Concept." We suggest this concept of grazing, or eating six smaller meals a day, to help you achieve your nutritional goals. It's a great way to fuel and hydrate throughout the day. By having six smaller meals spaced about two to three hours apart throughout the day, it allows you to enjoy a high level of energy all day long. You will rarely find yourself in a famished state, where you gorge yourself at any particular meal. Another benefit is that if the opportunity arises, you are always ready from an energy perspective to squeeze in a workout at lunchtime, or before or after work.

The concept of grazing is a great way to learn how to fuel and hydrate before, during, and after training. The smaller meals will help us to better prepare and understand how to fuel and hydrate for our training sessions.

Fueling and Hydration Before, During, and After Training

What are the best foods to eat before, during, and after a training session? How much should you eat before a morning training session, or after a late-night workout? These are all great questions, and we're going to help you answer them.

What are the best fueling and hydration sources conducive to a morning workout, or to help us recover properly from a training session? The important thing to remember is that we are all unique athletes, and what works for one may not work for another, from the type of food to its consistency (solids versus liquids).

The first step is to come up with a plan and then test it. Simple? Yes!

Fueling and Hydration Before and During Training

Upon waking, you should have an 8-ounce glass of water, preferably with lemon, to rehydrate yourself from sleeping overnight. This is the case whether you intend to train or not.

Additionally, your body uses glycogen during sleep, and you must replenish this glycogen even without consideration of a training session. To replenish the glycogen used overnight, most athletes will require about 200 to 400 calories in the form of hydration or fueling again, depending on your size. You can think of this as your normal breakfast, and one of your six smaller meals for the day.

If you do have a planned training session in the morning, you will want to consider whether you need to take in any further fueling or hydration before or during the session. As we mentioned in Chapter 8, for most workouts of 75 minutes or less, we really only need to consume water during the session.

If the training session will be longer than 75 minutes, then we suggest adding some additional calories beforehand in the form of liquids (hydration calories) or fueling. Again, depending on the size of the athlete and the estimated length and intensity of the training session, you should consume about one-third to one-half of the calories you expect to expend hourly during the session.

In terms of your hydration, you can start by determining your hydration needs by performing the Sweat Rate Test in Chapter 8. This will give you a good indication of how much hydration your body requires, based on a 75 percent intensity level and a particular room or outside temperature. You can also perform this test at higher- or lower-intensity levels to determine your hydration needs at those intensities. This is important information and will help you to hydrate properly before and during your training.

For example, if your training session is more than 75 minutes and you expect to burn about 800 calories per hour during the session, you will want to try to have at least an additional 260 to 400 (one-third to one-half) calories before or during the session. These can be in the form of all liquid calories, or some liquid and some solid calories. This typically depends on the athlete and what works well for him or her.

If you do your training immediately after work, then you need to be sure you've had one of your smaller meals approximately two hours before that session. This can be in the form of liquids or solids, depending on what works best for you. This assumes you had lunch in the early afternoon, and won't train until around 6 or 7 p.m. This will prepare you for a well-fueled and -hydrated training session. Again, based on the length of the training session (75+ minutes), you may need to have additional calories through hydration or fueling during the session.

Fueling and Hydration After Training

Within a 45-minute window after completing your training session, you need to replenish your glycogen stores and repair muscle tissue with ample amounts of carbohydrates and protein. If you are one of those athletes who can do a two-hour workout in the morning, then you need to take this into consideration when determining how many calories to take in after your workout. This will help your body to recover from the workout, as well as set you up for the next day's training.

Please consider the following popular fueling and hydration suggestions for before, during, and after training:

Pre-, During, and Post-Workout Fueling

The best sources of fueling are simple carbohydrates. They require the least amount of digestion compared to fats and protein, and they get into the bloodstream more quickly, so you'll need less digestion time between your meal and your workout:

Energy bar

Energy gel (these can be caffeinated)

Banana

Oatmeal with nuts

Yogurt with granola and fruit

Cottage cheese with melon

Toast/bagel, plain, or with almond, peanut, or soy butter

Waffles with jelly or fruit

Ensure, Boost, or protein shake

Pre-, During, and Post-Workout Hydration

The best sources of hydration are energy drinks with carbohydrates and electrolytes, like sodium. It's best to have about 8 ounces of water upon waking, and then another 8 to 12 ounces (or 150 calories) of one of the following:

Energy drinks like GU Brew, Gatorade Endurance, Hammer Nutrition, Enervit, and other calorie sources

Recovery drinks/shakes like GU Recovery, Gatorade Recovery, Muscle Milk, or Hammer Products

Orange, grapefruit, apple or other fruit juices

Sample Pre-, During, and Post-Fueling and Hydration Plan

Lisa Lubbock gets up at 5 a.m. to begin a one-hour, higher-intensity run session at 6 a.m. Using an estimate of 600 calories expended during this session, here is a sample of her pre-, during, and post-workout fueling and hydration:

Pre-Workout

Fueling and Hydration Source, Amount	Calories
Water with lemon, 8 oz.	0
Coffee (black), 8 oz.	0
Energy drink, 16 oz.	100
English muffin (light), 1	100
Peanut butter, 1 Tbsp.	100
Total pre-workout calories	**300**

During Workout

Fueling and Hydration Source, Amount	Calories
Water, 12 oz.	0
Total during workout calories	**0**

Post-Workout

Fueling and Hydration Source, Amount	Calories
Banana, large	100
GU Recovery Brew (2 scoops), 16–24 oz.	250
Total post-workout calories	**350**

Summary Totals

Total calories consumed (pre-, during, post-)	650
Less calories expended	(600)
Net calories after exercise	50

If Lisa were to continue the rest of her day by eating the remaining five smaller meals of approximately 345 calories each, she would arrive at her desired net calories for the day (1,776, per the example above, using her active BMR).

There is a lot of data about nutrition out there, and a lot of information to make this topic even more confusing and complex. However, what we have found is that the approach for every athlete is unique, and it's best that you try to modify your diet and nutrition over time. Too big of a change all at once, and you probably won't stick with it. With a modest-enough change, it can gradually become a habit. Before you know it, you will have transformed your daily nutrition and developed your body into the best form for you!

Following is the tenth of ten motivating profiles of an inspiring Half Iron-Distance Triathlete.

HALF IRON-DISTANCE SUCCESS STORY:
JIM COLBY

Jim Colby started training and racing Olympic Distance triathlons back when he lived in London in the late 1990s, but then drifted away from the fitness lifestyle for many years. Finally, in about 2010, heavier and less fit, he began to find his way back into the fitness lifestyle.

Upon turning fifty he started racing again, focusing on the Sprint and up to the Half Iron-Distance. By 2012, Jim was back into a great training groove, enjoying the fitness lifestyle, and having amazing success at the races.

Among his many accomplishments since turning fifty, Jim took a whopping 31 minutes off his previous best Half Iron-Distance time and, by doing so, won a qualifying slot to the Ironman 70.3 World Championship in Henderson, Nevada. Jim has also recently set new personal records in the half marathon, full marathon, and Sprint triathlon, and he completed his first full Iron-Distance Triathlon.

Jim's favorite Half Iron-Distance event is the Muskoka 70.3, which is held in September in Muskoka, Ontario. This classic event is located in a truly scenic location, and, having grown up in Canada, it's even more special for Jim. It was an especially memorable day for him in 2012, when he was awarded his slot to the World Championships by none other than Canadian triathlon great Lisa Bentley.

Jim Colby has a very busy family and professional life, with plenty of responsibilities. He has a demanding job as the assistant treasurer of a large corporation, and he is married with two children. Now that his children are of college age and have left home, he does have more free time; however, Jim still takes an active interest in his kids' activities. As an example, Jim and his wife frequently travel to attend their son's college swim events on weekends.

The IronFit training approach has obviously worked very well for Jim Colby. His string of personal records and breakthrough performances are a testament to that. Jim is extremely consistent with his training, and wisely uses the rest day / slide day approach to coordinate his training schedule with his family and work responsibilities.

Watch for Jim Colby at the races this coming season, as he continues to lower his times, achieve his goals, and enjoy the great endurance sports lifestyle.

CHAPTER 12

Perfecting Technique

The only way of finding the limits of the
possible is by going beyond them
into the impossible.

—Arthur C. Clarke

Most athletes come to the sport of triathlon from one of the three disciplines: a swimming, cycling, or running background. This usually requires them to learn at least one or two new sports, if not all three. This can be most challenging, and sometimes frustrating, to say the least—especially in a very technique-oriented sport like swimming.

Even most veteran triathletes have a weakness in at least one of the three disciplines, and can benefit from taking the time to focus on technique, and turn that weakness into a strength.

The beauty of the sport of triathlon is that there are a lot of resources to help you learn proper technique in all three disciplines. There are books like this one, and there are good swimming, cycling, running, and triathlon coaches to help you perfect your technique.

Swimming Technique

Let's start with the most difficult sport to learn as an adult or newcomer—swimming. As veteran triathletes know, swimming is a very technique-oriented sport and requires consistent focus and attention in order to improve. It's rare to see an adult athlete jump into a pool for the first time and swim well without ever working on form and technique. And if you are not focusing on your technique, you should be.

From the novice to the veteran triathlete, there are great benefits to improving your technique in swimming. If you can learn to swim more efficiently and expend less energy, you will not only see improvement in your swim times, but also your overall performance in a triathlon. What happens in the swim can greatly affect your performance in the bike and run, both positively and negatively.

The Five Most Common Flaws in Freestyle Swimming

The five most common flaws we see with our coached athletes in swimming freestyle are (1) incorrect body and head position; (2) lack of rotation and improper breathing; (3) poor recovery portion of the stroke; (4) incorrect entry and extension portion of the stroke; and (5) weak catch and pull portion of the stroke.

1. Body/Head Position: A lot of swimmers hold their head too high in the water, causing drag and improper breathing and kicking. When holding your head too high, you have to compensate for lack of balance in the water (i.e., you are sinking!) by kicking harder to keep yourself afloat. This becomes a very tiring exercise if all your oxygen is used to fuel your leg muscles while dragging them through the water.

Proper Technique: Your head should always be in alignment with your spine and relaxed in the water. Envision having perfect posture with your ear aligned over your shoulder, your chin slightly back and down, and your chest out. This is good posture. We like to teach our athletes to envision a stick on a conveyer belt coming straight up from the bottom of the pool. If you were to push off the wall on your chest, the stick should be centered on your sternum. A level body position is obtained by balancing on your chest as you rotate from armpit to armpit.

2. Body Rotation and Breathing: A common problem for a lot of swimmers is that they don't rotate enough through their torso and hips, or they only rotate to one side—usually their breathing side. Some swimmers rotate completely onto their side, almost on their back, ending up with their thumb pointing toward the ceiling. This often happens when swimmers attempt to breathe by turning or lifting their head out of the water. This is called over-rotation.

Proper Technique: Your hips should rotate to almost 90° while your shoulders rotate about 45°. The breath is taken when the hips are rotated to the side by keeping your head and ear in the water and pulling your chin toward your shoulder and keeping one half of your goggles in the water and the other half out.

3. Arm Recovery Portion of Stroke: A common flaw in the recovery is the arm crossing over the midline (at twelve o'clock) in front. This is usually caused by lack of body rotation, incorrect body rotation, or leading the recovery with the hand.

Proper Technique: A proper recovery begins with the pinkie exiting the water first as you raise the elbow up and point toward the ceiling as it follows the line of your body. The hand should remain relaxed, with your fingers slightly apart as you lead the recovery with your elbow. Once your hand gets beyond your head, then extend your hand and forearm out from your shoulder and enter it into the water.

4. Entry and Extension Portion of Stroke: The most common issue we see is swimmers dropping or relaxing their shoulder upon entry, which causes their elbow to drop lower than their hand. The arm is then not fully extended.

Proper Technique: The hand should enter the water with a slight medial rotation and be driven slightly downward in the water while the shoulder remains high. (**Tip:** To keep a high shoulder, try shrugging it.) This means the hand is turned slightly so the fingertips enter the water first, with the thumb slightly down. The arm continues until it is fully extended and pointed downward, without hyperextension at the elbow.

5. Catch and Pull Portion of Stroke: The most common issue we see here is that swimmers push the arm straight down without any vertical elbow bend. This causes upward movement of your body in the water instead of forward movement. The other flaw is not finishing your stroke, or allowing the hand to exit the water too soon, resulting in pushing less water behind you and, ultimately, less forward movement.

Proper Technique: After the arm has fully extended in front, the first movement while keeping your shoulder high, or shrugged as we say, is to bend at your elbow as you reach your hand toward the bottom of the pool.

At that point, your arm from your elbow down becomes perpendicular to the floor of the pool. This creates a paddle from the middle of your bicep through the tips of your fingers—the catch. The pull phase begins as you pull your hand down the midline of your body toward your belly button, and finishes with the push or extension of your arm (similar to a tricep extension), so that your hand finishes next to your thigh.

Suggested Corrective Swim Drills

The following three drills include progressions that will help you to correct the most common flaws in swimming, mentioned above.

1. **Kick with Kickboard**

   With your face down, hold your hands flat on the kickboard, squeeze your arms to your ears, and kick flat on your chest with a slow exhalation. You can exhale through your mouth, nose, or both, but avoid holding your breath even for a second.

   Stretch through your belly and feel the slight pressure on your chest and armpits as you allow your head to relax into the water. You can wear fins while you do this drill if you are not proficient at kicking. This will set up the correct head and body positions in the water. You can just raise your head straight up when you need to take a breath, as this is not the focus of this drill.

   Second Progression: Perform this drill again, but with only one hand flat on the kickboard and the other hand at your side, with a focus on your breathing. Rotate your hips and torso so your belly button faces the side of the pool, but the head remains facing the bottom of the pool and the pressure remains on your armpit (not your back) as you kick your way down the pool. Switch arms on the return length. Start each breath by turning your head, not lifting it, to the opposite side of the arm on the kickboard. Keep your ear in the water as you turn, and bring your chin toward your shoulder, keeping one half of your goggles in the water. You want to look behind you to breathe so that you see the side of the pool or lane line, not the ceiling.

This may seem like a very basic drill, and it is. However, most swimmers can benefit by understanding how to relax in the water by stretching through their abs and torso and "getting long" in the water. A good understanding of proper head and body position to master balance and breathing in the water will go a long way, and this progression of drills will help you do that.

2. **Kick on Side with Four Progressions**
   You can perform this drill with fins if your kick is not proficient. Start with one arm extended in front, palm down about 6 to 10 inches deep in the water, and the other arm relaxed at your side, with your hand on the front of your thigh. Force your head and arm downward as though you were swimming downhill in the water. Your belly button should be facing the side of the pool, with slight pressure on your armpit and lats. Shrug your shoulder and begin kicking all the way down the lane, simply turning your head to breathe as needed. Switch arms on the return length.

   Second Progression: Perform the same drill as above, except when you take a breath, continue with one full stroke with the arm that is at your side; that is, begin with the recovery and then take a full stroke, only stopping again with your arm at your thigh. Do not take a breath during the stroke; you should have taken one before you started. We want to learn to rotate our torso and hips without moving our head. Repeat with the other arm extended on the return length.

   Third Progression: We will perform two strokes on one side, then rotate and perform two strokes on the other side. Again, only breathe before you begin the recovery, and on the first stroke only. Be sure you rotate fully between each stroke, and keep the lead arm in front in the palm-down position until the recovering hand reaches it.

   Fourth Progression: We call this "delayed swimming." We will perform one stroke on each side, making sure we exchange arms out front and fully rotate to each side. Try breathing to one side on one length and switch breathing sides on the return length. You should be focused on leading the stroke with the rotation of your hips and torso.

We recommend trying the third and fourth progressions both with and without fins.

3. **One-Arm Drill with Your Arm at Your Side**

    This is one of our favorite drills because it serves many purposes; in fact, it hits all of the common flaws of swimming from body position, to rotation, to recovery, to entry and extension, and to catch and pull. You can perform this drill with fins, as it is very difficult for most swimmers. As you progress, though, try it without fins to see how you do.

    Start with one arm at your side and the other arm out in front. Rotate your hips opposite the arm that is extended, push off the wall, and start kicking. Take a breath to the opposite side of the extended arm, bring your head back down into the water before you begin to rotate your hips and torso, and take a full stroke with the extended arm. You finish by ending up back in the starting position—arm extended and hips rotated to the opposite side of the extended arm.

    Continue stroking down the length with that arm before you switch arms on the return length. It's as though you are swimming with only one arm.

    Second Progression: Perform this drill the same way, except add "fingertip drag" during the recovery portion of the stroke. Fingertip drag is when you raise your elbow straight up along your body line and then relax your hand under your elbow while keeping your fingertips in contact with the water through entry. This helps to maintain a relaxed recovery and high elbow, as well as keeping a nice, tight streamline throughout the stroke.

    Third Progression: Perform two strokes with one arm and then switch and perform two strokes with the other arm, with a smooth transition from one arm to the other. The opposite arm remains at the side during the two strokes.

    This sequence of drills can be challenging, so there is no shame in using fins to help while working toward being able to perform them without fins.

These three basic drills with their progressions will help you to correct your inefficiencies, build your technique, and take your swimming to the next level.

Open-Water Swimming

Most triathletes find a big difference between swimming in a clean, clear pool with a lane line versus swimming in an open body of water that can be dark, murky, and lacking lane lines. Here are a few suggestions to help you master the open-water swim:

1. **Befriend the Enemy**

   The best way to get comfortable in the open water is to practice swimming in the open water. As the race season nears, get some of your friends, grab your wet suit, and get to the open water for some practice. Because swimming is the first leg of the race, the anxiety level is very high for everyone, from the experienced swimmer to the beginner. You need to overcome any fears and minimize your anxiety in the water, and the only way you're going to do that is to practice.

   Sign up for some local open-water swims well before your first race, and make it a priority. This will help you to get comfortable swimming in a crowd.

   Tip: Play it safe in open water. Always swim with a buddy and in the presence of a competent lifeguard.

2. **Practice with Your Wet Suit**

   Sometimes the anxiety a triathlete experiences is simply from the tightness of the wet suit and the uncomfortable, restricting feeling of it around your neck, arms, and shoulders. Because most triathletes haven't worn their wet suit since the last time they took it off at their last race a year ago, it's an unnatural feeling and absolutely can cause anxiety.

   You can practice with your wet suit in a pool, but we suggest not doing so for more than 10 to 20 minutes, as you can easily overheat.

Tip: After using your wet suit in a pool, rinse it out well with non-chlorinated water to help preserve it.

Melanie remembers racing the Lubbock, Texas, 70.3 as her first race of the season one year, and even as an experienced swimmer and triathlete, she experienced a panic attack about 100 yards into the swim. She attributes her attack to the feeling of being choked by the wet suit. She did the breast stroke to regain her calmness, and then continued on without ill effect. Believe us, it can and does happen to everyone—from the very experienced racer to the novice. Focus on staying relaxed and controlling your breathing.

3. **Sighting**

    What's the biggest issue for most triathletes in open water? You guessed it: swimming in a straight line!

    If you have any imbalances in your stroke or breathing, you are more than likely going to swim off course and cost yourself extra yards of unnecessary swimming. To avoid this, practice breathing bilaterally so you're comfortable with using this technique if you need help to get your bearings on race day. This will help to accommodate a course that is clockwise or counterclockwise. Secondly, try to even out your stroke in the pool by practicing the drills we have presented earlier in this chapter.

    The most efficient way to sight is to raise your head as little as possible and try to find a landmark on shore, or a buoy ahead of you, immediately before you turn your head to take a breath. This technique works really well in a calm lake. If the swim is an ocean swim, you may have to time your sighting so you are at the top of a wave or swell to see the shore or buoy.

    If you are having trouble mastering the sighting, we recommend taking a few simple breast strokes to pop your head out of the water and make sure you are headed in the right direction. You want to avoid sighting too often, as it can be very tiring, but you also don't want to wait to sight until you have swum way off course.

4. **Drafting**

    Drafting is legal in the swim portion of a triathlon, so do it if the opportunity presents itself. Drafting is when you get right behind or alongside another swimmer to "catch that swimmer's draft." The effects of drafting can mean up to 15 to 20 percent less effort on your part. The issue with drafting is that you can get lulled into swimming at a slower pace than you intended, or are capable of, because you have relied on someone in front of you to set the pace. It's important to know when it's time to pass that person and catch up to a faster swimmer. Optimally, you want to swim behind someone who is just slightly faster than you.

A Masters Swim session is a good time to practice your drafting, but don't touch the toes of the swimmer in front you (not cool!). It's not good swimming etiquette in the pool.

Cycling Technique

The bicycle was invented in the mid-1800s, and although the design aesthetics and some electronics are new, the basic mechanical concepts remain the same, even in this modern day. You still have to power it with your physical body! Cycling technique is much more important than having the latest and greatest bike.

To avoid wasted energy and inefficiency, you need to have a bike that fits you. If you haven't already done so, you should have a good professional bike fit done for your bike. Fit on the bike is a key factor in affecting your power. Once you have done that, then the next step is to work on developing good riding technique.

The most common issues for triathletes in cycling are maintaining good posture on the bike, "spinning" the pedals instead of mashing them, and effective gearing. Other skills necessary for good cycling are proper technique for climbing, descending, cornering, and braking.

Each and every time you ride, no matter what your experience level, an opportunity presents itself to practice and develop your techniques in the following key areas:

1. **Good Posture**
   Just like with swimming, correct posture is important for good cycling, especially as you get tired and start to lose focus, your back starts to round, and you begin to use your arms instead of your core to maintain good balance and form.

A good way to start on the bike is to sit straight up and then fall forward, bending at your hips with a straight back. Allow your hands between your thumb and forefinger to fall onto the hoods of your brakes with a soft grip and slightly bent elbows. Imagine you are shaking someone's hand, which is the position your arm should be in.

2. **Cadence**

A lot of athletes who come from a running background, and triathletes in general, have a tendency to "mash the gears"; that is, they push down very hard, usually with their toe down and heel up, in a gear that is too difficult. If you have ever watched the Tour de France, you will have noticed the cyclists' smooth cadence around the pedals; they are spinning circles, with a lot of power coming from their glutes, hamstrings, and quads, and very little from their knee down.

In general, you should spin circles and stay mostly in the range of about 75 to 105 revolutions per minute (rpm). When you climb a big hill, it's normal for your cadence to drop under 80 rpm, but you want to try to maintain a higher cadence for as long as possible. While descending you may not be pedaling at all, or at a higher cadence of over 100 rpm. And on a long stretch of flat road, most athletes are most efficient at about 90 rpm, when maintaining a moderate Z2 heart rate, and at about 80 rpm when maintaining a higher-intensity Z4 heart rate. There are many different opinions as to what cadences are ideal, but this is what we find works best for most triathletes.

If your cadence is consistently too high, you are not taking full advantage of your power, and you're probably giving up speed. If your cadence is too low, you are probably pushing too difficult a gear, which means you are wearing out your muscles and may even risk injury. We suggest you generally try to stay within that 75 to 105 rpm range, depending on the terrain and targeted heart rate level, and find the optimal level for you.

3. **Climbing Technique**

To be a good cyclist and triathlete, you need to know how to climb hills without wasting a lot of energy. If you are riding a tri bike, the positioning can make climbing a lot more difficult. On a road bike you can sit back farther on the seat and use your hamstrings and glutes to gain power while seated. On a tri bike in the time-trial position, you don't have as much room to push back farther on the seat.

When you approach a hill, you want to shift into a lower gear, possibly even less of a gear than you think you need. You don't want to get stuck having to shift to a lower gear in the middle of the hill, as you risk dropping your chain. Obviously, as you reach the midpoint of the climb, your cadence will gradually drop, but the goal is to try to maintain speed and cadence. Try to perfect the seated position in climbing first before you attempt the standing position. You want to maintain an upright position to maximize your lung capacity and avoid bringing your chest and head down to the handlebars (hunching over).

To stand during a hill climb, you must first shift one or two gears up and then stand. You want to rock the bike in a straight line by pulling up on one side and pushing down with your pedal on the other side. Your pelvis should be forward so you are not standing straight up on your pedals. You want to straighten your arms slightly and keep your upper body still. You should be in a position that feels like your knees are going to hit your handlebars. Keep your wrists flexible and don't grip the handlebars too tightly.

Tip: Generally, for a hill that takes 1 minute or less to climb, you should be able to remain seated and power over the hill. For a climb that takes about 1 to 4 minutes, you will want to try to remain seated for about two-thirds of it, and then stand for the last third of the climb. And for climbs that will take more than 4 minutes, alternate between sitting and standing to help keep your leg muscles fresher.

4. **Descending**

This is the fun part of cycling for most triathletes. You want to put your weight flat on the seat centered over the rear tire. If you have aero bars or drops, and you are fully comfortable with them, now is the time to put them to use. Keep your pedals at the three and nine o'clock positions to be as aerodynamic as possible, and to avoid anything coming up from the road and hitting your pedals. If you are not comfortable in this position, keep your hands on the brake hoods and feather your brakes so you can control your speed.

The best way to learn how to climb and descend hills is to start practicing on smaller hills and then gradually work your way to bigger hills. Practice doing it repeatedly, and eventually you will befriend the enemy. The hill repeat sessions in the training programs in Chapter 5 are a great opportunity to practice your hill climbing and descending.

5. **Cornering**

This is a fun skill to learn, and once you do you will realize how much extra distance you have been traveling on your bike. As you approach a turn or corner, you want to try and maintain speed, depending on the severity. To do this, you want to straighten the outer leg so it's at the bottom of the pedal stroke and the inner leg is bent, with your knee at a 90° angle. Avoid steering the bike into the turn, but rather use your body weight and knee to lean into the turn. If possible, you want to "cut the apex" of the turn, or ideal line, to keep the shortest distance around it.

6. **Braking**

Braking is a key component of cycling in training and racing, as anything can happen out there. Cars can cut you off, and pedestrians may not see you and walk right in your path. You need to be ready to come to a complete stop when situations like this arise. To do so, push your weight back on the seat and grab both brakes hard at the same time. It's important to know the front brake alone provides the fastest stopping power. However, you have to learn how to apply the front brake hard without having the rear wheel lift off the ground. You do this by keeping both arms stiff and using them to decelerate while getting your center of gravity far back by pushing back on the seat. You should practice making hard and long stops while training in a safe area, and get comfortable with both of them.

Suggested Corrective Bike Drills

The following drills will help you to correct the most common cycling errors and develop better cycling technique. For each of these drills, focus on keeping your back flat, keeping your buttocks flat on the seat, and keeping your legs straight, with knees slightly in.

1. **90 Circles**
   Start by spinning the pedals with both legs, but focusing mentally on just one leg. With that leg, count 30 circles (or pedal strokes) and visualize 30 perfect circles with that foot. Then, focus on the other leg and visualize 30 perfect circles with that foot, still keeping both feet moving on your pedals. Finally, for 30 more circles, focus on both feet and visualize both feet spinning 30 perfect circles.

2. **Single-Leg Pedaling**
   This is another great drill to help you learn how to properly spin circles with your pedals. You can keep the other leg clipped in and avoid applying any pressure around the pedals with that leg, or take it out and just place it on top of the pedal. You should notice much more flexion of your ankle while maintaining even pressure around the pedal, and much more of an even, circular movement of the foot. This exercise identifies which leg is weaker, as well as any weak spots in the spin cycle. A great—and funny—visualization for this is to envision scraping dog poop off the bottom of your shoe. You can also visualize pulling your heel out of the back of your shoe through the three o'clock to the nine o'clock positions of the pedal stroke.
   Try to keep a cadence of 90 rpm with the one leg, and do this drill for 60 seconds with each leg.

3. **High Cadence Cycling**
   Try spinning with very low resistance for 1 minute at each cadence—100, 105, and 110+ rpm—during a 30- to 60-minute recovery cycle. This will help you to learn to stay flat on your seat, maintain good balance, and spin smoothly.

Try these drills as part of your warm-up to a workout, or during your high-rpm sessions, which you will find in the training programs in Chapter 5.

Running Technique

Running is such an instinctive thing for most of us. As children, after we learned to crawl and then walk, we ran! What could be more basic, right? But then why do so many of us get it wrong? Again, we go back to maintaining simple good posture. Leaning too far forward or too far back will cause inefficiencies and ultimately injuries in running. There are many philosophies of running out there, from running heel to toe, to running on your toes, to striking with your entire foot.

The best concept is to run with good posture, a neutral pelvic posture, head in alignment with your spine (ear over your shoulder), and shoulders relaxed. A good visualization is to picture a marionette with relaxed legs, chest up and out, and pelvis neutral, attaining a look of running tall. Your foot strike or stride, then, is really determined by the range of motion through your hips.

Two helpful tools to help you visualize good running are the "Two Strings" Approach and "Bounce-less Running."

"Two Strings" Approach

Visualize one string attached to the very top of your head, gently pulling you upward. Then visualize another string coming out of the middle of your chest, pulling you slightly forward. Visualize yourself "running tall" in an upright position while your shoulders remain relaxed. From this position, bend your elbows, raising your forearms and hands so they are parallel to the floor. Close your fingers and rest your thumb softly on your forefinger. This approach produces an improved running posture that will help you to maximize your power in running.

Bounce-less Running

If you are running from your hips down, you are probably experiencing minimal bounce in your running. You can determine if you are running "bounce-less" by identifying an object like a tree or pole in front of you, and watching it to see if it appears to be steady, or if it appears to be moving up and down. If you are over-striding, you may find yourself running with a lot of bounce, or if you are under-striding, you may be applying too much of a straight downward pressure into the ground.

The goal is to run with forward momentum as you leave the ground behind you, and avoid bouncing or loping. If you are outside, identify an object off in the distance. If you find that it is bouncing in your view, begin reducing the upward push in your running gait, until the bouncing stops. You can also do this by starting with the "two strings" approach, and then, in front of a mirror on a treadmill, practice running with a stable pelvis so you do not bounce.

Hill Running—Ascending and Descending

The idea of running hills can be very daunting from ascending to descending. The issue is usually technique related, and can cause either discomfort or possible injury.

While ascending, we find that many athletes try to take large, bounding steps up the hill, which is inefficient and can cause injury. We find the best way to approach hills is to lean slightly forward and shorten your stride a bit, while increasing your leg turnover. Pick a point about 20 feet in front of you to focus on, and run to that point. Then keep repeating this until you are at the top of the hill.

While descending a hill, a lot of athletes find it more difficult to control their form. Many runners will come over a hill and then let their arms and legs flail as they descend, or they will take too large of a stride and run out of control. This is wasted energy, and can cause excessive stress on the leg joints and, ultimately, injury. This is of particular concern for the athlete who is more prone to injury. As is the case with ascending, when descending it is best to shorten your stride, increase your leg turnover, and run in an efficient and controlled manner.

Suggested Corrective Run Drills

To help you find that neutral pelvis and good posture, we like to start with a few drills to loosen up your lower back, hips, and pelvis, and get you running with good form.

1. **Leg Swings Front to Back and Side to Side**
   Start in a standing position with a chair or wall to your side so that you can use it to hold with one hand. Raise your knee straight up, beyond perpendicular to the ground, and then swing the leg back behind you as far as you are comfortable and then forward again. Keep the leg relaxed and foot in dorsiflexion (flexion of the foot in an upward direction) as you envision a pendulum, with your hips being at the center of it. Repeat this ten times with each leg. Then turn to your side and raise your leg straight out to the side as far as is comfortable for you and let it swing in front, across your body. Repeat this ten times with one leg and then with the other leg.

2. **Lateral Crossovers**
   Start with hips and shoulders facing forward; then take the left leg and cross it behind your right leg, and then bring it in front of your right leg, and repeat for 15 to 30 seconds. Then repeat with the right leg leading the exercise.

3. **High Knee with and without Knee Grab**
   Start by coming forward onto the ball of your left foot and raise your right knee, grabbing it with both hands. Release the knee and repeat by coming forward onto the ball of your right foot and raising the left knee and grabbing with both hands. Repeat for 30 seconds. This is a great drill to work on your balance as well.

AN IRONFIT MOMENT

Gait Analysis

If you are still having issues with your running after practicing these drills and techniques, you may also want to consider having a gait analysis done by a competent professional. There are many sports trainers, podiatrists, chiropractors, physical therapists, and running stores with excellent training and abilities in gait analysis. A good running store will also be able to recommend the best running shoes to help you to perfect your gait.

Progress this drill simply to a high knee lift, alternating legs while maintaining good posture. As you raise your knee, avoid dropping your hip on the opposite side by keeping your pelvis stable.

These are great warm-up drills to help you loosen up your back, pelvis, and hips, and get you running with good form and technique.

We hope the above technique tips and corrective drills will help you to improve your swimming, cycling, and running, no matter if you are a novice or already an experienced triathlete. When it comes to technique, keep learning and keep challenging yourself to improve.

CHAPTER 13

Mental Training: Powerful Secrets to Self-Confidence

Nothing contributes so much to tranquilize
the mind as a steady purpose—a point on
which the soul may fix its intellectual eye.

—Mary Shelley

I n this chapter we present nine successful mental training tools to help you to stay motivated, focused, and confident throughout our sixteen-week training programs, and especially on race day. We have worked with hundreds of successful athletes for many years, developing, testing, and fine-tuning these powerful tools for training and racing success. These are not just theories. All have been successfully battle-tested by athletes at all competitive levels.

There will be rough patches ahead. Every day in our sixteen-week journey will not be perfect. There are sure to be hurdles, both physical and mental, along the way. When you encounter these hurdles, remember to turn back to this chapter, review our suggestions, and put them to work for you.

Following is a summary of our nine suggested techniques and approaches:

1. **Posting Goals**
   Probably the single most successful motivational technique we have used with our coached athletes is posting goals. We start by listing our coached athletes' goals prominently at the very top of their training schedules, so they see them every day. We encourage them to take the power of goals to another level by posting them at locations in their home or place of work, to be reminded of them frequently.

What we are talking about here is actually creating little signs with your goals written on them. A simple example of one might be as follows:

Eagleman

Sub 5 Hours

Top 3 AG

This athlete plans to race in the Eagleman 70.3 race in Maryland in June, and has the goals of both finishing with a time under five hours and placing in the top three in his age group.

These can be primary goals or stretch goals (see Chapter 9), whichever you find motivates you the most.

One of the most productive places to post goals is on your bathroom mirror, as that will be the first thing many athletes will see each day. Other popular places include your work area or your workout area.

There is a wonderful motivating power to posting goals. It keeps us focused on what we want to achieve, and it helps us to make wise decisions each and every day that will positively affect our ability to achieve our goals.

2. **The Family Meeting**

We encourage our coached athletes to have a "family meeting" early in your Half Iron-Distance journey. Bring everyone in your family together and let them know what you are in the process of doing and how important it is to you. Let them know that you will try very hard not to let this journey be a burden on them and apologize in advance just in case it does from time to time. Finally, ask for their support in achieving your dream.

There is nothing more important we can do to help make our Half Iron-Distance journey a success than to get the early buy-in and support from our loved ones. It will head off so many possible issues down the road, and it will really maximize your chances for success.

Once you've had your successful family meeting, we encourage you to have one with your "work family" and your "family of friends" as well—with anyone in your life who may be affected by your decision.

Not only will this "grease the wheels" for your Half Iron-Distance success, but you may also be surprised by the level of support you will get from these people in your life. You may be especially surprised at the impact you will have on them. Your positive example of taking on such a challenging and worthy goal, and following through on it, will be of value to them all.

3. **Energy Givers and Energy Takers**
Some people just do not share your excitement for your goals, or your general enthusiasm for life. They choose to be negative and will throw as much cold water on you as they can. Sometimes these people are even family members, which makes it extra difficult, because these are the people you would hope would be the most supportive of you and your goals.

But if that's the case, you cannot let them win; you just have to deal with the challenge as best you can. To the extent possible, try to minimize your valuable time with "energy takers" and try to maximize your time with "energy givers."

Try the following exercise:
Write down the names of the three biggest energy givers and the three biggest energy takers currently in your life. Then, next to each name, write out three specific action steps about how you can increase your time and exposure with each of the three energy givers and decrease your time and exposure with each of the three energy takers. Then, throughout your sixteen-week training pro-gram, follow through on these action steps.

4. **Deep Belly Breathing**
An effective way to calm your pre-race or any other type of anxiety is through proper relaxed breathing. Learning to breathe properly also provides many additional health benefits, from relaxation and stress reduction to energizing and healing. We can learn to breathe much more deeply to bring about positive change in our training and performances.

Deep belly breathing is a technique that we encourage many of our coached athletes to use with their racing and training. You start by lying on the floor, with one hand on your solar plexus and the other at or below your belly button. With your tongue on the roof of your mouth, exhale through your mouth with relaxed lips before you begin an inhalation through your nose, attempting to bring the breath all the way to your lower abdomen. Then, hold your breath for a count of 3 seconds before you exhale through your mouth for at least 6 to 10 seconds. Try at a minimum to exhale for twice as long as your inhalation. You can also do this in a sitting position while maintaining very good posture.

If you start doing this type of breathing a couple of times per day, with five to six belly breaths each time, you will become very comfortable with the technique, and be able to work its benefits in many situations. Use it to reduce pre-race nervousness, or any other time you could benefit from calming and relaxing your mind and body.

5. **Stay Mentally Sharp by Multiplying Two Two-Digit Numbers**
This a great tool to stay mentally sharp. Simply take two two-digit numbers and multiply them together in your head without using any assistance (like calculators, paper, pencil or pen, and fingers or toes). This is a completely mental exercise. Pick a couple of numbers now and give it a try.

Here's a sample test for you: What is the product of 56 x 13?

If you are like most smart people, you'll be able to do it, but it will take good focus. Once you think you have the answer, check it on a calculator and see if you were correct. If not, try it again in your head until you get to the correct answer on your own. Make it a habit, and do this every day. Select two two-digit numbers and multiply them in your head. Check the answer, and keep doing it until you arrive at the correct answer on your own.

A great time to do this is while you are preparing to start a workout session. This will help to get you alert and mentally dialed in.

Another suggestion: Make this an ongoing game that you play every day with a friend or your spouse or partner. Take turns coming up with the two numbers every other day. Make this mental exercise part of your daily routine. By the way, the answer to the above example is: 56 x 13 = 728. We hope you got it!

6. **The Positive Self-Talk Game**

   We tend to believe what we hear. If we constantly talk negatively, especially about ourselves, it wears us down over time, and we may even start to believe it. By doing so, we fail to be the positive people we aspire to be.

   This is not a helpful mind-set for an endurance athlete. We need to be one of those very positive "glass half full" people. By doing so, we can roll with the punches, power our way through the rough patches, and persevere no matter how great the challenge.

   If you are prone to negative self-talk, we encourage you to try the positive self-talk game. It takes two to play, so it's best to do it with a good friend or your spouse or partner, who preferably also wants to work on this in his or her own life.

   The game goes as follows: Anytime one of you catches the other one engaged in negative self-talk, you call the person on it. The person called on it must then say something positive about himself or herself, and repeat it aloud five times. The positive thing that the person says must be true, and it has to be spoken with sincerity.

   Here's an example: Don is playing the game with Melanie, and she catches Don saying, "My swim was terrible this morning. I don't know why I even bother." When Melanie calls Don on it, he has to say something positive about himself with sincerity, and repeat it five times. Don chooses to repeat the following five times: "While my swim sessions can be off once in a while, my swimming performance generally gets better and better."

7. **The Countdown**

   "The Countdown" is another great technique for both reducing pre-race anxiety and improving your race-day performance.

   We are often surprised by how many athletes closely follow their training plans for several months, get in the best form of their lives, and then just sort of show up at their race location without any plan for the crucial last couple of days. We see these athletes all of the time at the races. They are the ones who look like deer in the headlights. Their nervousness takes over, and they kind of wander through the pre-race registration and other activities, wasting a lot of time, forgetting important steps, and losing focus.

We encourage our coached athletes to write out a chronological list of activities, with exactly what they plan to do and when they plan to do it, over the final forty-eight to seventy-two hours before their big race. Actually write out a detailed schedule of when you will be traveling, when and where you will eat, when you will sleep, when you plan to visit registration, when you plan to organize your race equipment, when you plan to do your last couple of training sessions, and all of the other little activities you need to efficiently complete, right up until the time you enter the water on the morning of your race.

By doing this, we eliminate a large amount of pre-race stress. We also prevent ourselves from being pulled into activities that will not support our racing success. There are no deer-in-the-headlights moments. All you need to do is methodically and calmly work your way through your chronological list. You don't have to keep stressing over the thought of *What have I forgotten to do?* because you know that you haven't forgotten a thing. It's all right there on your "Countdown" schedule.

Second, your race will actually be more successful because you will not miss or forget anything in your pre-race plan. You will accomplish everything you need to accomplish, with minimal stress, and you will be able to maintain the confident and calm feeling we all want to have on race day.

8. **"Have a Great Race"**
It's so important to be in that confident and calm state of mind to be ready to race at your best. Some athletes allow themselves to get into overly aggressive and irritable moods on race morning. We suppose this may be a helpful state of mind for some sports, but it's not for triathlon. This type of negative energy will work against us in the long run. On race morning we want to have smiles on our faces and be in a positive, confident, and calm state of mind.

If you find that you have a difficult time doing this, we encourage you to turn your focus outward to your fellow athletes and spread some positive energy. The amazing thing about spreading positive energy is that the more you give, the more you get back; as a result, you will become calmer and more confident.

Start by frequently wishing your competitors well, especially when you cross paths on race morning. There is no better time to do this than at the often-stressful swim start. Don can recall many times when he was treading water in a crowded group of swimmers, awaiting the starting gun. Sometimes those last couple of minutes can seem very long. The most aggressive swimmers are up front, bumping elbows, bumping legs, all in total silence. It feels like you can cut the stress with a knife.

In moments like this, Don likes to turn to the swimmers around him and call out, in his most positive and sincere voice, "Have a great race out there today, guys!" It's amazing how the mood immediately changes. Next thing you know, everybody is wishing each other well and spreading positive energy. From all directions you can hear athletes saying things like, "Have a great race," "Good luck out there today," and "Have a good one, guys." A truly positive vibe replaces all the stress that existed.

Try this approach in your very next race to help you to achieve that confident and calm state of mind.

9. **"Nobody Cares"**

We have a little joke we like to say sometimes when our coached athletes express high levels of pre-race nervousness and anxiety. We say with a smile, "Don't you realize that nobody cares?" The reaction is usually surprise at first, followed by a smile when they realize we are joking to lighten the mood.

Yet there lies a nugget of truth here that needs to be understood and used to your advantage. The truth is that if your goal is to break five hours in your Half Iron-Distance triathlon, the only people who really care about this goal are you and perhaps your coach, if you have one. The reality is that nobody else really does care. Any pressure coming from that number "sub 5 hours" is 100 percent coming from the 8-inch space between your ears.

Even your family and friends don't really have any personal connection with that goal. Bottom line: Your true friends want you to enjoy your race and have a positive experience. That's all they care about. And if they are not your friends, you shouldn't care about what they think anyway. That's just wasted energy. When we come to realize this simple truth, we can let go of this stress.

Next time you are at the starting line, remind yourself of the following fact: *If you have the health, the fitness, the freedom, and the personal resources to enjoy the luxury of racing a Half Iron-Distance triathlon on a Sunday morning, then you have already won life's lottery. All you need to do now is enjoy it.*

We hope the above nine techniques prove helpful to you in the weeks ahead. Take the ones that fit your situation the best and put them to work for you in your Half Iron-Distance journey.

CHAPTER 14

Building and Maintaining Excellent Health

The mind's first step to self-awareness must
be through the body.

—George Sheehan

n this chapter we present strategies to help you maintain good health and
stay injury-free as you pursue your Half Iron-Distance dream. The importance of body awareness and early detection of potential injuries is par-
amount to maintaining good health and being able to follow a consistent
training program. We will present tips on how to assemble your optimal
"health team," explain why athletes often become injured in the first place,
provide injury-prevention tips, and offer suggestions on how to spot the
early warning signs of injury.

Assembling Your "Health Team"

We encourage all new athletes we begin working with to have a complete
physical from their primary-care physician as the very first step. This will
give you a baseline of some of the common things you should know about
your body: blood pressure, cholesterol level and breakdown, red and white
blood cell counts, glucose, vitamin levels, and other benchmark data. For
our athletes under fifty, a physician will typically recommend a physical
every two to three years. For those fifty years or older, usually a doctor will
recommend a physical every year.

This is simply a wise health decision for anyone. Melanie remembers a
story about one of her Masters swimmers in his sixties who was experiencing some health issues. She asked him if he had regular physicals, and was
appalled to learn that he didn't even have a regular primary-care physician;

in fact, the last time he'd had a physical was in high school! Based on her recommendation of a sports physician, he went for his first physical. After he started getting regular annual physicals, the doctor identified a serious male health issue. Luckily for him, it was detected early enough to treat successfully and without ill effect. Today he is healthier than ever, and racing the Half and full Iron-Distance races.

We realize that most athletes see themselves as very fit and healthy individuals, and, for the most part, that's true. However, with various factors like heredity, age, and training, things can happen, and you need to have professionals who are familiar with you and your health to address any issues as they arise.

We suggest the following for your optimal health team:

- **Sports physician:** Get a recommendation from a fellow athlete, friend, or coach for a highly endorsed sports physician. A good sports physician is familiar with athletic-type injuries and understands the athlete's perspective on training and racing. Schedule a physical with the doctor to get a baseline of your numbers, from an EKG to your cholesterol level. This is important should you suffer an injury and have to repeat these tests. Your doctor will see right away if anything varies from your baseline.
- **Orthopedist:** Your sports physician will usually have an affiliation with an orthopedist or, more than likely, have one in his or her medical group. This is a great asset if you should suffer a fall or break. Your sports physician can communicate your health history easily to an orthopedist, and bring the orthopedist up to date very quickly so you aren't starting from scratch with a new doctor.
- **ART provider:** Locate an ART (Active Release Techniques) provider—either a chiropractor, physical therapist, or massage therapist—in your area, who can treat you when you have an overuse injury that requires soft tissue work, as opposed to taking anti-inflammatory or other medication. Sometimes improving blood flow and reducing inflammation to an injured area is all you need to recover. This type of treatment will help you to do that.
- **Physical therapist:** A good physical therapist is a must. Again, start with your sports physician or orthopedist, who will more than

likely have an affiliation with a physical therapist or group. As we train and age, we develop weaknesses that can result in injury. It's fine to treat the injury, but a good physical therapist will help you to identify where the weakness is, and develop a strategy through exercise to help you build strength where you need it and avoid the injury going forward.

Once you have these specialists assembled, you will be prepared to address any physical issues when they arise.

Another aspect of our health is the ability to recognize when a potential injury exists—or what we like to call "listening to your body." For example, if you have consistent pain lasting more than a few days, it's probably time to see a doctor before it progresses and becomes more severe. The worst thing to do is to "train through" an injury in hopes that it will go away. In some cases, this may work, but in most cases, not so.

Why We Sometimes Become Injured

There are many reasons athletes become injured in training and racing, but from our own experience, we have found the following to be the most common:

- **Warm-up and cooldown:** Lack of a proper warm-up to prepare your body for an intense cardio or strength-training session, or not cooling down afterward, can lead to an injury.
- **Micro and macro training cycles:** Not following a proper training cycle strategy from your weekly training cycle to your annual training cycle can cause an injury (e.g., not tapering enough for a race, or doing two races back-to-back without allowing your body enough time to recover). (See Chapter 3.)
- **"Too much, too soon":** Failing to allow your body to gradually adapt to increasing time or mileage in any of the three disciplines can and usually will result in an injury. This also applies when athletes take some time off for whatever reason (e.g., they became ill and didn't work out for three to five days) and then

immediately come back to exercising right where they left off, instead of taking a gradual approach to getting back on schedule (see "Adjusting Training Program for Missed Workouts" on page 82). A good coach can help you through that process. (See Chapters 3 and 5.)

- **Training that's too intensive:** Too much training at too high an intensity level or heart rate, and failing to incorporate proper recovery days between these sessions, can lead to stagnation as well as injury. (See Chapters 2 and 4.)
- **Cross-training:** Not using cross-training to effectively work through potential injuries; instead of listening to your body when you feel an injury coming on, and backing off for a few days, you continue your normal training. For instance, instead of hopping on the ARC trainer, elliptical trainer, or stationary bike to help cross-train your way through a running injury, you run hill repeats with your friends; now you've exacerbated the situation rather than keeping a potential injury under wraps.
- **Improper technique:** Practicing with improper technique or form in any of the three disciplines (see Chapter 12) will most likely cause issues and result in an injury at some point.

What we have learned from our own experiences, as well as those of our coached athletes, is that as an athlete gets older (forty-plus), injuries take longer to heal, and the body takes longer to recover from workouts. It's especially important that forty-plus athletes realize they are no longer twenty-five and can no longer jump out of bed and go meet their buddies for a 10-mile run on little more than a cup of coffee. Nor should forty-plus athletes decide to match someone else's run or bike pace knowing they are much faster or further along in their training. Remember, you may feel good when you do it, and that's great, but often we see an injury pop up two to three days later after doing something like that.

These are the types of misguided decisions that will get you injured and off your training very quickly.

Preventing Overuse and Other Injuries

The typical injuries in endurance sports are overuse injuries resulting from repetitive-type movements that come from running, cycling, and swimming for long distances. Our recommendation is to continually listen to your body and follow a good protocol of self-myofascial release, proper warm-up and cooldown, icing, and stretching.

Here's how to approach and use these tools to prevent injuries and keep you training consistently:

- **Self-myofascial release tools:** Various density foam rollers, the body stick, spikey massage balls, and even the basic tennis or golf ball.

  These gadgets can be used to help loosen muscles, reduce inflammation, and bring healing to injured areas.

  We recommend you incorporate the use of any of these tools before or after a cardio workout to help the recovery process.

- **Icing:** If you experience inflammation from overuse, a great and easy tool is simple icing.

  Make a pack of ice and place with compression on the area for 10 to 20 minutes. Avoid burning of the skin from icing by placing a wet paper towel between the ice bag and your skin if you don't have a specific icing bag. You want to do this immediately after your workout and then again before retiring to bed.

- **Warm-up and cooldown:** It is particularly important as you get older to do at least a 5- to 10-minute warm-up and cooldown before and after any cardio or strength-training activity.

  Either walk, easy jog, or bike for at least 10 minutes to allow your core body temperature to rise so your muscles are prepared for the effort, whether it is further cardio or strength training. (Also see Chapters 6 and 8 concerning warm-up routines.)

  And just as important as warming up before, it's also important to cool down your body after a cardio or strength-training session. Again, you can do some easy jogging, walking, or cycling.

  Tip: A great cooldown routine is simply to walk at a moderate pace for 5 to 10 minutes immediately after training.

AN IRONFIT MOMENT

Compression Garments

Both a blessing and a curse, triathlon has become the petri dish for all types of new equipment, from racing and training gear to nutritional supplements and everything in between. A more-recent phenomenon is compression gear, including tops, shorts, long tights, calf sleeves, and socks. While you can find opinions at both ends of the spectrum, from good to noncommittal, for the most part our athletes' experiences (and our own) have been very positive.

Compression garments help to regulate your body at the correct temperature so you can maximize your performance while holding the muscles in place, thereby reducing damage. They also help to increase blood flow, bringing quicker delivery of nutrients to the muscles and faster removal of waste products from the muscles. And lastly, the right amount of compression can help to stimulate the muscles during training, racing, and recovery.

- **Stretching:** In addition to using self-myofascial release tools, it is important that after your cardio or strength activity, you also incorporate a regular stretching routine. You want to work especially on those areas that seem to give you the most issues, such as your quadriceps, glutes, hamstrings, calves, back, shoulders, and neck. Refer to Chapter 6 for some great stretching exercises.
- **Adequate rest:** We often take this subject lightly, but it is very important to get adequate sleep in order to absorb the training and allow your body to recover from your training sessions.

    A good indicator to determine whether you are recovered from a training session is your "resting" heart rate, which is your heart rate upon waking, before you even hop out of bed. Try taking your resting heart rate for a week straight by leaving your heart rate monitor next to your bed; or, if you can, manually take your pulse using your watch to determine your heart rate. If you are healthy, recovering well from training, and getting adequate sleep, your resting heart rate should be fairly consistent every morning. (For example, if you find your normal resting heart rate is 50 beats per minute for a few days straight, but then one day it's 55 BPM, this 10 percent increase may indicate several possibilities: You may be coming down with a cold/illness; you haven't recovered from the previous day's training session; or you haven't been getting enough sleep in the days prior.) Once you determine your normal resting heart rate, test it every morning and use it to hear what your body is trying to tell you.

Early Warning Signs

What we have found from coaching athletes is that many tend to have a "no pain, no gain" mentality. There is a difference between just pushing yourself hard and actually hurting yourself. If all of a sudden after a long run you wake up the next day and feel pain in your plantar, what do you do? We all know athletes that have had plantar fasciitis, and feeling that pain the day after a long run is a good indication something is brewing and you need to address it.

A few of the most common warning signs in each of the three disciplines are as follows:

- **Swimming:** Nagging deltoid, shoulder, and neck pain
- **Cycling:** Nagging back, shoulder, and neck pain
- **Running:** Nagging foot, calf, hip, or back pain

All of these early warning signs can and may lead to an injury if you don't address them head-on. Sometimes, as we've mentioned, it's related to your form or technique. You can address this with a good coach or specialist in that field. Other times, it's an accumulation of the training (overuse), and you may need to back off a bit on training time, duration, or intensity to allow your body to recover.

Sometimes, an active recovery is called for, and can work if the injury is identified quickly. There are many ways to cross-train through an injury without having to interrupt your training, and a good sports physician, chiropractor, or physical therapist will help you to determine when it's appropriate and when it's not. A good coach will help you to modify your training appropriately, as well.

In this chapter we have discussed the concept of assembling our optimal health team, explained many of the reasons why athletes often become injured, provided injury-prevention tips, and offered suggestions on how to spot the early warning signs of injury. Ultimately, we want to be athletes for life, so learning to work *with* your body and understand when it's telling you something is a key factor in having longevity in the sport of triathlon and athletics in general.

CHAPTER 15

Recovery and Maintenance Training

Work spares us from three evils:
boredom, vice, and need.

—Voltaire

You did it! You accomplished your Half Iron-Distance dream. Congratulations!

Now what?

This chapter presents specific training guidelines for the period immediately following the Half Iron-Distance Triathlon, as well as a suggested maintenance training program and approach for the off-season.

The Two Weeks After

Triathletes tend to be extreme people. We usually find that many of them are so excited and elated after completing their first Half Iron-Distance Triathlon that they want to race again on the very next weekend. Or, some want to completely rest, put their feet up, and not move a finger for a few weeks. Of course, neither extreme is good.

We risk injury if we race too soon after finishing a big event. Sometimes we feel so euphoric after a big accomplishment that we don't feel our body's need for recovery and rejuvenation. If we let our enthusiasm get the best of us and we race again too soon, we set ourselves up for, at best, a disappointing "flat" performance, and, at worst, a possible injury.

If, however, we completely stop training for a while, we don't allow our bodies an opportunity to "work the race out of our system." We will stiffen up and rapidly decondition. Our bodies are not made to be sedentary. They need to move, and our muscles need to work to properly recover and get back to 100 percent.

What we need to do after our Half Iron-Distance race is to have two proper recovery weeks. The first week will be sort of a "reverse taper." We will gradually build our low-intensity aerobic time in each of the three sports. Then, in the second week, we will return to a more-stabilized level of moderate-intensity aerobic time in each of the three sports.

From there, we suggest two possible directions:

1. If you are not planning to race again for a while—say, a couple of months or more—the second week of training will become our model week for our off-season training, and we will repeat this moderate-volume week throughout the off-season months. Then, when we are ready to go back to more-specific training for our next race, we are perfectly positioned to do so, with a solid aerobic base in all three sports.

2. The other possible direction is relevant when we are still within our competitive season. In that case, we would go right from the second week into our specific training program for our next race. Once we have completed the two weeks, we are ready to do so. Our bodies have recovered from our Half Iron-Distance, and our aerobic base has been firmed up. We're good to go!

Following are our suggested training programs for the two weeks after the Half Iron-Distance Triathlon for each of the Competitive, Intermediate, and "Just Finish" athletes.

As per our discussion above, if no other races are planned for the near term, the second week of each program can become the model week for the off-season maintenance program.

Competitive Athlete: Two-Week Recovery / Off-Season Maintenance Program (Note: Swims #1 through 6 can be found on page 49):

COMPETITIVE PROGRAM
RECOVERY / OFF-SEASON MAINTENANCE

WEEK 1	SWIM	BIKE	RUN
M	#1—Optional easy	Rest Day / Slide Day	Rest Day / Slide Day
Tu	Off	Off	45 min. Z1-easy
W	#2	Trans: 45 min. Z1 to Z2 (QC)	15 min. Z1 to Z2
Th	Off	45 to 60 min. Z1 to Z2	Off
F	#3	Off	45 to 60 min. Z1 to Z2
Sat	Off	1:00 to 1:15 hr. Z1 to Z2	Off
Sun	Off	Off	45 to 60 min. Z1 to Z2
Totals: 7:00 to 9:00 hrs.	2:00 to 3:00 hrs.	2:30 to 3:00 hrs.	2:30 to 3:00 hrs.

WEEK 2	SWIM	BIKE	RUN
M	#4—Optional	Rest Day / Slide Day	Rest Day / Slide Day
Tu	Off	Off	60 min. Z2
W	#5	Trans: 45 min. Z2 (QC)	15 to 30 min. Z2
Th	Off	45 to 60 min. Z2	Off
F	#6	Off	45 to 60 min. Z2
Sat	Off	1:30 to 2:15 hr. Z2	Off
Sun	Off	Optional: 60 min. Z1 (100+ rpm)	1:00 to 1:30 hr. Z1 to Z2
Totals: 8:00 to 12:00 hrs.	2:00 to 3:00 hrs.	3:00 to 5:00 hrs.	3:00 to 4:00 hrs.

Intermediate Athlete: Two-Week Recovery / Off-Season Maintenance Program (Note: Swims #1 through 4 can be found on page 62):

INTERMEDIATE PROGRAM
RECOVERY / OFF-SEASON MAINTENANCE

WEEK 1	SWIM	BIKE	RUN
M	Off	Rest Day / Slide Day	Rest Day / Slide Day
Tu	#1	Off	30 to 45 min. Z1-easy
W	Off	Trans: 30 min. Z1 to Z2 (QC)	15 min. Z1 to Z2
Th	#2	45 min. Z1 to Z2	Off
F	Off	Rest Day / Slide Day	Rest Day / Slide Day
Sat	Off	45 to 75 min. Z1 to Z2	Off
Sun	Off	Off	45 to 60 min. Z1 to Z2
Totals: 5:00 to 6:00 hrs.	1:30 hrs.	2:00 to 2:30 hrs.	1:30 to 2:00 hrs.

WEEK 2	SWIM	BIKE	RUN
M	Off	Rest Day / Slide Day	Rest Day / Slide Day
Tu	#3	Off	45 to 60 min. Z2
W	Off	Trans: 45 min. Z2 (QC)	15 min. Z2
Th	#4	45 to 60 min. Z2	Off
F	Off	Rest Day / Slide Day	Rest Day / Slide Day
Sat	Off	1:00 to 2:00 hr. Z2	Off
Sun	Off	Off	1:00 to 1:30 hr. Z1 to Z2
Totals: 6:00 to 8:00 hrs.	1:30 hrs.	2:30 to 3:45 hrs.	2:00 to 2:45 hrs.

"Just Finish" Athlete: Two-Week Recovery / Off-Season Maintenance Program (Note: Swims #1 through 4 can be found on page 72):

INTERMEDIATE PROGRAM
RECOVERY / OFF-SEASON MAINTENANCE

WEEK 1	SWIM	BIKE	RUN
M	Off	Rest Day / Slide Day	Rest Day / Slide Day
Tu	#1	Off	30 min. Z1—easy
W	Off	Trans: 15 min. Z1 to Z2 (QC)	15 min. Z1 to Z2
Th	#2	30 min. Z1 to Z2	Off
F	Off	Rest Day / Slide Day	Rest Day / Slide Day
Sat	Off	45 min. Z1 to Z2	Off
Sun	Off	Off	45 min. Z1 to Z2
Totals: 4:30 hrs.	1:30 hrs.	1:30 hrs.	1:30 hrs.

WEEK 2	SWIM	BIKE	RUN
M	Off	Rest Day / Slide Day	Rest Day / Slide Day
Tu	#3	Off	30 to 45 min. Z2
W	Off	Trans: 15 to 30 min. Z2 (QC)	15 min. Z2
Th	#4	30 to 45 min. Z2	Off
F	Off	Rest Day / Slide Day	Rest Day / Slide Day
Sat	Off	45 to 90 min. Z2	Off
Sun	Off	Off	45 to 75 min. Z1 to Z2
Totals: 4:30 to 6:30 hrs.	1:30 hrs.	1:30 to 2:45 hrs.	1:30 to 2:15 hrs.

AN IRONFIT MOMENT

Beware of the Post-Race Blues

After focusing so intensely on a great and worthy goal, many athletes feel a mental letdown in the weeks and months following its accomplishment. If this happens to you, don't worry; it happens to the best of us. We are goal-oriented people, and when we don't have a goal, we can easily drift. This is why the best cure for the "post-race blues" is another worthy challenge. Set a new goal and commit to it. As soon as you do, everything will start to improve for the better. It's amazing how registering for a race can have such an impact—but for people like us, it does.

It doesn't need to be as big of a goal as your recent accomplishment—any worthy goal will do, as long as you feel excited and motivated by it. The time frame is important, too; not too soon, but not too far away, either. For most athletes, something in the three- to six-month time frame works best.

Maintenance Training and Off-Season Focus

In addition to using the second week of any of the above three programs as your model for the off-season, please consider the following suggestions to get the greatest benefit from your off-season training:

1. **Focus on your weakest link:** We all have a tendency to focus our off-season training on the sport we like the best and forget about the sport we like the least. It happens with all three sports, but the most common example we see of this is with swimming. We coach a large Masters Swimming program, and there are some triathletes we know who are not particularly fond of swimming. They love triathlon, but look at swimming as a necessary evil. After their last race in the late summer, they instantly disappear from the pool, not to appear again until the following spring.

   The problem with this approach is that their weakness remains their weakness. When they start up the following spring, their already-weak swim is now even weaker. This cycle goes on and on, year after year, and the result is no swimming improvement.

223

We encourage our coached athletes to do just the opposite. As we like to say, "Befriend the enemy." We suggest that if they are not fond of swimming, then they should throw themselves into it even more. Take lessons. Spend more time focusing on drills. And here's the big one: Enter some winter Masters Swimming meets.

Those who take us up on our advice enter the next spring's triathlon season with their swim stronger and more efficient than ever. Their swim confidence is at an all-time high, too. Instead of dreading their open-water swim races to come, they can't wait to try out their newly developed swimming abilities.

As we like to say to our more-competitive coached athletes with respect to their off-season training: "Let's turn our weaknesses into strengths, and let's turn our strengths into weapons."

2. **Functional strength and core training:** The off-season is often the best time to focus on strength and core training. Because our overall swim, bike, and run training time is reduced, most athletes find they have a little more availability in their schedule for this important area. Focusing on functional strength and core training in the off-season will have you entering the next racing season stronger and more injury-proof.

   The functional strength and core training program in Chapter 6 details exactly what you need to do in the off-season.

3. **Stay lean:** Many athletes put on excess weight in the off-season. If you are already at a healthy weight, it's not a big issue if you gain a few pounds during the off-season. A few extra pounds can be safely shaved off when training shifts from the off-season to the preseason. But we are often amazed at how some athletes can put on ten to twenty pounds (or even more) in the off-season. Please don't let this happen to you. It is not healthy, and this weight cannot be safely taken off in a short period of time. Use the approaches and suggestions in Chapter 11, and stay lean and healthy year-round.

4. **Substitute in other endurance sports:** For a fun change of pace, substitute in different endurance sports activities for some of your

off-season training sessions. Some great options include cross-country skiing, mountain biking, mountain climbing, and hiking.

5. **Give back:** Life has been good to you. You achieved your Half Iron-Distance goal this year; now offer a helping hand to someone else. Inspire someone you know to become healthier. Help someone to run his or her first race, or volunteer at a local triathlon event. Doing so will make your Half Iron-Distance achievement even greater.

We hope this book contributes to the success and enjoyment of your Half Iron-Distance journey. Keep up the great work, and we hope to see you at the finish line!

Acknowledgments

We wish to thank the following individuals: Jonathan Beverly, Kellie Brown, Matthew Chiarolanzio, Patience Cogar, Jim Colby, Maureen Cullen, Debbie Debiasse, Tom Debiasse, David Drucker, Jen Gonyea, Craig Gruber, Yvonne Hernandez, Jeff Kellogg, Lynn Kellogg, Laura Litwin, Jen Luebke, Kimberly Mitchell, Adriana Nelson, Beth Poore, Francis Quinn, Sean Reilly, Tom Robertson, Shannon Schlageter, Robert Serling, Suzy Serpico, Jessi Stensland, Keith Wallman, Carl Wernicke, and Andrew Winter.

Appendix A: Additional Maximum Heart Rate Estimation Formulas

In addition to the popular "220 Minus Your Age" method presented in Chapter 4, following are two additional maximum heart rate formula approaches for your consideration:

Additional Formula #1

On his website (www.marathon-training-schedule.com), world-class endurance athlete and coach Marius Bakken writes the following: "In 2002 they did some research at the University of New Mexico. They took 43 (!) different formulas and tested which one was the most accurate. The result? This formula beat the rest:

1. Multiply your age with 0.685.
2. Take 205.6 and subtract the result of 0.685 x age.
3. You get a pretty accurate measurement of your max heart rate.

An example: For a thirty-five-year-old, that would mean: 205.6 – (0.685 x 35) = 182 in max rate."

We have tested this formula with some of our athletes and found (at least with our limited sample) that these results were more accurate. In general, the estimates for maximum heart rate by this formula are a little lower than those estimated by the "220 Minus Your Age" method in the younger ages, but then they catch up and pass the "220 Minus Your Age" formula at about forty-eight years.

Following are a few age comparisons for the two formulas:

AGE (YEARS)	"220 MINUS AGE"	"THE 205.6 FORMULA"
20	200 BPM	192 BPM
30	190 BPM	185 BPM
40	180 BPM	178 BPM
50	170 BPM	171 BPM
60	160 BPM	165 BPM

Additional Formula #2

In an article by Paul Keegan ("We Won't Let Him Hurt You") in the February 1998 issue of *Outside* magazine, the great Mark Allen's (six-time winner of the Ironman World Championship) approach to estimating maximum heart rates is presented: "Subtract your age from 180, and then adjust that number to reflect your particular circumstances. If you're recovering from a major illness or taking medication, subtract 10; if regular exercise is a hazy memory, subtract 5; if you've been working out consistently for two years or less, stick with 180 minus your age; if you've been exercising without injury for more than two years, add 5."

According to Paul Keegan, Mark Allen recommends an aerobic training range of 60 to 80 percent of the number yielded by this formula.

Appendix B: Glossary

Abs: Abdominal muscles.

Aerobic Energy System: An energy system that primarily uses oxygen and stored fat to power physical activity. This system can support activity for prolonged periods, as stored fat and oxygen are available in almost endless supply. Even a highly trained athlete with body fat percentages in the single digits has more than enough stored fat for several ultra-distance races back-to-back.

Anaerobic Energy System: An energy system that primarily uses glycogen (stored sugar) to power physical activity. This system can support activity for relatively short periods of time, as the body stores sugar in relatively small quantities.

Basal Metabolic Rate (BMR): The number of calories necessary to consume each day to allow our bodies to function normally and maintain current body weight. This book also refers to "active BMR," which is an athlete's BMR plus the additional calories needed to support normal daily activities, but not including the calories used in training and racing.

Body Mass Index (BMI): A relative measure of body height to body weight for purposes of determining a healthy or unhealthy weight.

BOSU Ball (acronym for "both sides utilized"): This is an inflated "half-ball" with a flat side and a half-dome side. This popular piece of equipment is primarily used to develop balance and stability on an uneven and unstable surface.

Brick Session: *See* Transition Sessions.

Calorie: A calorie is a basic unit of energy. Our bodies require energy to perform almost all functions, and get this energy in the form of calories. Carbohydrates and proteins have about 4 calories per gram, while fat has about 9 calories per gram.

Carbohydrate Loading: Various dietary approaches for the purpose of increasing glycogen stores prior to an endurance race.

Cooldown: A lower-intensity activity that helps the body to gradually and safely transition from a relatively higher-intensity activity.

Core Muscles: Includes abdominals, back, buttocks, pelvic floor, and hips.

Dumbbells: Handheld exercise weights available in various coatings from plastic to metal and various weights from one pound up to fifty-plus pounds.

Easy Eight: A 5-minute warm-up routine presented in this book that includes eight specific pre-exercise movements.

Electrolytes: Common examples of electrolytes are sodium, potassium, chloride, and carbon dioxide. Your cells need them to function properly and to keep your body's fluids in balance.

Foam Roller: This piece of exercise equipment is made of hard foam and is usually 36 inches long and 6 inches in diameter, with varying densities, used for self-myofascial release.

45-Minute Window: The time period of opportunity after a training session to jump-start the replenishment of glycogen stores.

Fueling: Within the context of endurance sports, this term refers to the process of consuming calories before, during, and after training and racing to build and maintain high levels of energy and to boost recovery.

Fueling Logistics: The means by which athletes access their needed calories during competition.

Glutes: Abbreviation for the gluteus maximus, medius, and minimus muscle group.

Glycogen: The form in which the body stores sugar (carbohydrates) for the purpose of powering muscle activity.

Hydrating: Within the context of endurance sports, this term refers to the process of drinking fluids before, during, and after training and racing to support optimal performance, safety, and good health.

Hydration Logistics: The means by which athletes access their needed fluids during competition.

Kettle Bells: These are handheld weights, but unlike dumbbells, the center of mass is extended beyond the hand. This facilitates ballistic and swinging movements. Like dumbbells, they are available in various coatings and weights.

Lactate Threshold: The heart rate level at which lactate begins to accumulate at a faster rate in the muscles than the body can clear.

Medicine Ball: This is a round, weighted ball with a rubberized or leather coating used in core and functional strength training exercises. It is available in various weights, from one to twenty pounds.

Overload Principle: According to the American Council on Exercise: "One of the principles of human performance that states that beneficial adaptations occur in response to demands applied to the body at levels beyond a certain threshold (overload), but within the limits of tolerance and safety."

Quads: Abbreviation for the muscles of the quadriceps.

Repetitions (Reps): The number of times an exercise movement is repeated within an exercise set.

Sets: A specific grouping of repetitions of a specific exercise movement. Typically, there will be one to three sets of each exercise within a specific exercise program.

75-Minute Fueling Guideline: The approximate point in a workout when water alone is not enough for most athletes to maintain the same performance level. Adequate calories, in addition to hydration, are needed.

Stability Ball (aka, Swiss Ball): This round, inflated exercise ball is the most popular and widely used piece of core-training equipment. It is important that it's properly sized to fit your height.

Stretch Cords and Resistance Tubing: These are rubber or plastic cords, usually with handles, and available in various resistances.

Sweat Rate Test: A physical test performed by an athlete to help determine his or her hydration needs while training and racing.

T1: The transition between the swim and cycling phases of a triathlon.

T2: The transition between the cycling and running phases of a triathlon.

Taper Phase: A pre-race training period of decreasing training volume for the purpose of having the athlete rested and energized for competition.

Training Volume: The combination of training duration, frequency, and intensity.

Transition Sessions (aka, Brick Sessions): Training sessions that involve two sports separated by a brief period in which the athlete changes from the clothing and equipment of one sport to that of the other.

VO2 Max: A measure of an athlete's ability to process oxygen and convert it to energy.

Warm-up: A movement routine that prepares the athlete's body for training or racing by raising our core body temperature and lubricating our joints and tendons.

Watts-Based Training: A training approach for cycling that involves measuring intensity by produced wattage.

Appendix C: References

Books

The books listed here have been very helpful to us over the years, providing a great deal of information as we compiled our research for this book. They may prove useful to you, as well.

Be Iron Fit: Time-Efficient Training Secrets for Ultimate Fitness, 2nd Edition. Don Fink. Lyons Press, 2010.

The Big Book of Endurance Training and Racing. Philip Maffetone and Mark Allen. Skyhorse Publishing, 2010.

Core Performance Endurance. Mark Verstegen and Pete Williams. Rodale Inc., 2007.

Endurance Sports Nutrition: Strategies for Training, Racing, and Recovery, 2nd Edition. Suzanne Girard Eberle, MS, RD. Human Kinetics, 2007.

Heart Rate Training. Roy Benson and Declan Connolly. Human Kinetics, 2011.

Instant Relief: Tell Me Where It Hurts and I'll Tell You What to Do. Peggy Brill and Susan Suffes. Bantam, 2007.

IronFit Strength Training and Nutrition for Endurance Athletes. Don Fink and Melanie Fink. Lyons Press, 2013.

Ironman 70.3: Training for the Middle Distance. Henry Ash and Marlies Penker. Meyer & Meyer Sport (UK) Ltd., 2008.

Lifestyle & Weight Management Consultant Manual. Richard T. Cotton. American Council on Exercise, 1996.

Mastering the Marathon: Time-Efficient Training Secrets for the 40-plus Athlete. Don Fink. Lyons Press, 2010.

The Perfect Distance: Training for Long-Course Triathlons. Tom Rodgers. VeloPress, 2007.

Personal Trainer Manual: The Resource for Fitness Professionals. Richard T. Cotton. American Council on Exercise, 1997.

The Power Meter Handbook: A User's Guide for Cyclists and Triathletes. Joe Friel. VeloPress, 2012.

Program Design for Personal Trainers: Bridging the Theory into Application. Douglas S. Brooks, MS. Human Kinetics, 1997.

Sports Nutrition for Endurance Athletes, 2nd Edition. Monique Ryan, MS, RD, LDN. VeloPress, 2007.

Training and Racing with a Power Meter, 2nd Edition. Hunter Allen and Andrew Coggan, PhD. VeloPress, 2010.

Training Lactate Pulse-Rate. Peter G. J. M. Janssen. Polar Electro Oy, 1987.

The Triathlete's Training Bible. Joe Friel. VeloPress, 2009.

Triathlon Science. Joe Friel and Jim Vance. Human Kinetics, 2013.

Suggested Web Links

Active Release Technique: www.activerelease.com
American Council on Exercise: www.acefitness.org
British Triathlon: www.britishtriathlon.org
Challenge-Family Triathlon Series: www.challenge-family.com
HITS Triathlon Series: www.hitstriathlonseries.com
IronFit: www.IronFit.com
Ironman70.3 Triathlon Series: www.ironman.com
Jessi Stensland: www.gojessi.com
Live Strong: www.livestrong.com
Lose It: www.loseit.com
My Fitness Pal: www.myfitnesspal.com
Revolution 3 Triathlon Series: www.rev3tri.com
Running in the USA: www.runningintheusa.com
Running Times Magazine: www.runningtimes.com
USA Triathlon: www.usatriathlon.org
US Masters Swimming: www.usms.com
Triathlete Magazine: www.triathlete.competitor.com
Triathlon Australia: www.triathlon.org.au
Triathlon Canada: www.triathloncanada.com
Triathlon New Zealand: www.triathlon.org.nz

Tri Find: www.trifind.com
Tri Life Photos: www.TriLifePhotos.com
220 Triathlon: www.220triathlon.com
Weight Watchers: www.weightwatchers.com
Yvonne Hernandez: www.bbasports.com

Index

A

American Council on Exercise, 24

B

Be Iron Fit (Fink and Fink), viii, ix, 2–3
Benedict, Francis Gano, 173
Brown, Kellie, 163
Buffalo Springs Lake Race in Texas, 1

C

Cambridge, Cary, 172–73
Challenge-Family Series races, 1
coaches, importance of, 161
Cogar, Patience, 149–50
Colby, Jim, 183–84
Competitive Program, 11–12, 14, 15, 16–17, 44–46, 48–57
Cullen, Maureen, 8–9
cycling
  90 circles, 197
  bikes, 193
  braking, 196
  cadence, 194, 197
  climbing technique, 194–95
  cornering, 196
  cutoff times, 148–49
  cycling power hill repeats, 10, 17–18
  descending, 195–96
  flying bike mount, 125
  good posture, 193–94
  high cadence cycling, 197
  high-rpm cycling spins, 11, 19–20
  injuries and early warning signs, 216
  planning bike course breaks, 146
  power meters on bikes, 80–81
  professional bike fit, 159
  single-leg pedaling, 197
  spinning circles, 20, 194, 197
  suggested corrective bike drills, 197
  techniques, 193–97
  watts-based training, 36, 80–81

E

Eagleman Race in Maryland, 1
European Championship, 1
exercises
  Abs and Back Stretch over Stability Ball with Arms Overhead, 89
  Advanced: Abs-Stability Ball Pass from Hands to Feet with Raised Torso, 98
  Advanced: Alternating Arm Chest Flys with Stretch Cords, Standing on One Leg, 101
  Advanced: Back Lunge of BOSU with Overhead Reach Using Dumbbell, 99
  Advanced: Bicycles over BOSU with Legs Raised, 111–12
  Advanced: Dead Lifts with Dumbbells to Calf Raise on One Leg, 94–95
  Advanced: Get-ups off Floor with Medicine Ball Overhead, 107
  Advanced: Jump Squats on the BOSU, 106
  Advanced: One-Arm Chest Press over Stability Ball with Rotation, 93–94
  Advanced: One-Leg Split/Squat with Elevated Leg and Two Kettle Bells or Dumbbells, 101–2
  Advanced: One-Leg Squat with Dumbbells, 93
  Advanced: Planks on Toes with One Leg Raised, 103
  Advanced: Rear Deltoid Flys, with One-Leg Squat in Stork Position, 95–96
  Advanced: Side Lunge onto BOSU with One-Arm Front Raise, 105
  Advanced: Side Lunge with Ax Chop on BOSU using Kettle Ball, 104

Advanced: Squat on One Leg, Curl and Press, 108

Advanced: Squat with Overhead Raises using Kettle Bell, 110–11

Advanced: Straight-Leg Push-up with One Leg Raised, 97, 102

Advanced: Swimming on BOSU, 109

Advanced: Transverse Lunge onto BOSU with Stretch Cord or Cable Row, 100

Basic: Abs-Open and Close Triangles, 97

Basic: Back Lunge with Overhead Reach Using Dumbbell, 98

Basic: Chest Flys with Stretch Cords in Lunge Position, 100

Basic: Chest Press over Stability Ball with Hip Extension, 93

Basic: Dead Lifts with Dumbbells, 94

Basic: Get-ups off the BOSU with Arms at your Sides, 106–7

Basic: Jump Squats onto Step or Box, 106

Basic: Obliques over BOSU, 111

Basic: One-Leg Split/Squat with Elevated Leg, 101

Basic: Overhead Raises with Stretch Cords or Bands, 110

Basic: Planks with Rollout on Knees and Forearms on Stability Ball, 103

Basic: Rear Deltoid Flys in a Stork Position, 95

Basic: Side Lunge with Front Raise, 105

Basic: Squat to Curl and Press, 108

Basic: Squat with Ax Chop on BOSU using Medicine Ball, 104

Basic: Squats with Dumbbells–Stability Ball against the Wall, 92

Basic: Straight-Leg or Bent-Knee Push-up, 96, 102

Basic: Superman on BOSU, 109

Basic: Transverse Lunge with Stretch Cord or Cable Row, 99

Calf Stretch, 113

Chest Openers, 86

competitive season, 90, 91–92, 108–12

Easy Eight warm-up routine, 85–89, 144

Forward Lunge with Elbow inside Knee, 87–88

Intermediate: Abs-Stability Ball Pass from Hands to Feet, 97–98

Intermediate: Back Lunge off Step with Overhead Reach Using Dumbbell, 98

Intermediate: Chest Flys with Stretch Cords, Standing on One Leg, 100

Intermediate: Chest Press over Stability Ball, Alternating Arms, 93

Intermediate: Dead Lifts with Dumbbells to Calf Raise, 94

Intermediate: Get-ups off BOSU with Arms Raised, 107

Intermediate: Jump Squats onto BOSU, 106

Intermediate: Obliques over BOSU with One Leg Raised, 111

Intermediate: One-Leg Split/Squat with Elevated Leg and Kettle Bell, 101

Intermediate: Overhead Raises with Stretch Cords or Bands in Lunge Position, 110

Intermediate: Planks on Toes and Forearms on Stability Ball, 103

Intermediate: Rear Deltoid Flys in Stork Position, Alternating Arms, 95

Intermediate: Side Lunge onto Step with Front Raise, 105

Intermediate: Squat on BOSU, Curl and Press, 108

Intermediate: Squat with Ax Chop on BOSU using Kettle Ball, 104

Intermediate: Squats with Dumbbells– on Bosu, 92

Intermediate: Straight-Leg or Bent-Knee Traveling Push-up, 96, 102

Intermediate: Superman on BOSU with Arms Overhead, 109
Intermediate: Transverse Lunge onto Step with Stretch Cord or Cable Row, 100
Kneeling Stretch, 88, 114
McKenzie Press-up, 88
off-season, 90, 91, 92–103
Pelvic Circles in Standing Position, 85–86
Piriformis, Glutes to Hamstring, 114–15
preseason, 90, 91, 104–7
Press-ups, 114
Quad, Psoas, and Hip Flexor, 113–14
Shoulder Stretch, 115
Squatting Groin Stretch, 113
Three-Position Lunge (Front, 45°, Side) with Opposite Arm Raise, 86–87
Torso Rotation over Stability Ball, 89
weights, 90

F

fueling and hydration
    after training, 180–83
    average nutritional ratios for pre-race, 139
    bathroom breaks, 143
    Boost, 140
    calorie sources, 136–38
    calories, 135–38
    carbohydrate loading, 141
    carbohydrates, protein, and fat, 136–37
    determining race fueling needs, 135–36
    determining race hydration needs, 132–34, 180
    energy bars, 126, 137, 140
    energy drinks, 137, 140, 142, 143, 181
    energy gels, 126, 137, 142, 143, 168, 181
    Enervit, 181
    Ensure, 140
    examples of race fueling and hydration plans, 137–38, 140–42

Gatorade Endurance, 181
Gatorade Recovery, 181
GU Brew, 181
GU Chomps, 137
Gu Recovery, 181
Hammer Nutrition, 181
Hammer Products, 181
Muscle Milk, 181
nutritional ratio data, 136–37
popular food items for pre-race, 140
pre-, during, and post-workout fueling, 181
pre-, during, and post-workout hydration, 181
pre-race fueling and hydration, 138–42
pre-race fueling data, 139
pre-race hydration data, 139
race fueling data, 136
sample pre-, during, and post-fueling and hydration plan, 181–83
the 75 Minute Guideline, 135
sodium and electrolyte replacement, 142–43
Sweat Race Test, 132–34, 180
before and during training, 179–80

G

Galloway, Jeff, 147
gear/equipment
    aero bars on bikes, 165–66
    bento boxes, 125–26
    bike cleats, 165
    bike frames, 160–61
    bike pedals, 165
    bike seats, 165
    bike shoes, 125, 126, 165
    bikes, 164
    CompuTrainer, 159
    cool new products, 162
    deep rim or disc racing wheels, 160
    drinking system and bike bottles, 125, 165

elastic shoelaces, 125
foam roller, body stick, massage balls, and basic tennis or golf balls, 214
heart rate monitors, 35, 38, 40, 158
helmets, 160, 164–65
race gear bags, 119
race wheels on bikes, 160, 166
running caps, 168
running shoes, 125, 167
socks, 124, 167–68
sunglasses, 121, 126, 166
sunscreen and sunblock, 124–25, 168
swim caps, 164
swim goggles, 163–64
tips on bike gear, 164–67
tips on run gear, 167–68
tips on swim gear, 162–64
tire-changing gear, 166
top five products needed for speed, 158–60
top three products that may be a waste of money for some, 160–62
tri suits, 121, 124, 162, 168
water bottles, 125, 165
wet suits or speed suits, 121, 124, 159–60, 162–63, 191–92
goal setting, 151–54
Gonyea, Jen, 115–16
Gruber, Craig, 126–27

H
Half Iron-Distance Triathlon
big ten time-management tips, 4–7
for busy athletes, viii, 3
exploding popularity of, viii, 2, 8
and a healthy lifestyle balance, viii, 3–8
and heart rate training, ix, 35–41
includes a 1.2-mile swim, a 56-mile bike, and a 13.1 mile run, viii, 1
and its future, 8
logistically accessible, 3–4

sixteen-week Half Iron-Distance Training programs, 44–83
success stories, 8–9, 22–23, 33–34, 42–43, 115–16, 126–27, 149–50, 156–57, 169–70, 183–84
and time and money, 2–8
half marathons, 30–31, 32–33
Harris, James Arthur, 173
health issues
adequate rest, 215–16
age differences and injuries, 213
ART (Active Release Techniques) provider, 211
assembling your health team, 210–12
Boost, 140, 181
building and maintaining excellent health, 210–17
and compression garments, 215
cross-training, 213
early warning signs and injuries, 216–17
Ensure, 140, 181
having a complete physical from primary-care physician for new athletes, 210–12
icing, 214
improper technique, 213
injuries, 212–13
lack of proper warm-ups and cooldowns, 212, 214
micro and macro training cycles, 212
optimal body weight, 171–74
orthopedist, 211
physical therapist, 211–12
post-race blues, 223
preventing overuse and injuries, 214–16
self-myofascial release tools, 214
sports physician, 211
stretching, 215
too much, too soon, 212–13
training that is too extensive, 213

heart rate and heart rate zones
  aerobic *versus* anaerobic energy systems,
    37–38, 40, 130
  cycling heart rate zones, 39–40
  estimating maximum heart rate
    (MHR), 38–40
  gray zone, 40–41
  heart rate monitors, 35, 38, 40, 158
  heart rate zones, 35–41, 81, 129–30
  lactate threshold, 41
  resting heart rate, 215–16
  running heart rate zones, 39
  testing, 38
  and training, 35–41
  220 Minus Your Age method of
    testing, 38, 40
  Zones 1-4, 39–40, 129–30
HITS Series races, 1

I
Intermediate Program, 11–12, 44–46
Iron-Distance Triathlon (full), xiii–ix, 1, 2–8
Ironman 70.3 Series races, 1

J
junk training, ix, 35, 37, 38
"Just Finish" Program, 12, 14, 15, 16–17,
  19, 44–46

K
Kellogg, Jeff, 36
Kellogg, Lynn, 152, 159

L
Long Course. *See* Half Iron-Distance
  Triathlon
Lubbock, Lisa, 174, 175, 181–82
Luebke, Jen, 129

M
Masters Swimming Programs and Sessions,
  5, 18–19, 33, 193

mental training and self-confidence
  the countdown, 206–7
  deep belly breathing, 204–5
  energy givers and energy takers, 204
  family meeting, 203–4
  having a great race, 207–8
  the positive self-talk game, 206
  posting goals, 202–3
  realizing that nobody cares, 208–9
  staying mentally sharp by multiplying
    two-digit numbers, 205
  techniques and approaches, 202–9
Middle Distance. *See* Half Iron-Distance
  Triathlon

N
National Championships, 1
National Institutes of Health, 172
Nelson, Adriana, 25

O
Olympic Distance Triathlon, 2, 30–32,
  33, 79
optimal body weight
  basal metabolic rate (BMR), 173–74,
    175, 176
  body mass index (BMI), 171–73, 176
  determining optimal calories per
    pound, 174
  11 calories per body pound, 176–77
  estimated calorie ranges, 175–76
  500 calories per day reduction in
    weight, 176
  14 calories per body pound, 174, 175
  grazing concept or eating six smaller
    meals a day, 178
  and the Harris-Benedict Equation,
    173, 176
  Live Strong website, 178
  Lose It website, 178
  My Fitness Pal website, 178
  net calories after exercise, 175–76

online calorie-tracking applications,
175–76, 178
optimal daily calories to lose weight,
176–77
strategy to obtain and maintain optimal
weight, 177–78
and VO2 max (maximum oxygen
uptake), 177
Weight Watchers website, 178

R
race schedule website, 2
race selection, 154–56
race strategies
course segmentation strategy and
approach, 144–45
fueling and hydration, 128, 132–43
the "90-95-100" perceived effort
approach, 131
planning bike course breaks and aid
stations, 146
race warm-up strategy and approach,
143–44
run/walk approach, 147
smile and make friends, 145–46
special race strategy tips for "Just Finish"
athletes, 145–49
strategy for maintaining proper intensity
level during the race, 128, 129–30
swimming buoy to buoy, 146
time segmentation for finishing under
the cutoff time, 147–49
Reilly, Sean, 22–23
Rev 3 Series races, 1
running
bounce-less running, 198–99
gait analysis, 200
good posture, 198, 199–201
high knee with and without knee grab,
200–201
hill running—ascending and
descending, 199

injuries and early warning signs, 216
lateral crossovers, 200
leg swings front to back and side to
side, 200
suggested corrective run drills, 199–201
techniques, 198–201
two-strings approach, 198, 199
Running the USA, 33

S
salt and electrolyte tablets, 142–43
Schlageter, Shannon, 33
Serling, Robert, 169–70
Serpico, Suzy, 118
sixteen-week Half Iron-Distance Training
programs
adjusting training program for a half
marathon, 79
adjusting training program for a Sprint
or Olympic Distance Triathlon, 79
adjusting training program for an open-
water swim, 78
adjusting training program for the "Mom
Shift," 83
Competitive Training Program: Base-
Building Phase, Weeks 1–8, 49–53
Competitive Training Program: Peak
Training and Taper Phase, Weeks
9–16, 53–58
Competitive Training Program for
experienced athlete, 44–45, 48–58
cross-training through injury, 83
guidelines for adjusting the training
programs for practice races, missed
workouts, and other situations, 78–83
Intermediate Training Program: Base-
Building Phase, Weeks 1–8, 58–61
Intermediate Training Program: Peak
Training and Taper Phase, Weeks
9–16, 63–68
Intermediate Training Program: Swim
Sessions, 61–62

"Just Finish" Training Program, 44–45, 68–77

"Just Finish" Training Program: Base Building Phase, Weeks 1–8, 68–71

"Just Finish" Training Program: Peak Training and Taper Phase, Weeks 9–16, 73–77

"Just Finish" Training Program: Swim Sessions, 72–73

"Just Finish" Training Program using the heart rate training system, 81

swim sessions, 47–48

Sprint Distance Triathlon, 30–32, 33, 79

Standard Distance Triathlon. *See* Olympic Distance Triathlon

swimming

arm recovery portion of stroke, 187

befriending the enemy, 191

body/head position, 186

body rotation and breathing, 186–87

catch and pull portion of stroke, 187–88

cutoff times, 148

drafting, 192–93

entry and extension portion of stroke, 187

five most common flaws in freestyle swimming, 186–88

injuries and early warning signs, 216

kick on side with four progressions, 189–90

kick with kickboard, 188–89

one-arm drill with your arm at your side, 190

open-water swimming, 19, 30–31, 33, 191–93

practicing with your wet suit, 191–92

sighting, 192

suggested corrective swim drills, 188–91

swim sessions in sixteen-week training programs, 47–48

techniques, 185–93

T

time management

commuting and completing errands via running and cycling, 7

indoor training options, 4

laying out clothes and equipment in advance, 6

lunchtime workouts, 5

Mom Shift, 5–6, 83

morning workouts, 4–5

power naps, 6

sacrificing the perfect to get the good, 7

training in time, not miles, 4

training

"A Race" training cycles, 28–29, 30

alternating long and longer runs, 10, 15

annual training cycle, 29

competitive athlete: two week recovery/ off season maintenance program, 220

crucial training principles, ix, 24–27

eight key workouts, 10–21

eight essential training sessions, ix–x, 10–21

focusing on your weakest link, 223–24

"415-20-45 Brick," 10, 12–14

functional strength and core training, x, 84–85, 90–112, 224

higher-intensity bike and run sessions, 10, 16–17

inspiring others, 225

intermediate athlete: two-week recovery/off-season maintenance program, 221

IronFit swim approach: masters, drills, intervals, and open water, 10, 18–19

"Just Finish" athlete: two-week recovery/ off-season maintenance program, 221

maintenance training and off-season focus, 223–25

overload principle, 24–25

principle of training cycles, 27–29

principles of training volume, duration, frequency, and intensity, 26–27
recovery and maintenance training, 218–25
sixteen-week training programs, ix–x, 44–83
staying lean, 224
strategic rest days/slide days, 11, 20–21
stretching and flexibility routine, x, 84, 85, 112–15
substituting other endurance sports, 224–25
training phases, 29
training races, 30–33
two proper recovery weeks after the race, 218–22
warm-up routines, x, 85–89
weekly training cycle, 27–28
transitions
  attaching items to your bike, 125–26
  bathroom breaks, 124, 143
  bike-to-run transition sessions (T2), 11–14, 117–23
  changing tents, 162
  filming your transition practice sessions, 123
  flying bike mount, 125
  how and when to practice transitions, 122–23
  keeping transitions as simple as possible, 123–24

knowing the rules, 124
mastering transitions, 17–26
more time-saving transition tips, 123–26
often referred to as the Fourth Sport, 117
race gear, 122–23
running with your bike, 126
shoes on pedals, 125
socks or no socks, 124
swim-to-bike transition (T1), 12, 117–23
top down/bottom up approach to speedy transitions, 120–21
transition area setups, 118–21
the Transition Game, 122
transition sessions (bricks), 10, 11–14
transition times, 117–18
walk-through of the transition areas and visualization, 119–20
wet-suit strippers, 124

U
US Masters Swimming, 33
USA Triathlon, 2, 8, 33

W
watts-based training, 36, 80–81
Wernicke, Carl, 156–57
Wildflower Race in California, 1
Winter, Andrew, 42–43

About the Authors

Don Fink is an internationally known triathlon and running coach/trainer and author of the popular endurance sports training books, *Be IronFit: Time-Efficient Training Secrets for Ultimate Fitness* (2004); *Be Iron Fit*, 2nd Edition (2010); *Mastering the Marathon: Time-Efficient Training Secrets for the 40-Plus Athlete* (2010); and *IronFit Strength Training and Nutrition for Endurance Athletes* (2013), all published by Globe Pequot Press. Among his credentials, Don is a certified personal trainer by the American Council on Exercise (ACE), and a professional member of the National Strength

Don Fink, Melanie Fink, and Sheena
Lynn Kellogg/www.trilifephotos.com

and Conditioning Association (NSCA). Don and his wife, Melanie, train endurance athletes on five continents through their business, IronFit (www .IronFit.com). Don and Melanie have utilized their innovative approaches to coach hundreds of athletes to personal best times and breakthrough performances in triathlon, marathon, and other sports.

In addition to being an endurance sports coach/trainer, Don Fink is also an elite athlete. He has raced over thirty Ironman triathlons (2.4-mile swim, 112-mile bike, and 26.2-mile run) and has many age-group victories and course records to his credit. Don's time of 9:08 at the 2004 Ironman Florida is one of the fastest times ever recorded by an athlete in the 45–49 age group. Don also placed in the top three overall in the 2002 Ultraman World Championship (6.2-mile swim, 270-mile bike, and 52.4-mile run) on the Big Island of Hawaii.

Among Melanie's credentials, she is a certified personal trainer by the American Council on Exercise (ACE) and a regional council member of USA Triathlon Mid-Atlantic. Melanie coauthored the popular endurance sports training book *IronFit Strength Training and Nutrition for Endurance Athletes* (2013). In addition to being a sports coach/trainer and Masters Swimming coach, Melanie Fink is also an elite athlete. She has many age-group and overall victories in triathlon and open-water swimming competitions, has completed twelve Iron-distance triathlons (including the Hawaii Ironman, twice), and completed Ultraman Canada (6.2-mile swim, 270-mile bike, and 52.4-mile run) in Penticton, British Columbia.

Don and Melanie Fink live in Morris County, New Jersey.

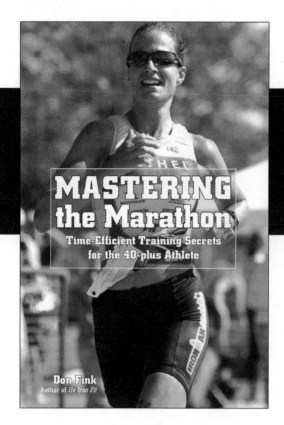